THE FAMILY
DOG

BARRON'S

THE FAMILY
DOG

AN OWNER'S GUIDE TO ALL ASPECTS OF
CARING FOR YOUR DOG

CONSULTANT EDITOR:

DAVID TAYLOR BVMS, FRCVS, FZS

BARRON'S

First edition for the United States, its territories, possessions, and dependencies, the Philippine Republic, and Canada published by Barron's Educational Series, Inc., 2001

Originally published in English by HarperCollins*Publishers* Ltd under the title:
COLLINS FAMILY DOG

Publisher's note: Throughout this book, we have referred to "he" rather than "she." This is just to avoid writing he/she all the time, or the rather impersonal "it."

All inquiries should be addressed to:
Barron's Educational Series, Inc.
250 Wireless Boulevard
Hauppauge, New York 11788
http://www.barronseduc.com

International Standard Book No. 0-7641-1708-4

Library of Congress Catalog Card No. 00-105304

Contents

Part One

The right dog for you

CHAPTER ONE – *Robert Killick*
Choosing a dog *12*

CHAPTER TWO – *Robert Killick*
The perfect puppy *24*

Part Two

Good dog behavior

CHAPTER THREE – *Nick Henderson*
Communicating with your dog *42*

CHAPTER FOUR – *Nick Henderson*
Curing common problems *52*

CHAPTER FIVE – *Nick Henderson*
Training is fun *62*

Part Three

Caring for your dog

CHAPTER SIX – *Robert Killick*
Daily care 82

CHAPTER SEVEN – *David Taylor*
Health care 98

Part Four

Advanced dog activities

CHAPTER EIGHT – *Robert Killick*
Showing your dog 136

CHAPTER NINE – *Robert Killick*
Breeding 144

Part Five

Popular dog breeds

CHAPTER TEN – *Robert Killick*
Dog breed guide 154

ACKNOWLEDGMENTS 190
USEFUL ADDRESSES 190
INDEX 191

Consultant editor

David Taylor BVMS, FRCVS, FZS

David Taylor is a well-known veterinarian,
broadcaster, and the author of over thirty books, including six
volumes of autobiography, some of which formed the basis for
three series of the BBC television drama, *One by One*.

He has also written the *Small Pets Handbook* and *Collins Family
Pet Guides: Rabbit*. The founder of the International Zoo Veterinary
Group, he has exotic patients across the world, ranging from
crocodiles to killer whales and giant pandas. He lives in Richmond,
Surrey, England, with his wife, four cats, and a hamster named "Fudge."

Contributors

Robert Killick

Robert Killick is a prominent breeder and exhibitor of Welsh Terriers, winning at the major Championship shows. He has a Judge's Diploma (Credit) and judges all breeds at Open Show level and his own breed at Championship level.

After a lifetime in the theater as a stage manager, director, and actor, he turned to freelance journalism. In 1990 he became a weekly columnist for the UK canine newspaper, *Our Dogs*. He also writes monthly columns in *Dogworld USA*, the world's largest circulating dog magazine, and the Swedish magazine *Hundesport*, and is a feature writer for *Dogs Today* in the UK.

In 1994 his poems were published by the American National Library of Poetry for which he received the award of "Poet of Merit" from the International Society of Poets, and he was nominated for "Poet of the Year" in 1995.

Nick Henderson
BSc (Edinburgh), MRCVS

Nick Henderson qualified as a veterinarian with a degree in veterinary science from Edinburgh University. Since then he has played an active role in the veterinary profession, being a founding member of the British Small Animal Veterinary Association, lifetime President of the Veterinary Marketing Association, and author of a number of books, among them several paperbacks on pet care (Corgi), *Cats – an Intelligent Owner's Guide* (Faber and Faber), *Cats and Cat Care* (David & Charles), *Rabies – The Facts You Need to Know* (Barrie and Jenkins), *The Book of Dogs* (Albany Books), and *The Book of Cats* (Albany Books).

Nick Henderson is an experienced broadcaster and has appeared on TV and radio both in the UK and the USA talking about pet care. He is now a professional consultant in both the human and animal health care sector.

Foreword

We enter the new millennium with the domestic dog as popular and remarkably useful an animal as ever. Whether as a decorative, loyal, amusing companion or a valued coworker, be it sniffing for contraband drugs or delectable truffles, guarding sheep or airfields, helping the blind or deaf, or simply helping to make folks feel better (for some time, scientists have recognized the therapeutic effects of canine pets in speeding the convalescence of human patients and actually lowering the blood pressure of people who pet them), dogs are undoubtedly most amazing animals.

It is a privilege as well as a pleasure to own one and that privilege demands that we take the trouble to understand their workings and their needs so that they, and we, can enjoy their lives in health and happiness. Innumerable books are available for the dog owner, novice, or professional breeder, but this is the first, in my view, that provides clear up-to-date information presented in a highly accessible style for the guidance and assistance of everyone who loves and admires our best friend.

David Taylor BVMS, FRCVS, FZS

The right dog for you

Buying a dog is a huge responsibility and one of the most important decisions that any family has to make. A dog is for life and he will become your responsibility for at least the next ten years; therefore, you should not rush into getting one without considering how he will fit into your lifestyle and what you can give him in return. Owning a dog is extremely rewarding but your furry friend will need regular exercise, feeding, grooming, and companionship, and you must be prepared to set aside some time every day to care for him and play with him.

Chapter One

CHOOSING A DOG

If you want a puppy, impulse buying is your worst enemy: Every puppy is small, pretty, and vulnerable, and it is so easy to fall for a little bundle of mischief without any consideration for the future – the puppy's future or your own. Buying a puppy or an adult

Above: *Owning a dog is very rewarding and you will receive many years of happy companionship and affection from your canine friends.*

dog is one of the most important purchases of a lifetime. You will be assuming control of another creature's life and he will be dependent on you for upwards of twelve years, so you are, in effect, buying a new member of the family.

Because of the importance of the decision, it is a good idea to consult with all the members of your family, from the youngest to the eldest, as each one will bear

some responsibility in different areas of the dog's life. Children should be closely involved, as the lessons they can learn from caring for a dog will stand them in good stead for the rest of their lives. Owning a dog now is likely to help them to be more caring to both animals and humans later on in their adult life.

Which breed?

There is a breed of dog that is suitable for every family. The American Kennel Club (AKC) registers 147 breeds of dog and obviously it will take a little research to discover which one is ideal for you, but all the effort is well worthwhile. Probably the first consideration is where you live and the size and style of the accommodations. All dogs love freedom and are suitable for country living with the exception of only some very small heavy-coated breeds, but not all dogs are suitable for city life. It would not be right to condemn a large dog such as a Saint Bernard or any of the larger hound breeds to life in a small apartment in a high-rise, but dogs, being what they are,

would adapt to the life. However, the fact remains that it would not be fair and would almost certainly lead to problems, particularly concerning behavior and temperament.

If you live in a neighborhood where the houses are quite close together, the neighbors must be respected. They have the legal right to peace and quiet, so a breed that is inclined to yap or bark for long periods is not suitable; nor would you want a breed that has the reputation for being aggressive to other dogs and too defensive of you and your family. Remember that unfortunately, not everyone likes dogs; therefore, you would not want to willingly introduce an element into your life that will bring aggravation.

Next, consider your own habits: If you are super neat, a dog with a thick double coat that tends to shed heavily would be a source of irritation. He would require daily grooming but would you have the time to do this? There are other considerations, such as whether the house is left empty for long periods. Is there a member of the family willing and able to walk the dog at least twice a day? Who will be responsible for feeding him and making sure that fresh water is always available?

FINDING A DOG

It has never been easier to find out about dogs, and the latest, most convenient, and complete way to do this is by using the Internet. It is simplicity itself to click on to the American Kennel Club's own web site or one of the others that relate to pets and link into the breed history, breed clubs, and the breeders themselves. It is possible to communicate with breeders and owners around the world and to download photographs and articles. The AKC will also provide you with the telephone numbers of any breeders close to where you live. However, if you are looking for one of the rarer dog breeds, you will have to be prepared to travel further afield.

There are literally thousands of books on breeds of dogs and there are many specialized bookshops dealing in the subject. The public libraries are also an excellent source of information, and if they haven't got a particular book, they will order it specially for you.

There are weekly newspapers devoted to purebred dogs, their care, exhibition, and breeding, as well as some monthly magazines publishing information on every aspect of owning pet dogs.

Purebred or mixed-breed?

At about this point you will have to decide whether you want to own a purebred dog or a mixed-breed. Some authorities claim that purebred dogs are less healthy than mixed-breeds or crossbreeds. Although this may be so with a few breeds, there is no scientific evidence that will prove the case generally. There are two reasons why a purebred dog is a purebred:

◆ The first is that his ancestry is known and recorded.

◆ Secondly, he breeds true; that is to say that if you mate a dog and a bitch of one breed, the resultant puppies will be replicas of their parents (color excepted).

One of the main advantages of a purebred dog is that within close parameters you will know the size to which he will grow. You will also know the sort of temperament he is likely to develop. However, buying a mixed-breed is a bit like a lottery – unless you have some specialized knowledge, the little creature at eight weeks might be a giant at eighteen months; he may have inherited some nasty genes from one of his parents that may not manifest themselves until he is two years old or even older.

The AKC, the Internet, and dog fancy magazines can all lead you to find the right purebred dog or puppy for you. Many prospective owners go to dog shows to seek out breeders but with today's All Breed Championship Shows, which are held over three days, you'd do well to find out in advance on which day your favorite breed is being exhibited. A telephone call to the AKC or a study of the dog fancy press will reveal the most convenient day; the smaller Open Shows that take place over one day may not schedule your particular breed.

■ **Left:** *No matter what sort of dog you choose, be it a purebred or a mixed-breed, it can enrich your life and become part of your family.*

Pet shops and puppy mills

There are traps into which the unwary can fall, and the selling of puppies and young dogs is now a multimillion dollar business; unfortunately, there are a few unscrupulous breeders, dealers, and retailers waiting for the gullible. Most people have seen on television and read in the national newspapers of "puppy mills." These are actually premises on which puppies are bred with no thought to their welfare, physically or mentally, and fed cheap and inferior foods with no veterinary attention. Their breeders are not concerned where they go or what happens to them after they leave their premises. The puppies can either be sold directly to the public via misrepresented newspaper ads, or they can go to dealers who will sell them by any method. Alternatively, they may be sold through pet shops.

It must be emphasized that these puppies do not have a good future, and it is most unlikely that the vendors will offer a "backup" in case of trouble. The puppy may become ill and his papers may be false. Therefore it is always wise to buy direct from a breeder who should be recognized by the AKC. Lastly, do not buy a puppy unless you see the mother!

Rescue dogs

Not everyone wants the problems associated with rearing a puppy and you may want a rescue or an adult dog. A network of breed rescue organizations exists to help you – a call to the local animal shelter will help you obtain the necessary information. There are many reasons for dogs to be in shelters: divorces, deaths, or simply an owner relocating.

A large number of these dogs come out of a happy home, are well trained, and can become a fully accepted older dog in any household. However, some have been ill treated and require tender loving care before they have confidence in their new home. Because of the difficulties, potential owners should be prepared for some searching questions before the dog is adopted. You may have to pay a small fee to cover expenses. It is also unusual for AKC registration papers to be made available; this is to stop the possibility of further abuse to the dog.

Of purebred dogs, Greyhounds have the biggest problem. Many racing Greyhounds are bred in the United States – far too many dogs for the market to absorb. As a result, numerous Greyhounds are abandoned by their owners if they don't make the grade. Contrary to some opinions, they can be easily trained not to chase small furry animals and can make extremely gentle and loving companions. There are special rescue organizations for the breed that not only place ex-racers but actually go to the racetracks and buy the animals back. These dogs are then placed for adoption.

NATIONAL ORGANIZATIONS

Organizations in the United States concerned with the protection of animals include the American Society for the Prevention of Cruelty to Animals (ASPCA), the Humane Society of the United States, and People for the Ethical Treatment of Animals (PETA). The ASPCA, which is devoted to protecting animals, was the first organization of its kind in the United States. The most important concern of the ASPCA is animal overpopulation. In order to reduce the number of homeless or unwanted house pets that are euthanized each year, the ASPCA advocates neutering, spaying, and animal adoption.

Above: *Giving a rescue dog a good home is a rewarding experience for both the dog and owner.*

Choosing a rescue dog

The problem when looking for a rescue dog is the beguiling eyes of the dogs. Every one will touch your heart but you must be practical. You will have decided on the most suitable size and how much time you are prepared to spend on grooming the coat. It is in the interests of the rescue center to match you with a suitable dog, so listen carefully to their advice, speak to the person who normally walks the dog in which you are interested, and ask them questions.

The dog may be suspicious at first, but don't worry – this is natural. He should come to you after about five minutes. However, if he shows any aggression, then beware. If he lies on his back urinating slightly, he is being submissive, which is acceptable in puppies but not in adult dogs. There is always a gamble with a rescue dog because his history is usually unknown, and great patience from the whole family will be needed.

1 Sit quietly without making direct eye contact with the dog but keeping an eye on him and his reactions to you.

2 Offer him a small treat or piece of food and watch his reaction. Does he snatch it or refuse it?

4 Put a leash on the dog and take him for a short walk. Note how he reacts to you. Then put him back in the kennel and invite him out again.

3 Ask the staff whether you can observe the dog's behavior when he is placed with other dogs.

THE RIGHT BREED FOR YOU

Breed	Temperament	Exercise
Labrador Retriever	Affable, tolerant, and easygoing with dogs and humans. Easily trained and learns quickly. Enjoys the company of children. A superb family and sporting dog.	An active dog. Needs lots of free running, walks, play, and retrieving games.
Golden Retriever	Gentle, biddable, and highly intelligent. A good sporting dog as well as an excellent family pet. Good with children and a great companion and gundog.	Needs frequent exercise and mental stimulation. Enjoys Flyball and Obedience.
Rottweiler	Intensely protective and highly intelligent, this is a good guard breed. Needs good socialization and kind but firm training. Not suitable to be left with young children.	Needs lots of walking (at least twice a day), free running, and games for stimulation.
German Shepherd Dog	Highly intelligent and a wonderful guard and herding dog, the German Shepherd makes a good family pet if it is trained and well socialized. Needs kind but firm handling.	Needs and enjoys as much exercise as it can get. Excels at Obedience and Agility training.
Jack Russell Terrier	Intelligent, alert, and always busy, this dog loves to hunt. An easily trained fun dog that loves to live within its family pack and is good with children. Affectionate and a watchful guard dog.	Needs lots of exercise with walks, free running, and playing stimulating, imaginative games.
Cavalier King Charles Spaniel	A gentle, docile, and intelligent little dog. Confident and fun loving with a friendly nature, it makes a good family pet and loves to play with children if they are not too rough.	Needs two short daily walks, free running, and play – less exercise than bigger spaniels.
Boxer	Exuberant, full of fun, loyal, and affectionate. A good guard dog and a loving family dog. Good with children but can be too boisterous with very young ones.	Enjoys exercise and needs lots of walks, free running, and games for mental stimulation.
Yorkshire Terrier	Playful, inquisitive, a good companion, and the perfect small pet, especially for the elderly. A spirited, game little dog that enjoys hunting and playing games.	At least two short walks a day plus playing games in the yard and running.
English Springer Spaniel	Gentle, loving, and good with children. Craves affection and hates to be left alone. Highly intelligent and easy to train. A loving family pet as well as a good sporting dog.	Needs plenty of free running, daily walks, and play. Excels at Agility and Flyball.
Cocker Spaniel	Gentle, intelligent, biddable, and easily trained. A good companion. Most suitable for adults. A happy sporting dog, good at retrieving.	Needs a lot of exercise, especially free running, as well as daily walks.
Poodle	Highly sensitive, loving, and intelligent, the Poodle can be easily trained and makes a delightful family pet. It is gentle with children and a good companion for all ages.	Has unbounded energy and loves exercise and playing games – can't get enough!
Dalmatian	Affectionate, anxious to please, and loves human company. Devoted, loyal, and very attached to children. A dog that is more suited to country than city life.	Boundless energy and needs a lot of exercise – as much as you can give.
Doberman Pinscher	Loyal, affectionate, intelligent, and easily trained, its power must be controlled and it needs kind but firm treatment.	An hour a day walking plus free running and games.
West Highland White Terrier	Intelligent, inquisitive, and mischievous with an independent spirit. A good family dog that loves to be involved in every activity. Relatively easy to train.	Naturally active and needs lots of exercise, especially free running and playing.

SELECTING THE RIGHT DOG

There is no magic formula for selecting the right dog from either a rescue center or from a litter of puppies at the breeder's kennels. It is best that the entire family go together to make a choice, as everybody, including the children, should be there to express their opinion. Staff at rescue centers are deeply concerned that the right dog goes to the right family, and they will ask you about your home and yard, whether there will be anybody at home during the day to look after the dog, and also whether you have any other pets. You will be shown dogs that have been carefully assessed and will be told candidly if, in the opinion of the kennel staff, there are likely to be any problems.

Before the dog is allowed to leave the kennel there will almost certainly be a home visit, as the rescue workers will wish to satisfy themselves that your home is suitable for the dog. They have to be sure that your yard is escape-proof if you want a terrier-type dog and that there are no steep stairs if you wish to adopt a big, elderly dog.

One of the most difficult tasks facing any dog lover is to walk along a corridor lined with kennels, each containing one or more dogs; their pleading eyes will touch all hearts and, in fact, it is often better to let the dog make the choice. Families looking for a pet will be allowed to be in a room with the dog and this is the moment to find out if the dog likes the family. Rescue workers often report how a dog may be indifferent to one family and yet go for another in a big way.

Dogs from rescue centers

There are disadvantages to getting a dog from an adoption center, the main one being that the dog is likely to have been a stray, either lost or abandoned by the previous owners, and nobody will have any idea of his previous life, how much training he has received, any illness he may have suffered, or whether he has been abused or ill treated in any way. The staff will have gone to considerable trouble to find and correct any behavior problems but in the privacy of a home the dog may lack confidence and be troubled by the unfamiliar atmosphere. New owners will require a lot of patience until the dog understands what is expected of him. It is, however, quite remarkable how quickly a rescue dog will attach himself to a new family if he is shown kindness.

The center should supply you with the dog's veterinary record so that in the event of illness or accident, your veterinarian will know what treatment has been administered. There will also be a record of your pet's vaccinations, which you will want to keep up to date. A dog's digestive system cannot cope with sudden changes of diet, and you should receive a small quantity of the dog's regular food. If you want to change his food, you should do it gradually over several days by increasing the amount of new food each day while reducing the old food.

■ **Left:** *With kind treatment and lots of tender loving care, a dog will soon settle into his new home. Try to involve him in family activities.*

Left: *You can usually find a dog breed that will be a good match for your personality and lifestyle. Jack Russells love to play tough and have boundless energy, whereas Border Terriers like lots of affection and are just as happy curling up next to you on the sofa as they are going out for a walk.*

Settling into a new home

■ **Above:** *A puppy will need smaller and more frequent meals than an adult dog, so feed him more often.*

When you pick up your rescue dog or puppy, there is a possibility that he may be carsick, as he might never have traveled in a car before. Although this can often be controlled, it is always advisable to consult your veterinarian on the subject. Do not be tempted to try home remedies; you must make sure that any medicine used won't harm the dog.

In his new home the dog must not be stressed; he should be allowed to find his own way. Put a basket or bed in a draft-free corner with something soft and comfortable for him to lie on.

This bed must be safe and secure, and once he goes to it for a rest, he must not be disturbed.

The children must not smother him with love to start with – a tickle under the chin, a pat on the head, and a few soothing words will be sufficient. He will let you know when he wants more. Be patient, take your time, and soon the dog will be your faithful companion.

Dogs like routine. Your dog will like to know that he is fed and taken out at the same time each day. He will have preferences for food but he should not be spoiled; otherwise, you may train him to eat only chicken! Try to persuade the children not to feed him treats at mealtimes as some dogs tend to become overweight.

The dog may have had some training or he may never have experienced it at all, so it would be an excellent idea to take him to a local training class. It can be a fun evening for your children, especially if your dog is to be trained in the AKC's Good Citizens program, which, when he passes simple tests, will win the children a certificate.

■ **Above:** *Let your children handle the new dog under your supervision. They will soon accept him.*

■ **Right:** *All dogs can benefit from going to a training class. Even if you own a rescued adult dog rather than a puppy, it is never too late to learn or to brush up on basic training.*

Purebred puppies

You may opt to start from scratch and buy a purebred puppy. If you have done your research you will have probably arrived at a short list of two or three breeds you like. You should now try to find a suitable breeder. You can do this by contacting them at a dog show, but bear in mind that many of the lesser-known breeds have only a few breeders in the country and you may have to wait or get on a waiting list for a puppy. The choice of the breeder is really important so if you don't like the breeder, do not buy a puppy from him or her. The ideal breeder has a policy of breeding sound dogs, both mentally and physically, will take advantage of all the modern veterinary technology as far as genetic tests are concerned, and will be interested in the puppy's future life. In fact, the purchase of a puppy can often be the start of a lifelong friendship.

You must be prepared for some searching questions about your lifestyle, and, in return, the good breeder will not be offended if you ask leading questions about their breeding history.

Genetic tests

From your research you will know which, if any, genetic anomalies your favorite breeds suffer. One of the most frequent in the larger dogs is hip dysplasia. The best breeders, however, have been working on this problem for many years and are succeeding in reducing the incidence in most breeds. Responsible breeders have their dogs' hips examined, radiographed (X-rayed), and evaluated by their veterinarian

WHICH SEX?

The choice between a dog and bitch is not easy. Bitches are presumed to be gentler and more biddable but the supporters of male animals claim they are more sensitive to their owner's feelings. Bitches of the larger breeds are probably better with small children, and dogs with teenagers. The main problem with bitches is that they come into season roughly every six to nine months and during this period they must be kept away from the males; otherwise, puppies will result. Dogs will scent a bitch in season, travel miles, and wait for an opportunity to mate with her. Spaying the bitch and castrating the male prevent the problem and do not affect the character of either.

before the animals are used for breeding. The veterinarian then submits the radiographs to the Orthopedic Foundation for Animals (OFA), which consists of a panel of veterinary orthopedic specialists. The panel reviews the radiographs and rates the animal's hips in relation to the breed. You may contact the OFA to learn the average hip ratings for the various breeds. Ask the breeder to show you the OFA hip certificates for the parents of the pup you are thinking about buying. If the parents' OFA evaluations are less than fair for its breed, you should not purchase the puppy.

Choosing a puppy

Take your family to see the puppies, which should be over eight weeks old, but make sure the children are under control. There is a possibility that the puppies have never encountered children before and might be disturbed, as will the breeder.

Always ask to see the puppies' mother. This will enable you not only to see the fully grown size of an adult dog but also, and more importantly, to make a quick judgment of her temperament.

Whichever sex you have decided upon, ask the breeder to remove the others and then examine each puppy. Look for any sort of discharge from the eyes, the mouth, the anus, or the vulva; if there is any, don't take that puppy. Any runt of the litter should also be discounted. Do not on any account be persuaded to buy a puppy at a lower price because "there is something minor wrong with it." Therein lies trouble. If everything looks good, watch for the most extroverted puppy, the one that approaches you full of curiosity and happiness, and ignore any that creep about apprehensively.

■ **Below:** *Never buy a puppy without seeing the mother first. This will help you to assess a pup's eventual size, appearance, and temperament.*

CHECKING OUT A PUPPY

When choosing a puppy, make sure you examine him thoroughly before committing to a purchase. Always look at the mouth, ears, nose, and anus or vulva for any signs of discharge. Watch the puppy carefully for reassurance that he is contented and well cared for. Stroke the puppy, play with him, and ask to see the mother.

1 Gently examine the puppy's anal regions for any telltale signs of discharge.

2 Fold back the earflap and check for any wax or discharge. They should not have an unpleasant smell.

3 Check the eyes for signs of discharge. They should be clear, bright, and alert.

4 Examine the mouth and teeth. They should be white and smooth with a correct bite.

The cost

For most people the expense of having a dog has to be thought about carefully. The costs of buying and owning a dog can be considerable. The initial cost of buying a purebred puppy depends very much on the breed but even if you acquire a crossbreed or a mixed-breed puppy you will still have to pay for his first vaccinations and, later on, for annual boosters. Veterinary care is not cheap and statistically, some dog breeds need more veterinary attention than others. Fortunately, some insurance companies specialize in insuring against illness and accidents in pets, thereby ensuring that you can afford to pay the veterinary fees. The cost of pet insurance varies and you will have to shop around to find the best deal for you, but paying the annual premium may save you a lot of money in the long run if your pet does ever have an accident or a serious illness.

A fact of life is that the bigger the dog, the more he eats, and a large dog can cost a lot to feed properly, although there are often cheaper alternatives to expensive dog foods. Another important element is professional grooming unless you are prepared to learn how to do it yourself. Breeds such as Old English Sheepdogs and Poodles can cost a lot of money to keep well groomed.

Taking your puppy home

The children will be very excited when you finally bring your new puppy home but you must try to keep them calm during the trip. The puppy is most unlikely to have been in a car before so have a soft blanket available, sit him on a lap, and stroke him gently. He may be carsick so you should have plenty of paper towels. Don't be angry with him if he gets sick; he doesn't know that he is doing anything wrong and he should be comforted to make him think that traveling in a car is a pleasurable experience.

At first reading, all this may seem to be an awful lot of trouble but the owning of the right breed of dog can really create enormous interest and bring to your family a closer understanding of nature.

Don't forget...

Discuss a "buy back" agreement with the breeder. Most reputable breeders will agree to take the puppy back if, for any reason, he is not suitable or your home conditions change so much that you cannot look after him.

Do not forget to get a signed and dated receipt when you hand

over the money. You should also inquire about whether the breeder has any information about insurance. Probably the best place to inquire about this is at the veterinarian.

The breeder should give you five or six days' free supply of the food normally fed. Keeping to the same food will help to prevent stomach upsets and enable you to change the diet slowly, if required.

■ **Above:** *When you get home, make sure your puppy has a warm, comfortable bed and some toys to play with. You don't need an actual basket – a cardboard box will do.*

■ **Left:** *When you bring your puppy home, wrap him in a blanket or towel and sit him on someone's lap in the car to make him feel more secure.*

REGISTERING YOUR PUPPY

Registering your dog with the American Kennel Club is important because you will not be able to show or breed your dog without full registration. The breeder pays the AKC for litter registration and receives an individual registration application for each pup in the litter. The breeder will provide you with the individual registration application and you pay the AKC to transfer the pup to your name as owner. Be sure to do this right away because there is a time limit. The

breeder can assign individual pups in the litter "full registration" or "limited registration." Limited registration documents that the dog is purebred, but restricts the animal from being exhibited at AKC-sanctioned shows or from registering any of its future offspring with the AKC. Limited registrations can later be changed to full registrations, but only the breeder has the authority to do this.

Chapter Two

THE PERFECT PUPPY

Every puppy is born perfect; it takes human beings to introduce imperfections. Like children, the first part of a puppy's life is the formative part. With puppies the first year is of ultimate importance but what constitutes a perfect puppy varies considerably. While some people are very tolerant of lively, active puppies, others like them to be calm and laid back. However, whichever you want, a puppy must always be treated with affection and firm kindness – hitting and harsh treatment of any kind are always counterproductive.

The perfect puppy should arrive in your house when he is between seven and nine weeks of age, although some unscrupulous breeders, puppy farmers, and dealers often try to sell them too young. However, the extra two weeks are of great importance to the young puppy because it is during this time that he will learn from his mother about his own identity in dog terms and also how he should behave with his own species. He also acquires just a little more strength and maturity that will allow him to settle into a new environment with minimal stress for both dog and owner. Ideally, you should

Left: Although puppies appear to have boundless energy and love playing, they spend a lot of time resting, too.

Above: Choosing a puppy is never an easy task as they all look appealing, but you must harden your heart and not be tempted to take more than one.

try to get a puppy from a breeder who allows the bitch to have her puppies in the house. In this way, they will be socialized from the moment they open their eyes and they will not be disturbed by the presence of people or any loud household noises, such as the vacuum cleaner, the television, and washing machine. An added advantage is that the litter is almost certain to have been trained to defecate on newspaper, which is of great help with later house-training.

BRINGING YOUR PUPPY HOME

Having made the decision to get a puppy, it can be great fun planning for his arrival. With the help of your children and other family members, you can decide what sort of things your new puppy will need. Dog fancy magazines are full of advertisements for suitable accessories. You may be lucky enough to have a really good pet shop close by where the added advantage is that a knowledgeable assistant will be able to point you in the right direction.

Your puppy will most certainly need just a few basic items of equipment, including a soft puppy collar, a leash, feeding and water bowls, some bedding and possibly a bed, and also some strong toys, including an artificial bone and hide chews to chew on.

Special grooming tools can be bought at a pet store or at one of the Championship Shows. There are always a large number of vendors selling items solely for dogs.

Getting your puppy

At least two people should pick up your new puppy and ideally he should travel home in the car on someone's lap. He may never have been in a car before and will be separated from his family and littermates for the first time so he will need lots of reassurance and comforting. Be sure to take a supply of paper towels with you as he may get carsick. Put a bottle of water and a bowl in the car in case he needs a drink. Don't let him out of the car at rest stops to relieve himself as these can be serious sources of infection.

Settling him in

The first important thing to impress on everybody is that the puppy should not be taken into a public place before having his course of vaccinations for fear of infection (see page 33). Second, give him his name and only use it with pleasant connotations. Your puppy should be given a place

▥ **Below:** *If buying a plastic basket, get a suitable size for a fully grown adult dog.*

that he can call his own – a warm, draft-free corner of the kitchen is ideal. You can invest in a hard, unchewable plastic bed lined with some soft bedding or machine-washable fleecy man-made fabric but this is not strictly necessary at this stage.

When puppies are very young, they often have a great liking for cardboard boxes, so turn a box upside down, cut an entry hole in it, and put in an old sweater. Your puppy will love it because he feels safe inside. He can also chew the box and it can be replaced at no expense. When he gets older, you can buy a proper chew-proof dog bed of adequate size.

Whenever he goes into his box,

▥ **Right:** *Puppies enjoy chewing on baskets and plastic beds so a cardboard box is a cheap and practical alternative. If your puppy chews one, throw it away and replace it with a new one.*

■ **Left:** *A puppy playpen will keep your puppy safe and secure.*

leave him in peace. Instruct the children that his bed is his private sanctuary and he must be allowed to sleep without being disturbed. Like a child, a puppy needs rest. It is during these periods that his body and bones develop. Whenever you put the puppy in his box, give him the command "*In your bed*" and he will soon understand what you mean.

Many people find that a puppy playpen is a very good idea. The puppy's box can be placed inside it with his toys. The floor can be covered with newspapers. A playpen will keep your puppy safe and out of the way of the children and family while still allowing him to be with you all and observe what is going on around him. He can rest or sleep, and the playpen can be moved from room to room if you wish.

For the first day or two, do not hassle the little dog; let him investigate his new home in his own time. Comfort and reassure him because he will feel lonely. Don't leave him alone in the house but be with him, talk to him, and play gently with him. This is an important socialization period and what you do now will set the pattern for the future, too. Don't give him any sweets and treats or he will suffer an upset stomach. Leave plenty of fresh water down for him and give him the food that he is used to eating.

Feeding your puppy

The breeder should give you a diet sheet together with a small supply of the food on which your puppy has been weaned. To avoid problems, stick to the regime as closely as possible. Puppies have tiny stomachs and should be fed only small amounts frequently – as many as four or five times a day. After two

or three weeks, reduce the number of feeding times to three and slightly increase the amounts given at each meal. Every breed will differ but by the time your puppy is five to six months he should be on two meals a day. Always feed the best food available, at the same time, and in the same place to establish a routine. A wide range of specially formulated food for

FEEDING TIPS

◆ It is always unwise to feed your puppy scraps from the table: If you don't start now, he won't bother you when you are eating.
◆ Don't offer him sweets, cookies, and cakes. Also, chocolate is toxic for dogs. All these treats are bad for his teeth and his weight.
◆ If your puppy does not eat his food immediately, don't leave it down for long in case insects contaminate it.
◆ Don't allow him to eat the cat's food or milk, nor should you feed them together.
◆ Don't feed him cow's milk while he is still very young. Some dogs react unfavorably to it and it may cause diarrhea. All he needs is water to do well.
◆ If he has a diet of complete dried food he will need plenty of water, so make sure he has a continuous supply and change or top it off frequently.
◆ If you introduce new foods, do this gradually so as not to upset his stomach.
◆ Don't give your puppy cooked chicken, lamb, or pork bones as these can splinter and cause serious injury. Hide chews will help with teething and cleaning teeth.
◆ Large knucklebones can be given but train your pup to give them up to you – young dogs can soon become overprotective of their food and treats. It is wise not to let the puppy have them for too long as he may manage to chew small pieces off that can eventually become impacted in his stomach.

■ **Right:** *A puppy needs small, regular meals while he is very young. A bowl of fresh water should always be available.*

puppies is available, including the complete dried foods, canned foods, and biscuits. Alternatively, cook some fresh meat and mix it with special puppy meal. However, the advantage of the commercial puppy foods you can buy is that they provide the right scientific balance of vital nutrients for a growing dog.

It is impossible to overestimate the importance of giving a dog the correct food. There are hundreds of brands from which to choose, so pay special attention to the manufacturers' recommendations and be sure not to overfeed your puppy. Dogs are running creatures

and should be slim with hard muscles. Even small dogs, such as Pekingeses, should not carry any excess weight. If you are unsure about how much food your pup should be eating, ask your veterinarian for advice.

Do not be tempted to give him extra supplements of vitamins or minerals unless it is on veterinary advice. The modern convenience foods are said to contain all the essential nutrients and therefore there is no need for supplements. Some experts believe that to reach their full potential, young adult dogs should have meat as part of their diet. Whichever type of food is offered, an unlimited amount of fresh water should always be available.

Nighttime

Missing the comforting presence of his fellow littermates, your puppy may cry during the first few nights, so tire him out by playing with him before he goes to sleep. Place a hot-water bottle under his bedding, put a ticking clock in

FEEDING GUIDELINES

Puppies have incredibly small stomachs and after weaning need small feeds frequently: four meals a day plus two puppy milk replacer meals. There is no way to know exactly how much to feed a puppy as every breed differs. A general guide using complete puppy food is 3/4 ounce (22 g) per 1 pound (450 g) of body weight daily, bearing in mind that medium-sized dogs double their birth weight every seven days, and larger dogs grow even faster. Every major specialized dog food manufacturing company gives guidelines and most have a telephone helpline. The best way to monitor progress is to weigh the puppy daily. Any loss of weight needs immediate investigation, so make sure he is getting his proper quota.

with him, and play the radio quietly – you are trying to fool him into believing that he is not alone.

It is best to place the box on a washable, noncarpeted floor and to surround it with newspaper in case the puppy needs to urinate during the night. Puppies rarely soil their bed.

If he howls during the night and you go to him, he will think you are answering his call, so steel your heart and try not to go. However, it is cruel to let him cry all night and if he is very persistent and cannot settle down, you may have to take him into your bedroom.

■ **Left:** *Puppies should not have too much exercise while they are young. A short walk or run will be sufficient.*

Put his box by the bed and comfort him by patting him from the bed, but on no account let him get up onto the bed because you may be setting a pattern that will be very difficult to change when he grows to his full size.

When he is relaxed, you can move his box a little closer to the door each night until it is outside, and then it can be taken back to the kitchen. However, if he does sleep upstairs, make sure that he cannot fall downstairs – his bones will not be calcified until he is about six months old and will break comparatively easily at this age. As a temporary precaution, place a child-proof gate at the top of the stairs. This can be used at the bottom of the stairs during the day to prevent him from climbing upstairs. If he does go with you, always carry him up and down as he is likely to injure himself if he falls.

■ **Left:** *Provide your puppy with a snug bed that he can call his own. Make it comfortable with some rugs or towels.*

House-training

Wherever you put the puppy's box, surround it with newspaper as he will not want to soil his own nest. When he is accustomed to using the paper, gradually remove some pieces and move the remainder toward the kitchen door. At the door it is then an easy matter to place it outside.

Every puppy will indicate that he wants to perform, but each one is different. One may turn in little circles, while another one will run back and forth sniffing.

Whenever your puppy indicates that he wants to relieve himself or finishes a meal or awakes from a sleep, put a collar and leash on him and take him outside to the place in the yard where you want him to go. Always use the same one or two words as a command and then praise him rapturously when he performs to order. Never chastise him severely when he makes a mistake in the house unless you catch him in the act. If so, use your voice, never your hand. He regards defecating, and where he wants to do it, as perfectly normal behavior and will not understand why you are punishing him.

There are some times when the puppy should be taken into the yard that will stimulate him to perform: first thing in the morning, after every meal, after any strenuous play, after a daytime nap, and before bed every evening. With the praise system, he should soon relate it to the required performance.

LIFE EXPECTANCY

Like their owners, dogs are living longer nowadays, but few will pass seventeen years, which is eighty-four human years. The record for canine longevity is claimed for a twenty-seven-and-a-quarter-year-old black Labrador that died in Great Britain, though there are less reliable reports of another dog tottering up to an incredible thirty-four years!

One year of the dog's life is equivalent to seven of human's, or so the saying goes, but it isn't true. A one-year-old bitch is mature and can have pups; a seven-year-old child cannot. Many dogs reach fifteen years of age but few folks celebrate their 105th birthday. A more realistic approach has been worked out by a French veterinarian, Dr. Lebeau. He has suggested that the first year of a dog's life equals fifteen human years, the second equals a further nine human years, and thereafter, each dog year counts for four human years. This provides us with the table shown below.

Age of dog	Equivalent age of a human
1 year	15 years
2 years	24 years
3 years	28 years
4 years	32 years
8 years	48 years
12 years	64 years
15 years	76 years
20 years	96 years

Cats and other pets

Do not force your new puppy to accept a cat. Holding a cat near a puppy so he can smell it is not advisable – the cat will object and it could be painful for the puppy if he gets scratched. Anyway, the cat will probably find a high place to keep out of the way for the first few days. Feed them both in

Below: *Dogs and cats can grow accustomed to each other and learn to live happily together, even sharing a bed and playing games.*

Above: *This Spaniel puppy is being introduced to a pet guinea pig. Neither animal seems stressed by the encounter but you should never leave your dog alone with a small pet.*

different places and don't let the puppy eat the cat's food; it may not suit his digestion. Sooner or later, the cat will venture close to the puppy, but if he gets too frisky the cat will defend itself. In this way, the puppy will soon learn to keep out of the cat's way.

In time it is usual for a dog and a cat to live together in harmony in the same house, even after a tense start. However, this does not mean that the dog will tolerate a strange cat running across the lawn.

Take special care to separate him from any pet rabbits, gerbils, hamsters, or other small animals, as they are a natural prey for a dog and it would be wise not to tempt him. When your puppy is a little older he can be introduced to any small pets under your supervision, and most dogs will learn to live alongside them.

Danger and hazards

CHECKLIST

Inside
- Fit gates at the top and bottom of flights of stairs
- Cover exposed cords and wires
- Unplug electrical appliances
- Cover outlets with plastic protector plugs
- Don't leave small chewable objects at ground level

Outside
- All fences should be high enough and secure
- Close gates securely
- Attach wire netting to the bottom of fencing
- Check for holes in netting and fencing
- Lock up poisons and sharp tools

Dogs like being outside if the weather suits them, and their yard becomes an extension of their territory. As puppies, they will explore every corner, so for obvious reasons you must make your yard escape-proof and remember that most puppies can squeeze through very small holes. As they grow, some of the taller breeds will jump 3–5 feet (1–1.5 m) if something attracts their attention. Securing wire netting on top of the fencing and then bending it over inward toward the dog's territory solves this particular problem.

Make sure also that any gates and yard doors close securely and cannot be opened by an inquisitive dog. Nor should there be a gap at the bottom under which the dog can crawl; if so, attach fairly strong wire netting to the gate or door at ground level.

Inside the house

There are danger points inside the house, too. When they are young, long, low dogs, such as Basset Hounds and Dachshunds, and large breeds, such as Wolfhounds, should not be allowed to go up and down stairs as their vertebrae can be overstressed, leading to spinal disk troubles in later life. A child gate at the bottom of the staircase will put an effective stop to this activity.

Electrical outlets, plugs, and trailing wires present an almost irresistible temptation to most inquisitive puppies, so cover the wires, unplug those that are not in use, and plug outlets with plastic protectors. You could even place a piece of furniture over the outlet.

With a puppy around, children have to learn to live on a higher level. Their habit of leaving their favorite toys on the floor will tempt the puppy who will pick up and chew any small plastic toy. This can be very dangerous as small pieces can lodge in the dog's stomach and even tear the lining, resulting in death or some very expensive veterinary treatment. Puppies also tend to frequently mark their territory with urine and clothes left on the floor are often targets.

▦ **Above:** *Small, low-slung dogs, such as Dachshunds, shouldn't be allowed to climb the stairs.*

▦ **Left:** *Don't leave temptation in your puppy's way. This Cocker Spaniel is chewing the TV remote control!*

Indoor kennels and travel crates

One of the great training aids is an indoor kennel, which can be a wooden box with a wire front, a plastic travel crate, or a simple wire cage. These are all available from pet stores and also from specialized vendors. It is easy to train your puppy to go into it happily by feeding him inside the crate; he will very soon enter willingly and the door can then be closed for a short while. This will prove of inestimable value if you want some peace to vacuum the carpet

■ **Left:** *A sturdy wooden box with a wire grill can be used for short periods or when traveling in the car.*

or to go shopping for an hour. However, do not keep him locked up for long. It is not cruel to crate dogs for short periods as

they like the security they experience inside it, but make sure that the container is of an adequate size. The dog should be able to stand up, stretch out, and lie on his side easily.

A travel crate is especially good in the car, where a wild young puppy leaping around at seventy miles an hour is not conducive to safe driving. It also offers security if your car is ever involved in an accident, as the car doors can fly open, releasing a frightened, loose dog who can become a danger to himself and to traffic.

■ **Left:** *For small dogs, such as these pretty Pomeranians, a plastic traveling crate is ideal for most car trips.*

■ **Above:** *A puppy can be caged in a wire crate fitted with a small rug or blanket and containing some of his favorite toys.*

At the veterinarian's

Tell your veterinarian that you are going to acquire a puppy and make sure he knows which breed so that he can find out in advance about any potential health problems before you take your new puppy in for his first visit. When the puppy has settled down after a couple of days you will need to introduce them to each other. However, do not put the puppy down on the sidewalk between your home and the veterinary clinic and, above all, do not set him down on the floor of the clinic. There may be other dogs waiting and because yours is a puppy, they are likely to be interested. Keep him well away from their inquisitive noses as there is a danger of infection, and most dogs visiting the veterinary clinic are there because there is something wrong with them.

between six and eight weeks of age, with a series of boosters approximately every two to three weeks, until twelve to twenty weeks of age, followed by annual revaccination. Vaccine recommendations vary according to disease, risk of exposure, type of vaccine used, individual animal, and the state in which you live.

■ **Left:** *The veterinarian will give your puppy a thorough examination and will look at his eyes, ears, nose, and mouth.*

Now is also the time to ask any questions that might be bothering you about your dog's diet, behavior, or health, and also about matters such as insurance.

■ **Below:** *When your puppy has his first vaccination, the veterinarian will check him all over to assess his general health.*

Vaccinations

The veterinarian will give your puppy a general examination and if your pup is healthy and old enough, he will receive his vaccinations. Several diseases are a threat to your dog's life: parvovirus, distemper, leptospirosis, hepatitis, Lyme disease, coronavirus, and rabies. It is essential that your dog is properly inoculated. Most veterinarians will perform the initial vaccination

GOOD SOCIAL SKILLS

Your dog needs good social skills if he is to become a well-behaved member of canine and human society. Thus, it is very important to socialize and train your puppy from the earliest age. This will help to prevent any behavior problems later on and make your dog more socially acceptable. Your dog must always be under complete control in any public place.

Leash training

The first essential accessories that you need are a collar and leash, in fact, two collars and leashes. Some trainers recommend that the first collar should be very light, like a cat collar, the wearing of which will not irritate the puppy. The leash can be made of light cloth, which is hardly noticeable. Thus, the puppy will learn to wear a collar without being aware of it. The second collar should be more substantial, probably made of leather, with a supple leather leash. An identification tag on which your name and telephone number have been engraved has to be attached to the collar your dog wears whenever he is outside your home. Do not engrave your dog's name on it; that would make it too easy for thieves.

Collars

A young puppy will need a lightweight collar made of nylon, soft leather, or fabric. He will grow out of it quite quickly so don't bother buying an expensive one.

DID YOU KNOW?

A traditional and most polite greeting in China when entering someone's home was to ask, "What is the honorable name of your dog?" This applied even where, as in most cases, no dog was owned. The old habit of keeping house dogs had declined and, instead, pottery figures of dogs were used to "guard" the dwelling. Nevertheless, the genteel etiquette of inquiring after the substitute pet continued up until recent years.

You can begin leash training almost as soon as the puppy arrives in the house. Let him run around wearing the collar for a

■ **Above:** *Let your puppy run around with the leash on to get him used to it but watch him carefully in case the leash gets caught on something.*

■ **Right:** *When a young puppy is old enough to take out after vaccinations, keep him on a leash in public places as there are always many distractions to tempt him away from you.*

little while and then add the light leash; he will quickly get accustomed to it trailing after him. Pick up the leash and follow him without applying any pressure to it. After a little while, assert some light pressure and try to guide him but don't make it so strong that he stops to fight it. Talk to him all the time in an encouraging way to boost his confidence.

Make certain that the collar is sufficiently tight that he cannot pull out of it, but at the same time it should not be so tight that it is strangling him. Continue the exercise outside in the yard. Make it fun and train in short bursts as puppies become easily bored, like young children.

If the teaching period lasts for too long, most puppies can think of something better to do.

When your puppy is ready to go out for a real walk, remember that all cars and trucks appear as huge, smelly, noisy monsters to him, so he may be afraid. Carry him in your arms around the block two or three times for a day or two before you put him down. Speak to him gently all the

■ **Left:** *To get your puppy used to traffic and sidewalks, carry him in your arms for a day or two before walking on the sidewalk.*

while; it will help to build up his confidence knowing that you are there to protect him. Never allow him to walk in any traffic areas without a collar and leash; a dog does not understand that cars can kill him and neither does he know or care that his presence on the road may cause an accident for which you can be held responsible.

■ **Above:** *Your pup may be reluctant to walk on the leash at first and may hang back. Don't get angry at him. Try to make it fun.*

Toys and games

A young dog needs lots of things to do and his brain needs to be stimulated. In the wild, he would be taught to track animals, to fight predators, and to catch prey. However, the domestic dog has none of these skills to learn and therefore you should provide alternatives. By doing so, you will minimize the chances of your puppy becoming bored and then engaging in destructive behavior. Toys and games are the answer; most dog toys are now virtually indestructible, though not totally, as you will soon find out. Dogs, particularly terriers, love squeaky toys and will not be content until they have found the squeak and killed it. Sometimes, however,

they may adopt a soft toy, which retrievers or spaniels will carry around in their mouth.

Do not play tug-of-war with a soft toy – you will be training your puppy to be destructive and possessive. All dogs can be taught to play with a ball but be careful that the ball is not too small. Dogs' jaws can open very wide and they can swallow quite large objects. If they should accidentally

■ **Below:** *Tug-of-war games are great fun for both dog and owner, but you must win the game more often than the dog does or he will never bring anything back. A powerful puppy, such as this Rottweiler, may be too strong for a child, and adult supervision is advisable.*

TOYS FOR PLAYING GAMES

1 Soft toys: Ideal for retrieving and exercises

2 Tug toys: Ideal for strong and boisterous dogs

3 Squeaky balls and toys: Fine for smaller dogs

4 Kongs: Ideal for mental stimulation when your dog is left alone

5 Rubber rings and toys: Perfect for tug and fetch

6 Frisbees and tennis balls: Ideal for playing outdoor fetch

Another good game is to teach your dog to find your child. Some dogs love to push a football with their nose, and kids can play kickball with their pet. Rubber rings are fun to throw and pull but the ultimate throwing game is with a Frisbee. Dogs get great exercise running and leaping for it.

Good pet shops will have a variety of toys, and you should choose those that are said to be indestructible with no metal or plastic. The "Kong" is particularly good – a hollow, unusually shaped ball that can be stuffed with small food treats. Your dog will chase it happily for hours, trying to get the food out. Nylon bones keep dogs occupied as well as keeping their teeth clean.

swallow a rubber or plastic ball, the repercussions can be very serious. Do not give your puppy an old shoe or slipper to chew and destroy – dogs notoriously ignore the difference between old and new shoes.

Throw a ball just in front of him, then make a fuss of him when he returns it and persuade him gently to drop it. When he is proficient at retrieving, hide the ball for him to find, close by to start with but gradually increasing the distance.

■ *Below: Most puppies enjoy playing "fetch" with a ball. It allows them to run freely and have some fun.*

Games you can play

Games for dogs are invariably those of catch, retrieve, and hide-and-seek. Dogs derive the most fun out of chasing and retrieving balls. However, you must make sure that the ball is not too small in case it slips down a dog's throat and chokes him. Start when your dog is a young puppy.

■ *Left: Reduce the risk of losing your best footwear by not giving your puppy any personal items to chew or play with, especially shoes, socks, and children's favorite toys.*

Socialization

When a puppy faces something he has never encountered before, his first instinct is to run, and it is up to you, his owner, to socialize him in such a way that he will not be afraid of anything. He should not be overprotected from any household noises, and it is a good idea to get him accustomed to the sound of such appliances as the vacuum cleaner, dishwasher, radio, television, and washing machine. In fact, even dropping a trash can cover about 15 feet (5 m) away from him is not a bad idea.

After his vaccinations, you must introduce him to the people who visit your house regularly: the mail carrier and the trash collector. Let your friends and neighbors handle him and, when he is old enough, take him into town or to

■ **Left:** *This West Highland White Terrier puppy is meeting some older dogs. Most adult dogs will not be aggressive to young puppies.*

the open-air market and let him mix with people, always on the leash and under your control.

Puppy socialization classes are a good way of getting him used to

meeting other dogs as well as a wide range of people. Ask your veterinarian for the details of the nearest class. They are now common in most areas.

■ **Left:** *If friends come to visit with their dogs, encourage them to handle and play with the puppy. It is important to introduce your puppy to as many new people as possible.*

■ **Right:** *Puppies will get most of their normal daily exercise requirements from general play and activity with you at home. Therefore, make sure that your walks aren't too long at first. Use them to help your new dog develop social skills and reinforce his training, especially leash training.*

Exercise

Young puppies get all the exercise they require from their own exuberance when running and playing, and there is no need for formal exercise. In fact, it could harm a puppy's development if he is forced into too much activity at too young an age. The age at which it is necessary varies from breed to breed, but the average is probably between five and six months – the breeder or your veterinarian can advise. For a large dog, such as an Irish Wolfhound, too much exercise can be harmful for a growing puppy whose bones are still growing. It is also a good idea to start taking your puppy for short walks on the leash.

You can teach your puppy some simple but essential commands, such as "*Sit*," "*Stay*," and "*Come*," at home. More formal training can begin when he is about six months of age and it is advisable to attend obedience classes at your local dog training school where there will be some knowledgeable trainers.

■ **Above:** *Like many other giant breeds, Irish Wolfhound puppies should not exercise excessively before the age of six months. Let them play in the yard rather than take them for long walks.*

Social responsibilities

Behavioral scientists have proved that the ownership of a dog is definitely beneficial to adults and particularly to children, but in the light of today's social attitudes, an owner must train a dog to fit into modern society's perception of what constitutes acceptable social behavior.

As a responsible dog owner, you must be certain to obey the dog ownership laws and regulations in your state. For example, your dog should be vaccinated against rabies and licensed by the animal control authorities in your county. You should be certain your dog is properly confined in your home or yard and that he does not run loose in the neighborhood or chase your neighbor's livestock. If your dog strays, he can encounter

trouble and become injured (accidental breedings, dog fights, hit by car) or damage property (knocking over trash cans or digging up gardens). Remember that you are legally responsible for your pet's activities, and if your dog causes an accident, damages property, or bites a person or animal, you are liable. Each county and state has laws and regulations pertaining to dog ownership and you need to become informed as to the specifics of the laws in your area.

Regulatory authorities are taking a stance on promoting clean beaches and parks and are also enforcing laws under which dog owners can be fined should they allow their dog to foul public places without picking up after them. There are many hygienic

methods of doing this and various gadgets can be obtained from pet shops to pick up dog feces.

Owners would be wise to always carry something with which to scoop up the dog mess, even if it's just a plastic bag, when they're out walking their dogs.

Every day thousands of dogs find their way to animal shelters. In the unlikely event that you lose your dog, you will want to be sure your pet has a permanent form of identification, such as microchip implantation or tattooing. A microchip can be read with a special scanner. It is about the size of a grain of rice and is assigned a unique number that is maintained in a data registry. Your veterinarian can microchip your dog. The procedure requires no anesthesia and is quick and simple.

Good dog behavior

When we take a dog into our family we want him to be acceptable to everyone who comes to our home, whether they are our friends, our children's friends, or callers on business. We do not want our new family member to be a nuisance to us or anyone else, either in the car or when walking on the street or in the country. Our dogs have to learn good manners and we have to teach them – by patient repetition, by watchfulness for instinctive behavior that has to be controlled, and by teaching the dog to trust us. First of all, we must understand the dog's senses, the way in which they work and how they are controlled.

Chapter Three

COMMUNICATING WITH YOUR DOG

The dog is probably the best communicator in the entire animal world; perhaps this is why, for thousands of years, dogs have been the favored companions and workmates of the human race. And from the earliest days of the dog/human relationship, dogs were not only used to help with hunting, guarding, and herding, but were also regarded with great affection.

Right: *We have taken over the role of pack leader and in return for shelter and food, dogs give us loyalty and affection.*

This relationship is supported by the finding of the skeleton of an elderly human, clasping the skeleton of a puppy of about five months. These remains were discovered at a burial site in Israel where the grave was estimated to be 12,000 years old. It may be that this puppy was in fact a tamed wolf. However, it has now been established that all modern dogs are descended from wolves that indirectly offered themselves to our ancient ancestors as suitable candidates for domestication by becoming part of a human community.

The man/dog relationship

Professor James Serpell wrote in his book, *The Domestic Dog* (Cambridge University Press), that all archaeological evidence indicates that the dog was the first species to be domesticated. There was a mutual advantage bargain to be made; the wolf that came in from the cold instinctively helped man in hunting and pulling down quarry and in tracking wounded animals. In return, gradually relinquishing its wild state, the wolf had the benefit of shelter and food and, eventually, shared company and a tolerable pack leader.

It is probable that relatively few wolves were domesticated in this way. Those wolves that did form a relationship with the primitive tribes would have mated with other like-minded wolves. Many generations of mating within this small gene pool would have gradually produced an animal that bore little resemblance physically or temperamentally to the wild wolf; the dog was emerging as a separate and individual animal. And the dog has never left man's side, at least in the Western world. Where there is a break in the dog-man relationship now, it is brought about by man's intransigence, never by the dog choosing to be wild again.

Although some dogs may, on impulse, break out of their homes, whether they are impelled by an overriding desire to seek a willing mate, or to revel in the fast chase of some quarry, these dogs will invariably come home again,

provided that they have not been injured in a traffic accident. A dog that has temporarily lost touch with his owner through yielding to the temptation to chase some quarry in the woods or through open country will usually return to the place where the owner and dog were last together, or to the place where the walk started. Very few dogs want to be on the run permanently, and there are, in current records of dogs rescued from cruel and neglectful homes, many examples of dogs that seem devoted to harsh and unkind owners.

In the United States, feral dogs – dogs that live and breed far away from the homes that once sheltered them – are not a significant problem, as are feral cats. Dogs rarely change their homes deliberately or voluntarily, by leaving one home and

applying at another for food and shelter, as many cats quite often do. So, can this very special relationship and devotion, as strong as ever today, be reinforced by the ease with which man and dog communicate and the pleasure that both species can take in their exchanges?

The reason why many families make the effort to have pets – and pet ownership, however enjoyable, can indeed be an effort in today's busy life – is because the dog can become the separate and inviolate confidant of the whole family.

Children can gain a tremendous amount of comfort and stability from having a canine best friend who shares their disappointments, misunderstandings, and troubles, yet never blames them, never tells their secrets, and never transfers his allegiance to any other person. This unique friendship is

▓ **Above:** *A sporting dog, such as this young retriever with a pheasant in his mouth, learns to work with his owner as part of the human pack.*

especially valuable in the modern world where many traditional human relationships are no longer permanent. The high level of mutual communication that we have with our dogs is the basis of real friendship on a special level between dogs and their owners.

DID YOU KNOW?

The Australian aborigines use dingoes (wild dogs) for warmth on cold nights by sleeping with them clasped in their arms. Women, when not carrying their young children, will often "wear" a dog draped across the lower back with the head and tail in the crook of their arms as a kidney warmer.

▓ **Left:** *Your dog will always be your devoted companion, giving you love and affection, and will never be judgmental.*

COMMUNICATION MECHANISMS

Dogs have many ways of communicating with us; they have voices, facial expressions, manipulation of ears and lips, body language, a neat use of paws, and a very visible signaling mechanism with their tails. Dogs usually have very acute hearing so that they can hear our slightest whisper. They use their warm pink tongues to dry tears or to beseech us to notice them; they will raise our spirits by playing simple games very enthusiastically, and their coats give us tactile pleasure. And dogs are closer to us than we will ever be to them; they have so many hours in which to watch us, to assess our facial expressions and our behavior, and to interpret our moods.

The dog's voice

Dogs have an extraordinary vocal repertoire; they can talk to us in a myriad of ways that we can interpret and understand, provided we take a close interest in them. The dog's vocalizations range from a murmur, usually directed straight to the human ear, to a whine, a pleading bark, a serious warning or an aggressive bark, an attention-seeking bark, a low growl or a very deep intense growl, and also a muted howl ranging in intensity over several notes. The latter, quite musical howl is usually made as a protest against strident noise from some outside source, such as some television commercials. The classic long howl is usually made from a sitting position with the dog's head and throat thrown back into an almost vertical line so that the voice travels as far as possible.

The howl, which is particularly annoying or distressing to the neighbors, is thought to be a rallying call to the pack, triggered by loneliness. Dogs do not howl when they're in pain; in fact, a dog suffering physical discomfort from an injury is almost always completely silent. Nor does a howling dog forecast a tragedy in the neighborhood. These two old-fashioned beliefs still surface sometimes, even among city people when they want to complain about noisy dogs causing them disturbance.

Singing is a talent only a few dogs express; some dogs vocalize in a cadence of notes when they are very pleased, such as when their owner has arrived home after an absence. These dogs can be taught to respond as a duet when their owners sing back to them, and both the dog and the human can enjoy this harmony. The murmur, made with mouth closed and straight into the human ear, is a demonstration of greeting and affection. Enjoy this spontaneous expression by your dog; he certainly will not murmur to a stranger or someone he is not fond of or does not trust to handle him gently. Puppies in the nest murmur into the mother's ear, which is usually turned back to allow maximum access; the puppy also relaxes the outer flap of its ear, one of the signs of

Left: *Dogs make a wide variety of sounds, ranging from barks and growls to howls and murmurs. Some dogs can even "sing" along with their lucky owners.*

pleasant submission. All puppies are born completely without hearing though they can vocalize at birth using the humming murmur for pleasure and satisfaction, usually while feeding from their mother, and also telling the world when they are unhappy, hungry, cold, or ill by using a thin, high-pitched wail.

The ear canals do not open until nearly three weeks after the birth. As soon as the puppies can hear they start to use their voices, ranging through sharp little barks at the arrival of the breeder and food, to growls and mini-roars when playing competitively with their littermates.

Whines

Your dog will direct his whine at you too. The whine is used to ask you to fulfill his need or wish of some kind, whether to have the door opened or for treats to be handed out. Enjoy the fact that your dog is communicating with you and also that you can interpret what he is asking for. You will not want to comply with every whined wish but when you do so, try to make it a happy time because your dog asked and you understood what he wanted.

If the request is obscure, make an effort to find out what the dog wants; touch this or that object and show the dog things that he normally uses. Is it the food dish, his leash, or a toy? You will get a very positive response of tail wagging, dancing on hind legs, or another expression of joy when you find the key to the pleading whine. Less vocal dogs will stand and stare silently at the object they want made available to them; these are usually serious canine requests but can also be converted into a game in which the dog has to tell you what he wants and then you grant the request.

Sound sensitivity

Howling in response to a loud noise or a particular musical sound, such as a strident trumpet or violin, seems to mean that this noise is actually painful to a dog's very sensitive hearing. Remember that dogs' ears are much more acute and more discerning than our own. Sound sensitivity of this degree may often coincide with a fear of fireworks and thunder.

Dogs can hear sounds on a much higher register than we can appreciate, so very high-pitched sounds can inflict actual pain. Dogs will often show fear and resentment, even anger, at some pieces of household equipment that make a painful sound for them. Many breeds with pricked-

Right: *You will soon recognize the sounds your dog makes and learn to understand what he is trying to tell you. His body language will also provide you with clues.*

Above: *A dog's hearing is extremely sensitive and many prick up their ears and swivel them to locate sounds.*

up, wide-open ears, such as the German Shepherd Dog, can suffer acutely in a household that is drenched with loud sounds.

Fear of thunder is made more acute if a family member is also nervous about the noise; being brave and not reacting to storms will help your dog and may help you too. Because his first instinct is to run away from an overpowering sound, provide a refuge when you know a noise is going to occur: either a covered crate that will insulate the dog from the noise, or perhaps access to a bedroom where he can dive under the bed, or even a closet that is insulated by its contents.

Try not to act with any urgency or fear but always make your actions quite matter-of-fact and calm, and then your dog will imitate your mood.

Deafness

While thinking about the sounds that can inspire fear in dogs, we must remember also that some puppies are born deaf, in one or both ears. White-coated dogs are more likely to be affected by this inherited fault. Even partially deaf dogs should not be bred.

Susceptible breeds, including Dalmatians, Border Collies, white Bull Terriers, and white Boxers, should be tested as puppies before they are sold at eight weeks old. The old-fashioned way of testing by dropping a tin dish behind the puppy is too inaccurate to be of any use in deciding the future of a puppy – the puppy may see the movement or feel the air vibration as the testing object falls. The

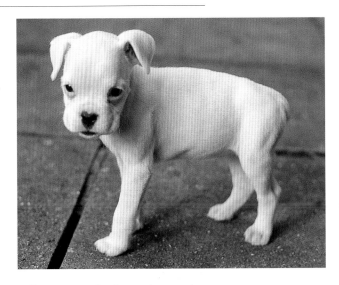

▥ **Right:** *White dogs, like this Boxer puppy, are susceptible to deafness.*

definitive computerized test, called the Brain-stem Auditory Response Test, is quite painless and can be used on puppies from five weeks of age. Your veterinarian can refer you to a specialist to test for hearing capacity.

In old age, dogs may lose some of their hearing capacity just as humans do, or chronic ear disease may have the same effect, but these dogs will usually know all they need to know about their owners and their way of life so partial deafness is not a tragedy for them. There should never be any need to shout at a dog.

Even stone-deaf puppies can be trained, by the use of human facial expressions, hand gestures, and body language, to be happy and safe companions.

Sight

Dogs that live in a human family keep their eyes on their owner and other caretakers all the time. Dogs watch us constantly; they can predict what we are going to do next, and even what we are thinking of doing. You have made, as your ancestors did long ago, a mutual agreement with the dog to live and work together. Your life has no secrets from your dog; even a half-asleep dog is well aware of everything you do and is poised to accompany you in whatever you choose,

▥ **Right:** *Dogs learn a lot about us and how to communicate and respond to us from our facial expressions and the hand signals we use.*

however boring an expedition it may be from the dog's natural inclination. Because your dog's eyes are almost always on you,

Right: *The dog's eyes are extremely expressive and are almost always on you. Respond with a smile and you will see his face soften.*

Right: *Whippets were bred for the chase and to focus on their prey, and thus their field of vision is very narrow (only 200 degrees).*

that the whole face softens: the lips spread instead of being tense, and the ears drop. It does you good to smile back. Both you and your dog are at peace with the world! And if you are not very happy at some time, then the knowledge that your dog has sympathy and comfort to offer you can be helpful and cheering.

However, a long, hard stare right into your dog's eyes is a challenge signal and should be used only when it is obvious that the dog is about to do something that is normally forbidden. Never "hard stare" an angry or a hostile dog or one that is defending his own territory. It is better to watch the dog with an oblique glance

while planning your next move.

A puppy's eyes are open and its sight is fully developed by about fourteen days after birth. Unless a dog has a particular sight defect, it can usually see better than humans in dim light or darkness. At a distance, dogs see moving objects best, so if you are calling your dog from a long distance, use hand signals.

A dog's field of vision

Dogs see differently than we do and they have a larger field of vision whereby they can see things to the sides and rear. Their accuracy in judging distance is determined by the amount of overlap.

enjoy the pleasant habit of some mutual smiles. When you catch your dog's eye, you will notice

The mouth

In both humans and dogs, the mouth is a very important organ of relationship. Young puppies will lick around the mouth of their mother to entreat her to disgorge partly digested food for them. Puppies playing together often use open-mouthed biting as part of their play strategy. They will also try to lick around the lip and chin area of their owners, and it may be that this impulse is the origin of leaping up to people's faces in greeting, a habit that we do not wish to encourage.

Some breeds, particularly retrievers, sometimes have the ability to produce a grin of greeting, with the open mouth showing the teeth, much like a human smile. We have to learn to differentiate between this grin and the true angry snarl grimace where more teeth are bared and the mouth is wide open.

■ **Left:** *Some dogs can smile and look happy. Just take a look at this cheerful Pomeranian!*

Scent recognition

Dogs have around fifty times the capacity for detecting scents as humans possess; scenting is very important to a dog's way of life. The enormous number of scent-detecting cells in the dog's nasal area allows it to detect a far wider range of smells than we can, and also enables dogs to be sensitive to faint scents. Dogs learn a great deal about their world and the other animals and the people who pass through it by savoring the distinctive scents that are left behind on the ground, on fallen leaves, and on gateposts. Dogs habitually do their own scent-marking by depositing urine and feces and also by leaving traces from the sweat glands on their feet. Another animal inspecting such a scenting post is like a human being reading the local newspaper – he instantly finds out what animal has been that way, how old he was, what species, where he was going, on what purpose, and whether the passing animal was looking for a mate, for food, or a place to burrow. Where several dogs are kept together in a household, it can be noticed that the leader of the dog pack will "countersign" urine deposits made by the other dogs, all the animals seeming to deliberately urinate on the same patch.

The scents of the dog's owner and the rest of the household are important to a dog, and an

■ **Left:** *Terriers and spaniels are more likely to be on the scent trail of their "prey" rather than checking which other dogs have strayed into their "territory."*

Right: *When dogs meet and greet each other, they do so by smell. Each will sniff the other dog.*

important means of recognition of a familiar person in different clothes or in an unusual place. This talent is also used by search-and-rescue dogs that are given their scent clue by being allowed to smell the sweat on a garment that the victim has used. Human footprints also emit individual smells, and an adult dog can successfully follow a trail on grass four hours after it was laid. Many dogs seem to dislike strong perfume, perhaps because it masks the natural scent that they need to recognize.

Tail signals

When a dog has its full tail, it is a very valuable adjunct both to communication with humans and with other dogs. A tail can be wagged in pleasure, particularly on greeting, but if it is held out stiffly behind the dog, it is usually part of an aggression pose. When a dog with a tail that is normally "teapot handle-style" is truly and happily relaxed, the tail will straighten out, all except for the last tiny curl.

Below: *Although the Staffordshire Bull Terrier is holding his tail up, it is held quite stiffly and, together with the fact that the ears are down, indicates that the dog is ready to take a defense posture. In contrast, the jaunty Jack* Russell is enthusiastically greeting the somewhat apprehensive Great Dane whose tail is drooping down between his legs. The terrier's tail is up and wagging and his ears are pricked as he jumps up at the larger dog.

HUMAN/DOG COMMUNICATION

In an ideal situation, we should start communicating with a new puppy while he is very young and still with the breeder and the rest of the litter. If you are able to visit the litter frequently, it is a good

■ **Above:** *The first meeting can often be a nervous and tentative affair as you and the puppy get to know each other better. Be patient, get down to his level, and let him sniff your hands and face. He will soon relax.*

idea to do so and once you have chosen your puppy, take every opportunity to get to know each other in order to build a firm foundation for a happy transfer to your own home. Ask if you and your children may hold the puppy; let him sniff at your faces and hands. Make sure as many people as possible talk to the puppy in gentle but natural voices. If

■ **Above:** *Puppies crave company and affection and will always respond with enthusiasm to their new owner.*

you have decided on a name, by all means use it, but if the choice is still open, just call the little dog "puppy." Most dogs will respond to "puppy," used occasionally, for their whole lives. Let your new puppy become familiar with the voices of all the members of your family. Always use a light and pleasant voice, never a deep resonance that could easily be confused with a growl.

Possibly the most important act of communication, once you have the new puppy in your home, is to call your puppy to you often. Always crouch down to receive him with open arms and make sure he knows that coming to you is worthwhile, either by giving him a small food reward or a lot of fuss and praise. This is the foundation of all human/dog communication so make it worthwhile to your dog!

■ **Left:** *Play with your puppy every day and praise him lavishly when he comes to you when you call him. Make a fuss over him and reward him with a hug or a favorite treat.*

Chapter Four

CURING COMMON PROBLEMS

We, as dog owners, can create some behavior problems in our dogs. We ask so much of them; we expect them to share our lives and our homes and cars, yet we also expect this pack-oriented animal to be content to be alone when we do not want canine company. We want the dog's services as a warning of intruders;

Right: *Boredom or lack of mental stimulation, especially in active breed types like the Boxer, can sometimes lead to destructive behavior.*

however, we do not want him to create any unnecessary noise, nor do we expect our dog to ruin any of our possessions. When a dog fails to live up to the canine image we have created, we say he has a

behavior problem, meaning the dog does not always behave in the way we want and expect.

A new industry, employing a large number of variously qualified animal behaviorists, has grown around the need to stop dogs from doing what comes naturally to them – chewing, gnawing, barking, and urine-marking on the dwarf conifers. It's possible to achieve modification of some of a dog's more annoying behavior traits if we try to analyze what is causing the behavior and why the dog finds it necessary to do it. Whatever the problem is, it's not done to annoy us, that's for sure. The dog does whatever he feels he must in the prevailing situation, and probably our annoyance at his behavior is only peripheral according to the dog.

The first night in your home

After all the fun and the cuddles and kisses of the day, your new puppy will find himself absolutely alone for the very first time in his life – no mother, no brothers and sisters, and not even the scent of where they have been. He is in a strange room with no familiar

noises, and he will feel abandoned, lonely, and frightened. Cruel, yes! You could say that, but you did make the rule – no dogs in the bedrooms – and you are starting as you plan to continue. As a side effect of this, however, you may be instilling into your puppy a

long-lasting insecurity, a phobia about being left alone.

Your most constructive plan alteration is to take the puppy into your bedroom, keeping him in a deep box or in the wire crate you have bought for him. Put the box beside your bed so that you

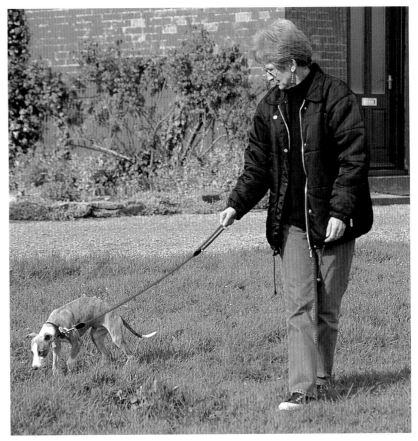

can just put a hand down to soothe the puppy when he cries. In this way there is no break in building trust and confidence between you and the puppy. He will surely wake up at first light, and you then have the opportunity to rush him outside so that you are continuing the house-training.

This first-thing-in-the-morning visit to the yard is the one that always gets immediate results, so capitalize on it. The puppy will enjoy a little game afterwards or you may want to feed him early. No matter; let the puppy shape your day while he is new to your home. When he has confidence in you and knows your rooms and your household scent, you may want to move him. However, in many ways it is advantageous to have your dog close to you at night anyway.

Right: *Always take your puppy out into the yard first thing in the morning.*

House soiling

It is both disconcerting and annoying to find that your dog, who may have been perfectly house-trained for a long time, has suddenly started to urinate or worse in the house, overnight or when you are out.

Is your dog unwell?

First of all, think illness. Are there any indications that the dog is not well? Is he perhaps drinking more? Does he have diarrhea? Is it inevitable that he cannot wait as long as you expect him to? Can you make it possible for him to get outside when he needs to? Have you made any change in the feeding plan? Is there the possibility that the formula of the food you give can have been altered? Then think

disturbance. Are there workmen or visitors in the house, or even another animal introduced? Are there any new noises from neighboring houses?

Many dogs are great creatures of routine and they can feel very disturbed by any domestic changes. Their expression of anxiety may be demonstrated in an intestinal disturbance. Watch carefully for a few days and then, if there is no improvement, consult your veterinarian.

Left: *Check that your dog's diet has not changed recently. This may cause him to soil inside the house.*

Build an outside run

It is a good idea, if at all possible, to create for your dog his own exit from the kitchen or the utility room in which you keep him when you are busy or out of the house. You could build a small yard-type well-fenced concrete run for the dog to which he has access through a dog door. He will soon learn how to utilize his run and he will also have an alternative environment for when you're out; quite the opposite to being shut inside the house. Our dog yard is also used as a clothes-drying area and for storing flowerpots, quite a dog's delight, but damage is surprisingly minimal.

Dogs that are house-trained will expect to go outside to relieve themselves when they need to do so, either overnight or when you are out during the daytime. You must be prepared to make some allowances, especially for the time in the fall when the house doors are shut again, having perhaps stood open practically all summer.

The dog has to ask to go out at this time, and younger dogs may find this concept difficult to grasp, so you may have to go back to an hourly or two-hourly routine of putting him out for a while until he adjusts.

Elderly dogs

Remember also the disabilities of old age: elderly dogs tend to drink more and they need to urinate in considerable quantities. If they also suffer from arthritis, they may find it difficult to get up from their beds. Understand and do not grumble but plan to make their life easier for them.

Male dogs

Some male dogs may perform urine marking indoors if they feel that some provocation warrants it – a bitch in season in the house or next door, or even a new baby coming into the home. In fact, any creature with a completely different smell may trigger the dog's need to mark the premises as his own.

Cleaning up

You must clean up all indoor mistakes thoroughly but do not use an ammonia-based product as that will compound the smell of urine. Supermarkets now sell a number of floor, upholstery, and carpet cleaners that are specially formulated for cleaning up our pets' mistakes and they do work very effectively.

Summary

You cannot eradicate the soiling behaviors mentioned other than by investigating the cause and doing what you can to alter the situation. You may well indicate to your dog that you are not pleased, but otherwise the dog should not be blamed.

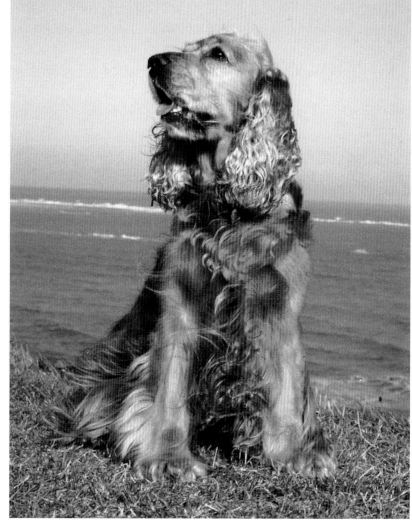

▐ **Left:** *You may have to face the fact that even though your elderly dog is still fairly fit and active, he may start to suffer from the ailments that come with old age. If he drinks more, he may find it difficult to hold his urine and may soil inside the house.*

Play-biting

It can be a great disappointment, especially to children, when their new puppy that they just long to cuddle just seems to be intent on biting them constantly. Those tiny sharp teeth can inflict some quite painful bites. You must train your puppy from the beginning that *biting is unacceptable!*

When you get your puppy at around eight weeks old, he should have his first set of baby teeth, but the second, and permanent, teeth will be coming through until he is about four months old.

The pain of teething causes the puppy to need to gnaw, unfortunately often at your hand or ankles. Tell your puppy, "*No!*" whenever he bites and be sure to have some hard nylon bones handy to push into the puppy's mouth to gnaw on. Our most recent puppy had a passion for undoing shoelaces – some twenty times a day we had to retie them! Then suddenly she stopped needing to do this and gave up the annoying habit – we never found out why. Perhaps it was a particular tooth that had eventually come in.

You should express displeasure at hand biting; a sharp "*Ouch!*" "*No!*" or probably overexaggerating the pain felt, as well as giving the puppy something more suitable to bite, will be the best deterrent.

■ **Above:** *Short-faced dogs like this Pug can find teething especially painful and you should check their mouths regularly for infection or damaged teeth.*

Never let this puppy-biting stop you from doing something you want or need to do to the puppy, such as handling or grooming him. If it is really necessary, you can resort to a basket muzzle, which you can put on at such times.

Your veterinarian or pet shop can supply a suitable muzzle, even for the difficult-to-fit short-faced breeds.

■ **Left:** *All puppies go through a spell of play-biting, especially when they are teething. When your puppy bites you, cry out in pain so that he realizes he is hurting you.*

EDIBLE CHEWS TO HELP WITH TEETHING

1 Treated real bone: Ideal for strong and boisterous dogs; will keep them occupied for a long time
2 Real hide strips: Strong taste and smell will tempt most dogs but they can become smelly over time
3 Rawhide strips, bones, and toys: Ideal for most dogs, and especially good for teething dogs; they won't damage the dog's mouth or teeth as they soften easily
4 Compressed chews and bones: Most dogs love these but don't give too many at a time as they can upset a puppy's tummy; they also crumble quickly

Car travel

It is absolutely essential that your new dog get used to car travel. Even if you have no need for a car yourself, you will inevitably have to take the dog to a veterinary clinic and perhaps further if you are referred to a specialist. Many taxi companies now refuse on principle to carry dogs because of the possibility of hair shedding – dogs do sometimes shed excessive quantities of hair through excitement or fear.

If a friend is kind enough to offer you transportation, you want to be confident that your dog will behave well in their car.

Your new puppy should ride home comfortably in someone's arms or, if the driver is alone, in a deep box placed in the front on the passenger's seat. It is safest to place the box on the backseat and secure it with a seat belt. Take the trouble to accustom the puppy to the car very gradually. Park the vehicle in the shade and let the puppy explore the car, then sit on the backseat and attract the puppy to sit with you, perhaps to fall asleep.

The car needs to be perceived as a restful, contented place, so try to keep the excitement rating low, as some dogs do tend to get overexcited when in the car and subsequently will behave badly.

You have to decide where the dog will travel when he is older. If you have chosen a large breed, you will probably consider buying one of the specially constructed and shaped dog crates that are designed to fit into the hatchback of a car. The advantage is that your dog will have plenty of

Right: *Let your puppy explore the car before you take him on a trip in it. Don't allow your puppy to run around in the car. For his own safety, he should be put in a crate either on the rear seat or in the back of the car. The crate should be well ventilated and always shielded from direct sunlight.*

room, and the wire construction of the crate will act as some protection for him if there should ever be a rear-end accident. A smaller dog can ride in a small crate placed on the backseat. In either system, the crate may be

Left: *A specially constructed wire crate that will fit snuggly into the back of a hatchback is a good investment. It will protect your dog, keeping him safe, when you're driving.*

Hard chews

Simulated bones and hard chews will keep most dogs happy for hours and are good for their teeth and jaws. They will bring relief to puppies that are teething.

covered with a light sheet to protect against sunlight and also to prevent the dog from watching the road and perhaps objecting to other dogs that are walking or riding past his car.

Drive very gently on the first few "learning" outings, going only a short distance at a time with a break for a talk and a cuddle at some point during the expedition. Maybe drive to a friend's house nearby and then give your puppy a little time to enjoy exploring their yard before getting back into the car for the return trip.

If you have a sport utility vehicle, the space needed to crate a very big dog on the backseat may be formidable. The answer is to buy a car harness for the dog, which will fasten onto the attachment for the seat belt. The fastening attaches to a comfortable harness but this must never be attached to a collar or neck chain.

Early in life many dogs tend to drool or be actually carsick. Dogs are best taken in the car on an empty stomach (very empty), possibly twelve or more hours

after their last meal. Then when the ride's over the dog can be fed as a "reward."

If the dog is distressed in the car, do not sympathize. Just clean him up and drive on. Hopefully, he will get over these carsickness reactions in quite a short time, just as children have to. In the meantime, fasten a waterproof bib around him so cleaning him up is not such a problem.

Home alone

Being alone in a room for a short time is another of the lessons that a puppy should learn in his first weeks in your home. Puppies need quiet and rest in any case, so being left alone in the kitchen or utility room is a good beginning. Make sure the "time out" is quite short and do not introduce any element of retribution for bad behavior.

Tidy up the room unobtrusively before putting the puppy in, remembering that he will walk off with and probably chew any object that you have recently handled and that has your scent on it. Line the puppy's crate with some soft material and leave a soft toy and a nylon chewing bone where they can be found. The door of the crate should be left open. Leave also a small untippable bowl of water. Perhaps leave the radio on, tuned to a talk station so the puppy hears a human voice. Put the puppy into the room, perhaps with a tiny piece of biscuit as a present, then quietly shut the door and walk away. No good-byes ever, whether you are going out for ten minutes or two hours.

▌ **Left:** *Get your dog accustomed to sitting quietly while you are busy doing other things. It's always a good idea to let him have something he can chew on, such as a nylon chewing bone.*

▌ **Above:** *No young puppy likes to be left at home alone. Don't leave him for too long and give him some toys and chews to keep him occupied.*

Dogs are natural pack animals and do not like to be left alone, but most have to endure this experience and they do come to accept it. If your puppy cries when you shut the door, just say, "*Quiet, quiet*" and walk away. When he has been quiet for, say, five minutes, open the door and let him out. Your behavior at this stage is critical. Do not make a great fuss over the puppy; just take this whole routine as an ordinary day-to-day experience. It is also probably a good idea to follow the "time out" by going into the room used with the puppy and finding something to do there, so that you and the puppy can be companionable together in a quiet situation and he does not link this room with always being left alone. The next day and every day, repeat this routine until the puppy accepts short periods of solitary confinement happily.

As the puppy grows, his owners will probably need to be away for longer periods. It is very important to make your exit and your return very low key. Having unobtrusively tidied the room in which the dog is to be left, making sure that all cabinets are firmly closed, shut the dog in, remembering to leave the radio on quietly, and possibly closing the blinds so that people cannot peer in. Just go, quietly and undemonstratively, without

SINS OF SOLITARY CONFINEMENT

It is really not fair to blame your dog for what he has done in your absence; certainly it is too late to think of a reprimand for something that may have been done an hour ago. So say nothing, but take note, and plan what you can do to prevent more damage from occurring again in the same place.

Table or chair legs chewed?
You can buy a liquid, unpleasant to taste but quite safe, to paint on wood. Probably the staff at your local veterinary practice can recommend a suitable product for you to use.

Cabinets open and contents scattered?
This is your fault! You must find a better way to close them.

Houseplants pulled down and chewed?
Move them to a safer place – the room where the puppy is going to have to stay alone needs to be stripped of all temptations.

House-training broken down?
If the dog cannot get outside, remember to put down some newspaper in the area that has been soiled.

any impassioned good-byes that will only make the dog feel that this is a big event.

Your return should be just the same: come into the house, take off your coat, and let your dog out

of confinement, but do not make too much fuss over him. It is a good idea if you both have a short walk around the yard together or a little play, but do nothing that will heighten his excitement.

The barking and/or howling problem

It is normal for dogs to bark a warning when they sense that there are intruders in their territory. Most of us want our dogs to warn us if there are strangers around or salesmen approaching the door. But dogs, even tiny dogs, seem to become incensed if anyone approaches their property, and a warning bark can become a tirade and escalate into a howl, and that is when the neighbors start to complain. We want the dog to bark but not to go on incessantly.

For advice on teaching your dog to stop barking and be quiet, turn to the training routine "Stop barking" on page 78.

▌ **Left:** *It is natural for a dog to bark as a warning to people approaching his territory, but he must not bark excessively or your neighbors may complain.*

If your dog barks when you are out, he may have good reason to bark – for instance, if the doorbell or the telephone rings. Having an answering machine on which you leave a message can be useful for calming your dog; he can hear your voice telling him to be quiet. What your callers may think is another matter! However, if your neighbors complain, you may want to point out that your dog's barking is actually a deterrent to potential intruders and is helping to protect their property, too. Persistent barkers may respond to more exercise, especially in busy urban situations where the dog can quickly acclimatize to noises that would cause him to bark if he were left at home alone.

Stop doing that!

There will always be times, within the house or out in the yard, when your dog starts to perform undesirable actions. Digging in the carpet, for instance, standing up on his hind legs to reach a full table of food, pulling at a cushion, or scratching at the back door – an endless list of unwanted behaviors. It is very useful to be able to stop the dog in his tracks without declaring your presence, and this is where an empty can or an already filled water pistol comes in handy. You can throw the can close to the dog without any intention of hitting him, or direct the water pistol at his hind end. It is the startle factor and the projectile that comes from an invisible source that do the trick. Try not to let the dog see the action you are taking. Magic works very well on dogs.

Jumping up

Excitement seems to project a dog into jumping up toward the face and mouth of newcomers, just as very young puppies jump up to the mouth of their mother to get her to disgorge food. It is embarrassing when a dog insists on jumping up on visitors when they have just arrived, but it is difficult to control an enthusiastic dog at this time. Work out a routine to suit you, your house, and your dog. Many people put the dog in the kitchen or another room before letting people in; say "*This way, this way,*" and the dog troops in, knowing that he must not be at the front door when it is opened. You are still making it clear that you have a dog to protect

Left: *If your dog bothers you and jumps up when you are sitting at the table eating or drinking, it is best just to look away and ignore him. If he cannot get your attention, he will soon give up and stop the behavior.*

Above: *Jumping up is an annoying habit – and potentially dangerous if you happen to own a large, boisterous dog. Discourage your dog from jumping up on you and shut him in another room when opening the door to visitors.*

you, as the visitor will be able to hear your commands to the dog. In many cases, it is advantageous to let the visitors enter the house and sit down, preferably at a table so that they have some protection when the dog does come in. Ask visitors not to interact with the dog at this stage, and not to make eye contact; let the atmosphere cool until all the excitement has died down. You may then want to put your dog into his crate where he can see and be seen, or perhaps attach a leash to his collar so that you can keep him at the *sit* and *down*, under your control while you talk to your guests.

Safety first

Beware of leaving any dog with guarding instincts alone with a visitor; he might object to the visitor harmlessly handling an object in the room – even an old magazine is sacrosanct to a dog guarding his owner's possessions.

Summary

Careful and thoughtful management of your dog early on will pay dividends later on; you should end up with a dog that enjoys life fully but also understands where he stands in the household hierarchy. And you will have the pleasure of knowing that your dog is obedient and anxious to please you but not clinging – a confident, happy dog, created by your sensitive and compassionate training.

USING DOG ABILITIES

Your dog is more agile and more clever than perhaps you will ever realize. Playing with dogs is fun for people, too; we get so little opportunity for carefree play! Dogs enjoy hide-and-seek and other games that stretch their mental powers; seeking hidden objects is well demonstrated by sniffer dogs that find secreted drugs or guns. Your dog, especially if he comes from one of the scenting breeds, can specialize in finding other objects, such as your car keys. Dogs enjoy solving puzzles too. As an exercise, block the way through a door with some boxes and see how your dog works out his own solution to creating an exit for himself.

You may even want to set up a mini Agility course in your yard: a flexible tunnel that the dog has to crawl through, a ladder to climb, and a suspended tire to jump through.

Wrestling with big dogs seems an irresistible game for the young and fit, but remember that a large dog will always win. It is better not to play rough games with dogs with dominant tendencies. Never end the game in such a way that your dog thinks he has won; always end when you say so. "*That's enough*" or "*Finish*" can be the words you use, but say them calmly, not on a note of panic. Reward the dog when he stops the game on command and bear in mind that you are playing with fire to allow such a game at all. However, it is not a good idea to put yourself in competition with the dog when he has all the attributes to win the contest.

Below: *Playing games such as hide-and-seek with your dog will stimulate his mind as well as exercise his body. Mental stimulation helps to prevent boredom and can prevent unwanted behavior problems from developing, many of which may be caused by having nothing to do. Try to make time to play with your dog every day.*

Chapter Five

TRAINING IS FUN

You can make training fun! Like any kind of education, whether it is designed for children or puppies, sometimes the going is hard and sometimes you or your dog may despair of ever getting it right, but the joy of having a well-mannered, happy dog that is a credit to you in any situation is a joy that can scarcely be matched.

The trained dog is a happier dog, too, not always getting into trouble because he has behaved badly without being aware that he is doing so; not always being shut away because he is a nuisance. The dog who has been trained to be a tolerable member of our society flourishes in the approval of his owner and his owner's friends.

The dog is unable to reason that because he is well trained he gets to go on a lot more outings than the badly behaved dog, but this is definitely the case. If you can trust your dog to behave well, he can go into the country, to parks, and interesting beaches. He can walk through spring woods, and visit all the places where he can meet other dogs. The trained dog has a wider social life, and so will you! If both you and your family take pleasure in obedience training, you may decide to take the skill to further lengths; for instance, you may want to join a local class for more advanced training or even proceed to competition level. However, this progression will have to be deferred until you and your puppy have mastered the initial kindergarten stage.

Get a language

Before you bring your new puppy into your home, draw up a short list of the words that you will use in training him. Make the words as simple as possible, easy to say, and distinctive from one another.

You may want to make your word for "*go and pass urine or defecate in the yard*" a special and secret code word, so that you can use it anywhere in public without any embarrassment. The Guide Dogs for the Blind Association uses the words "*Hurry up!*" – as good a phrase as any for the purpose. However, remember, if you adopt these words, not to use the phrase at any other time.

Your language list should then continue with the puppy's name, followed by "*Come!*" Usually, just calling his name will suffice, and you can use hand signals to back up your request.

Right: *Your dog or puppy will enjoy training sessions if you make them fun and keep them short. He will always be ready for walking on the leash.*

USEFUL COMMANDS

Here are some useful commands that you should use with your dog. You cannot teach your puppy all these words at once. Introduce them slowly and he will soon learn to respond.

- *"Bed"* (get in your bed!)
- *"Down"*
- *"Sit"*
- *"Stay"*
- *"Good dog"*
- *"Give it to me"*
- *"Come on"*
- *"Outside"*
- *"Quiet"* (to stop barking)

"No!" said sharply is a very important word, the one you will say when the puppy is about to do, or is actually doing, something that you do not wish him to do.

It's important to make sure that all the members of the family use the same words for the same actions, at least for a year or two. When the dog is an adult and is familiar with what he may or may not do, it's possible to vary the commands a little or, indeed, to do without commands at all.

Most dogs respond to a variety of names later in life – affectionate nicknames – on the basis that it doesn't matter what you call them as long as you call them!

House rules

In the early days of puppy owner-ship, you should decide what your dog is allowed to do with regard to such basics as going upstairs or not, lying on the furniture or not, or being temporarily enclosed in a crate when the family is busy, when high-powered cooking is going on in the kitchen, or when there is any crisis in the home. Decide what precautions you will always take when opening the front door so that there is no risk of the puppy slipping out. The entire family must agree on what is forbidden to the puppy; it is no good if most of the family keeps him off the sofa but Auntie allows him to snooze there with her in the afternoons.

Danger zones outside

Talk to the whole family about the hazards of the house and yard. What about taking the car out – could the puppy be underneath? Get into the habit of checking up on the puppy, always knowing where he is. What about callers leaving the gates open? Is the swimming pool securely fenced against puppy access? What about hazards within the yard: Are there insecticides, poisons, or slug or snail bait? These are very dangerous substances, whether they are put down for use or stored in a shed. If there is any possibility that the

Left: *It may look cute when your puppy climbs up to look out the window but when he becomes an adult and more conscious of territorial rights, damage may well be done. Do not tolerate "chair climbing."*

puppy could escape into your neighbors' yard, ask them if they will be kind enough not to use snail and slug bait. Reinforce your fencing, remembering that the puppy may dig underneath or, later on, go over the top.

Check also that there are no old cans of paint or varnish lying around, and that all the outside drains are properly covered. There is a case recorded of a puppy who got trapped in a drain while some boiling water from a washing machine flooded over him.

A puppy will always investigate everything he comes across, so never think that "he won't touch that" because the odds are that he will. It is not easy to keep a new puppy off your cherished flower borders or seedbeds. The easiest way is to make or buy very low wicker hurdles as temporary barriers. Puppies find great joy in digging up what you have just lovingly planted and bringing their trophies proudly in to you. Spring bulbs are very dangerous if chewed, as are buttercups, azaleas, foxgloves, and discarded foliage from shrub- or hedge-trimming. Knowing what your puppy is doing and stopping him from doing it can be a full-time occupation.

Tags and collars

Your puppy must wear a collar with an identification tag when he is away from home, but make sure that it is removed when he is in the yard or in your home, so there is no risk of his becoming caught on protruding branches and the like. Never leave a puppy or even an older dog confined alone in a room while wearing a collar. I know of one unfortunate dog that

got her collar caught on the brass doorknob of an old-fashioned cupboard and was in immediate danger of strangulation when she was discovered.

Danger zones inside

Indoors, train yourself to be tidy and to keep dangerous objects out of the puppy's reach. Do not leave your puppy alone where he can chew electrical cords and wires. Turn pot handles facing inward on the stove top so your dog cannot jump up and tip over a pot or skillet containing hot liquid or grease and burn himself. Some puppies are skillful at opening cabinets, so be sure they are tightly closed and that any

■ **Right:** *Another hard day working in the yard. Puppies love to explore and investigate and will happily dig up your flowerbeds and border plants. Train them not to do this at an early age.*

household cleaners or dangerous products are safely stored.

Buy a child gate for the stairs to prevent the puppy from going up. If he should accidentally climb the stairs, always help him to come down safely step by step. A tumble down the stairs at a young age could not only injure a young puppy, but also make him scared to climb steps later.

■ **Left:** *There are many hazards lurking in your home and yard. Almost everything in this garden shed poses some sort of danger to a dog. Never risk your dog having access to household or garden chemicals. It takes only a few seconds for him to lick a chemical or paint container or chew an electric cord.*

HOUSE-TRAINING

This is probably the subject that warrants priority in most households. However, it can also be the most difficult attribute to teach, although every dog varies in its ability to grasp what it is you want done because to the dog there are many built-in facets in the acts of urination and defecation. As we have said before, territory marking is important to both dogs and bitches, as is pack marking – eliminating on the same patch used by other dogs of the same breed or the same family. Male dogs do not usually use the leg-lifting marking stance for urination until they reach puberty, perhaps at twelve to eighteen months old. Bitches usually squat to urinate all their lives but may also lift a leg sometimes, especially when marking.

When you first bring your puppy into your home, carry him through into the yard and put him down on the patch that you would like to be used for elimination purposes. Try to pick somewhere near the house, as you will be spending quite a lot of time there! You may decide that cement is most easily cleaned, or you may want your puppy to use the grass. Remember that on clay soil bitch urine bleaches the grass in circles, but on chalk soil this is not noticeable.

Your puppy will be anxious to urinate after the trip and so you will get a successful result almost immediately. Now say the word you have decided upon and praise your puppy.

You have to start watching your puppy now so that if at all possible you can prevent him from soiling in the house. You must always keep the doors to your rooms shut unless you are actually in them, so the puppy does not have the opportunity to "mess all over the house," as complaining owners say.

Taking your puppy out

When a puppy, or a young adult, wakes up from sleep and right after feeding are good times to take the dog outside to relieve himself. Please note the emphasis is on taking the puppy out. This means that you go too, rain or shine! It is absolutely useless to push the puppy outside and then leave him to his own devices. He will not be learning anything, except perhaps to wonder why he was suddenly pushed outside in the cold. Go with your puppy; every hour on the hour is a good regime. Stay near the place you have chosen for the pup to use and say the words you have chosen. It takes time, but when learned, house-training is there for life, except perhaps in illness.

Using newspaper

If the weather is bad and the pup is very small, you may decide to use newspaper. This is what the litter would have used when it was still in the whelping box. Although this only postpones the job of house-training until later on, it can be helpful if the weather is bad. Remember that in the winter, when you heat your house, the air becomes dry, which makes your puppy thirsty. Your pet will need to have water available at all times. Remember also that your puppy has a small bladder and will have to urinate frequently, so be sure to change the newspapers often. To train your puppy to use the news-paper, do the following:

Right: *When a puppy, or a young adult, wakes up from sleep and right after feeding are good times to take the dog outside to relieve himself. Be patient! In the end, your puppy will know what to do!*

1 Placea a thick pile of newspaper near the back door.
2 When your puppy starts sniffing or running around in small circles (both indications that elimination is imminent), pick him up and put him on the newspaper.

Puppy crates

A folding crate made of plastic-coated wire is a modern blessing in helping to keep a puppy, or an older dog, safe and happy. These crates fold down to a flat pack in just a few seconds and are just as quickly erected wherever they are most needed. Puppies and grown dogs love their crates – they are to the dog the equivalent of the primitive den, a safe house from which the dog can see everything that goes on but is out of harm's

Left: *A puppy playpen or crate will not only keep your puppy safe for short periods, but will also stop him from soiling the house. A wire crate makes a wonderful substitute for a primitive den, and has the advantage that the puppy can see and be seen while being safe from harm.*

BE PATIENT

House-training can be a trying procedure; its success largely depends on a human watching the puppy for indications of its needs. Obviously, some breeds are quicker to learn and house-train than others – the smaller toy breeds are notoriously slow but the puddles are smaller! When you feel that you are not winning in the house-training race, remember that puppies are a great deal easier to train than human babies – a puppy does not produce involuntary urination during sleep after four weeks of age. Most puppies are house-trained by the time they are seven months old, while the human child takes quite a bit longer.

way. Comfortably furnished with fleece bedding, with possibly a rug thrown over the top to make the inside cozy, the door of the crate can stand open all day for the dog to use as he wishes, or it can be quickly shut and fastened if you want absolute assurance at any time that your dog is totally safe from any potential dangers or unsuitable encounters.

Your first experience of using the crate may well be on the puppy's first night in his new home. The crate may be set up in your living room or bedroom, possibly with a well-wrapped hot-water bottle for comfort, so you have the advantage of keeping the puppy within sight and yet not intruding too much on your own space. Remember that the puppy

will need to be given the opportunity to relieve himself. Every hour on the hour is a good time schedule to aim at when training your puppy. His natural instinct, and the regime that his mother instituted when he was with his littermates, is to get away from his bed for this purpose. If the crate you buy is a large one that will suit the puppy and be very useful for the rest of his life, then it should be possible, while he is still so small, to fill one end of the crate with some newspaper to serve as a place for elimination.

Below: *It may be a good idea, especially during periods of cold, wet weather, to train puppies to urinate on newspaper.*

GET DOWN TO TRAINING

Reward treats

Dogs respond well to food rewards and it's a good idea when training to keep some small treats in your hand or pocket. Use dried food, cheese cubes, or tiny pieces of cooked liver.

Literally! Bend or crouch down as near as you can to your puppy's height and communicate on his level. From time to time, pick him up to give him an opportunity to converse with you face to face but on your terms.

You are already training your puppy to interact with you and with other members of the family; the message he gets is that little food rewards and lots of petting and approval come from these people, as does the mutual play experience. Life is good with these people and they can be trusted not to hurt or tease him, and to create a secure environment as a basis for further socialization experiences. Let your puppy meet a wide variety of people and carry him outside the home so that he can see and hear the rush of traffic while he is safe in your arms. Until your veterinarian has completed his series of vaccinations and given them time to take effect, it is not a good idea to put your puppy down on sidewalks that are frequented by other dogs or take him to fields or parks used by other dogs.

HEAD COLLARS

A comfortable nylon head collar, such as the one shown below, will help you to control your dog when walking on the leash and in training. It doesn't hurt the dog, allows you to direct his head and body in the right direction, and prevents him from pulling.

1 To fit the head collar, push the noseloop over the dog's nose and jaw.

2 Put the collar band around the dog's neck and fasten it securely at the back.

■ **Below:** *Get down to your dog's level and praise him enthusiastically when he responds to your commands. Make him want to please you and come to you. If you wish, keep a small treat hidden in your hand.*

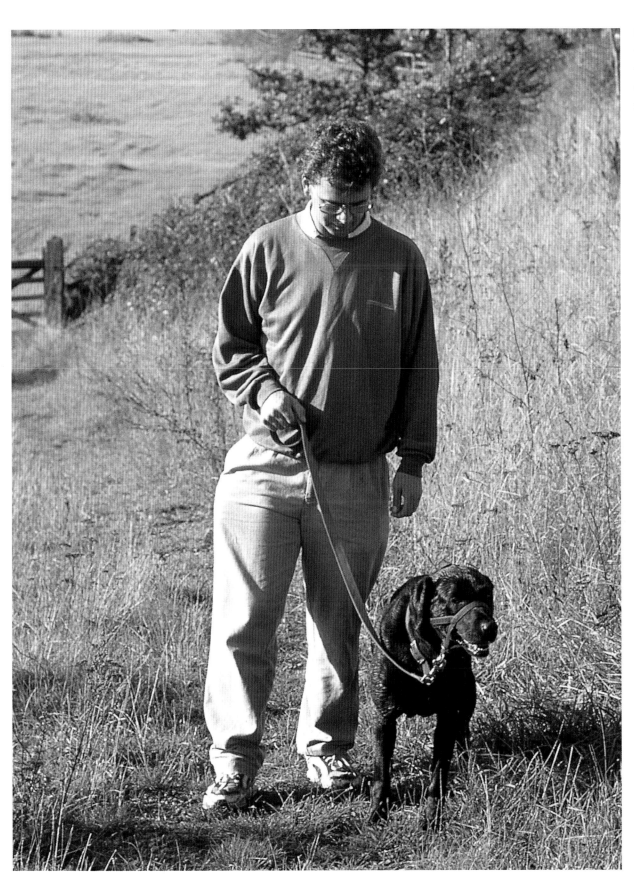

■ **Left:** *A well-trained dog who walks on the leash at your side without pulling is a pleasure to take for a walk.*

"Sit"

Teaching your dog to sit when he responds to your call is a very useful move, because the *sit* is a calming finish of the run or gallop

1 Kneel or crouch on the floor to be nearer your puppy's level.

2 Hold the reward over his head so that he must look up to see what you have for him. Tell him "*Sit.*"

3 He should go into the *sit* position naturally because he cannot look up without losing his balance. Give him the reward and praise him.

toward you. When your puppy comes in response to your call, the next thing he must learn is to *sit* on arrival, either in front of you at your feet or by your side. The puppy knows the attitude of *sit* well – he has been doing *sits* spontaneously since he was four weeks old. What you have to teach him is the word that you use when you want him to go into this position. A small reward will be necessary to get your puppy's attention initially; special dog treats are ideal. It's a good idea to teach this command while your puppy is still young and eager to respond. The *sit* is a position that dogs assume readily of their own accord many times a day. The head is held high, the front legs are straight, and the hind legs are folded in a jackknife position.

Training tips

◆ Never use force at any time when teaching your puppy any basic commands; it is unnecessary and unproductive. Some gentle pressure on the hindquarters is enough to show the puppy what you want him to do.
◆ Never give your puppy the reward until he has assumed the *sit* position or performed the behavior you want him to adopt.
◆ As he learns to comply with your command, do not always give the reward but continue to

Right: *Be careful not to hold the treat too high or you will encourage your dog to jump up to snatch the reward. Obviously, this is counterproductive.*

HEAD COLLAR – "SIT"

You can use a head collar to teach the dog to sit. Pull the leash gently forward and upward. As your dog's nose goes up, his rear end will go down. Say "*Sit*" when it touches the floor and reward him.

praise him and show that you are delighted with your smart puppy.
◆ If your puppy does not assume the *sit* position immediately, just run your hand down his back in a stroking action and press very lightly at his hip level so that he folds his legs correctly.
◆ Use the word "*Sit*" often so the puppy realizes what he has to do to get the reward. Then say, "*Good dog*" and give the reward.

"Stay"

When your dog will go into the *sit* and *down* positions when you ask him to, you can move on to teaching him to stay. This may be a difficult task as the dog's natural instinct is to be with his owner and you are going to ask him to remain at a distance from you, perhaps in distracting circumstances. It's best to put a collar and leash on your dog when teaching *stay* so that you have some control over him.

1 Begin with the dog in the *sit* position beside you. Hold your hand up, with the palm of your hand toward the dog, and give the command *"Stay,"* controlling the dog if need be by using the collar and leash every time he attempts to move.

2 Then move yourself, just one pace or two away, and continue giving the *stay* signal. Keep eye contact with the dog all the time. Praise him and then call him to you.

After a lot of practice you will be able to move a short distance away, and the dog will be comfortable that he still has the security of your presence even though you are standing away from him.

Training tips

◆ Do not forget to praise your dog when he has remained correctly in the *stay* position, and then you can formally break that control by using some release words of your choice – *"OK"* will do.
◆ Always give the command to break the *stay*. Never allow the dog to wander away, and do not do so yourself. Later you may want to introduce a distraction, such as some other person walking by, or another dog coming on the scene.
◆ If your dog "breaks" before you have released him from the *stay*, take

Left: *When you're teaching the* stay *at a distance in a public place, always use an extending leash.*

him back to the position he was in originally and start the exercise again. Perhaps you may wish to enhance the reward a little by offering a treat so that your dog realizes that complying with your wishes is well worthwhile.
◆ If you intend to train your dog up to competitive obedience level, he must learn to *stay* for fifteen to twenty minutes, probably along with other dogs but with their owners out of sight.

"Come when called"

When you start out on some more formal training for your puppy or, indeed, an older dog, try to arrange is so that he does not have the opportunity to get things wrong. Success always pays as far as puppies are concerned, and if your puppy comes straight to you when you call him, welcome him enthusiastically with cries of pleasure. Stroke him and pat his chest and flanks, but don't raise your hand above the puppy with the object of patting the top of his head, as a hand coming down toward a dog can be perceived as a frightening gesture. From time to time, but not every time, quickly produce from a hidden source – a pocket, for example – a tiny food reward.

If your puppy does not come to

TRAINING TIPS

◆ Keep the training sessions short. About ten minutes twice a day, preferably just before meals, is enough formal training while your puppy is young, but if you are teaching "*Come* when called," every time that you need or want to call the puppy is an opportunity for training him.

◆ Never chase a puppy as a game or because he is teasing you by not coming to your call. The odds will be in his favor as he is likely to be faster and more agile at dodging, and trying to catch a playful puppy can be very frustrating. The best thing to do in these circumstances is to walk away; this takes the advantage away from the puppy, who will find it more attractive to follow you in the end.

◆ The same tactics may be applied when an older dog will not return to you on an off-leash walk. If your dog has this tendency to test your patience and tolerance, practice calling him and putting him on the leash long before it is time to go home, and then after a short time let him off again. Repeat this process so that your dog does not associate the putting on of the leash with the end of fun.

1 First of all, tell your dog to sit. Raise your hand with a treat in it.

2 Move slowly away, with your hand raised, and keep your dog looking up at your hand.

3 Call your dog to you at the same time as you drop down to his level, which is similar to an invitation to play. Praise him enthusiastically when he reaches you and give him the treat.

you when you call him, then say nothing but walk away to another place and call him again from there. Remember that you are the clever one with devious ideas, so never let the puppy think that he can defy you or evade you. Nor should you ever get angry, shout, or deliver any physical punishment to a puppy no matter what he has done. Just arrange things so that the pup does get his task right and then reward him with lots of praise or even a treat because dogs learn by finding out what behavior pays best for them.

Remember that rewards work only if they are given within seconds of the puppy having done what you have asked him to do. Five minutes later is too late, as the puppy will not then connect what he did with the gaining of a reward, and you may in fact be rewarding behavior that you did not wish him to do.

▨ **Right:** *As soon as your dog comes to you when you call him, reward him with lots of praise. Pet him and give him a treat.*

RELUCTANT PUPPIES

If your puppy is incorrigibly naughty about coming when he is called, then try putting a collar on him and attaching a long line or piece of rope to it. If he takes no notice of your call, gently haul him in toward you by means of the line and then praise him and give him a reward within seconds of his arrival. All maneuvers must lead to the conclusion that coming to you when you call that magic name ends in good things.

1 Tell your dog to sit about 3 feet (1 m) away from you. When you have his attention, move back a little, making sure he doesn't move and the leash is slack.

Extending leashes

A lightweight modern extending leash is ideal for training your dog to come when called. You can gently reel it in as your dog comes to you.

2 Call him to you while gently retracting the lead and showing him the treat.

3 Reward him immediately with lots of praise and a treat.

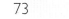

"Down"

With this command the puppy is required to fold his legs in the *sit* position, but also to extend his front legs until they are parallel with the ground. The neck is extended and the head is held up high. This is another "resting" pose that the dog does not mind doing when he understands what you want him to do.

It's important to limit the words that you use. Take care not to say "*Get down*" when you are reprimanding a dog that is jumping up to greet you.

If you ever want to take part in competitive obedience displays, your dog must be accustomed to a precise word of command for each action he performs.

Training tips

◆ Like the *sit*, this command will have to be repeated many times and in many different situations before it is imprinted on your dog's mind, but this is easy to practice wherever you may be.
◆ Remember the importance of body language and raise your hand, palm toward the dog, to reinforce the fact that he must stay in the *sit* or *down* position until you give your command to release him.
◆ When you are able to add *stay* to the *sit* or *down* exercise, you have taught the basics of training that you can elaborate on as you wish. Remember, you and your dog learn together; congratulate each other when you get it right.

1 Get the puppy to go into the *down* position by putting him first into the *sit*, holding a reward in the appropriate position above his head. Let him sniff the hand holding the reward.

2 Gradually lower and draw back the hand holding the reward, but keep the reward within your puppy's field of vision throughout.

3 When he moves his front legs forward to be nearer the reward, and his elbows touch the ground so that his body is extended, say "*Down*" and give him the reward. Praise him.

"Retrieve"

This is an action that comes naturally to many dogs; you can start your puppy playing retrieve games as early as eight weeks old. Start indoors, and reserve a specific playtime with the puppy, say about twenty minutes' play before a meal is due.

1 Show the puppy an interesting toy of a suitable size for him to pick up. Make sure that he gets the scent of the toy, and also your scent.

Training tips

◆ Praise and encourage the puppy when he brings back the toy and say "*Give it to me*" in a light, happy voice so that he knows that this is play. However, never say "*Give it to me*" when he runs off with something you did not intend him to have.

◆ If the puppy is reluctant to come back to where you are, use a long cord attached to his collar and gently pull him in to you. However, most young animals are eager to come to the person who has taken over as their foster mother or pack leader.

◆ If an older dog, who knows about retrieving, is available, it is useful to allow the dog to join in, but do not allow the toy to be picked up and pulled between the two animals, making every game a tug-of-war,

because this is not what you want.

◆ You can develop the *retrieve* indoors further by deliberately throwing the toy into a "difficult" place – under a cupboard or onto a low table. Your dog must find the toy by scent.

◆ When the playtime is over, make sure the object that has been played with is put in a drawer out of sight; this will make the dog more eager and interested for a game next time.

◆ Later, your retrieving game can move outside, adding even more interest. As your dog grows up and gets more confident, he may be reluctant to give the toy to you; the human player should crouch down, offering a small food reward in a hand held out to the dog and giving a lot of praise when the article is given up – the dog will usually drop the toy in front of you.

◆ Don't forget to use a happy voice and happy face to greet the dog. Even if he has not carried out the command as well as you would wish, never get angry or lose your temper.

Retrieving dummies

There is a range of dummies that are made for retrieving trials that you can buy in most pet stores.

2 Now send the toy skidding across the floor and give the command "*Go fetch.*" Almost certainly the puppy will chase after it.

3 As the puppy picks up the toy, say "*Come.*" When he brings it back to you, say, "*Give it to me*" and take it out of his mouth and praise him. Reward him, if you wish, with a treat.

Leash training

"Heeling" with your dog off the leash is a somewhat outmoded practice now, and this quasi-military exercise is no longer wanted or needed for the pet dog. What we are aiming for is a dog that will walk quietly at our side on a leash, not pulling too far forward or deviating backwards or from side to side. In today's heavy traffic conditions, it is almost never the action of a responsible owner to allow a dog to walk without any leash control on any type of road, even on a supposedly quiet country lane. It is essential that you train your dog from the earliest possible age to walk happily on a leash at your side. If your dog is a pleasure to walk, you will both enjoy going out together and he may even end up getting more exercise.

Make your dog a pleasure to walk

Start with the puppy on a light but firm leather collar. Never use any form of chain collar as it has been found that jerking on a check or choke chain can do serious damage to a dog's throat and larynx. For a few days, just attach the leash to your puppy's collar and leave it loose while he is eating or walking around the yard with you. Make the leash a pleasant thing, not something that your puppy feels obliged to fight. Start formal leash training when you are not going out anywhere! Inside the house or in the yard is ideal, but never when you are on some sort of errand.

Training tips

◆ When you have taught your dog to concentrate on what you want him to do regarding walking at your side, you will want to introduce a command to remind him – you can use the word "*Heel*" or "*Here*" or "*Steady*."
◆ When he has reached the stage of walking at your side on a

1 Start off by holding the leash in your left hand, with the puppy on your right side.

2 Hold a favorite squeaky toy or a food reward in your right hand to encourage him to move forward.

3 Don't forget to praise him and say "*Good dog*" when he gets it right, even for only a few steps.

public sidewalk, remember always to have a plastic bag in your pocket, ready to pick up any feces your dog may pass. Dispose of the bag in a discreet spot if there are no trash cans designated especially for this purpose in the area. You should even do this on open land if the feces has been dropped on a footpath where people habitually walk.

◆ Once your dog is walking steadily, use the *sit* command when you meet someone coming in the opposite direction or if a loose dog rushes up to you. Keep your dog in the *sit* position and continue to reassure him until the loose dog is reclaimed by its owner.

◆ Even if your puppy is really

Below: *If another dog approaches your puppy, keep him in the sit position and reassure him until the loose dog is reclaimed by his owner.*

small, never pick him up when confronted by another dog; the intruder may jump up and you could be caught off balance. Additionally, snatching your dog away from another dog tends to

build up into a nervous reaction to other dogs. Puppies are usually sacrosanct to adult dogs; a puppy is unlikely to be savaged but will be treated to a curious in-depth inspection.

Leashes

A leather handle with a chain that clips onto the collar is ideal for large dogs, but a heavy swinging chain can hurt a smaller dog.

Nylon leashes are light and are easily wrapped around your hand to bring the dog close to you for better control.

Cord and rope leashes are more comfortable to hold easily for strong pullers, but they do get wet and dirty.

4 Inevitably, the puppy will want to pull forward; this is when you turn around and walk the other way. The leash should always be slack, never taut.

HEAD COLLAR

The head collar below is an excellent one that gives the owner full control while teaching walking manners. It is also excellent for preventing a dog from lunging sideways at other dogs he passes in the street. By controlling your dog's head and nose, you can direct his whole body.

"Give it to me"

Whenever your dog succeeds in bringing a thrown or requested object back to you at your command, never go into tug-of-war mode. It may be a precious object you want back in one piece! Instead, praise your dog enthusiastically for coming back to you and encourage him to give it to you without having to fight for it. If you wish, you can reward him with a favorite treat.

1 When your dog brings an object back to you, don't try to pull it out of his mouth. Praise him lavishly and then tell him firmly to "*Sit.*"

2 When he is sitting in front of you, put your hand on the object and say "*Give.*" If necessary, open his mouth with your free hand. Praise him when you have the object.

"Stop barking"

It is useful to teach some dogs to stop barking and be quiet. Probably the most useful command is the word "*No!*" However, if the dog is barking as a warning of intruders, use calming words like "*All right, all right*" and then praise him if the barking was warranted.

1 When your dog barks, say "*No!*" and get him to go into the *sit* position. Dogs rarely continue barking when sitting.

2 When your dog sits down and stops barking, praise him enthusiastically and reward his good behavior with a favorite treat.

"Bed"

Sending a dog to bed should never be used as a punishment. Dogs love their beds and should regard them as a safe place where they can lie and sleep or sit and watch in safety and undisturbed. If you want him out of the way, tell your dog to get in his bed but do so in a happy voice and give him a treat or favorite toy; praise him when he has settled down. Make the bed comfortable with a rug or a soft blanket and position it in a draft-free place that is out of direct sunlight.

Right: *If you want your dog to get into his bed, just point to it and say "Bed" in a happy voice. Never send him to bed as a punishment for any bad behavior on his part.*

TRICKS TO TEACH YOUR DOG

Most dogs enjoy learning tricks and commands that stimulate them. Teaching your dog new things will strengthen your understanding of each other and enrich your lives.

"Give a paw"

This is an endearing action. Visitors dote on a dog that gives them a paw in a handshake gesture. You can encourage the voluntary paw giving that some dogs want to do; in others, you may have to pick up the paw several times. Reward your dog with lavish praise and a treat when the paw comes up naturally. Always practice this command from the *sit* position.

"Come on"

This is the command you will use in the yard or in open country when you want your dog to follow you without being on the leash. You must never be so confident in your training skills that you allow your dog off the leash on a road, not even on a country road where the traffic is very light.

Other tricks and commands

There are many commands and tricks you can teach your dog. He will show you the words he recognizes and you can work them into a trick.

Right: *When the dog offers you his paw, hold it lightly in your hand. Reward him with a treat.*

Caring for your dog

Your dog will become your lifelong companion and you will have to care for him on a daily basis. Not only will you have to feed, exercise, and groom him, but you will also have to play games with him and arrange for him to be well looked after if you go away on vacation. You also need to know how to keep your dog fit and healthy and thereby prevent many common health problems as well as how to treat them if they occur. In this section, there is expert practical advice on every aspect of looking after your dog.

Chapter Six

DAILY CARE

Recent studies have shown that one of the most important facets of a dog's life is his involvement in the life of the family; the more involved he is, the more integrated he will become, and the more he is spoken to, the more he will understand what is expected of him. The dog is a hierarchical animal and he is happiest when he knows his position within the pack – in this case, the human family with whom he lives.

Within the framework of his breed he will, almost certainly, wish to please his "pack leader."

It is not fair, however, for you to attempt to persuade a dog to do something or behave in a way to which he is not temperamentally suited; for instance, if he is not genetically a guard dog, he should not be forced into guarding. He will do his best but will be unhappy and this unhappiness may manifest itself in a way that's not typical of the breed.

The daily care of your dog is dependent on the breed and the purpose for which the dog was acquired. Thus, a companion dog will be treated differently than a dog that was acquired for showing, and he'll be treated differently than a dog that is a working gundog.

Below: *Grooming is just one of the many things that you will have to do for your dog. Children will enjoy helping.*

Your responsibilities

It is socially irresponsible to allow a dog to run free without the control of his owner. Such dogs can form packs and terrorize their entire neighborhood; their feces can contaminate the streets and can cause infections in humans. Most communities have specific laws that penalize dog owners if their dog is a public nuisance or danger.

A dog has to be trained to behave himself in human company as well as in canine company. This requires daily lessons. The length of time it takes depends on the skill of the teacher and the dog's intelligence.

So take your dog to training classes that specialize in teaching your dog good behavior. He will be taught everyday good manners, and children can enjoy learning, too. You can reinforce this training with daily, short training sessions at home.

In peak condition

To stay healthy, fit, and happy and to succeed in any activity, a dog needs to be operating at the peak of his condition, and this can be achieved only with the correct feeding, exercise, and mental stimulation for the breed. The show dog probably needs more attention at home than pet dogs and working dogs, for not only must he be trained to perform in the show ring, but he'll need more time spent on his presentation and grooming. The amount of time spent will depend on the type of coat. Lhasa Apsos and Afghan Hounds, for instance, require more grooming than most terriers.

However, whatever breed of dog you own, you must be prepared to exercise and play with him every day and to groom him at least once a week, depending on his coat type. He will also need to be fed a well-balanced diet that contains all the vital nutrients he needs for good health.

GENERAL HEALTH CARE

Any dog that comes from a caring breeder who pays due concern to the breed's genetic potential for anomalies should, with regular health care, lead a long and healthy life. For full health, the four main considerations for a dog are:

- Worming
- Correct feeding
- Correct exercise
- Mental stimulation.

Regular examinations

Examine your dog regularly. Whenever you groom him is a good time for this. Look especially at the eyes, ears, mouth, and genital area for any unusual discharges. If you do notice something out of the ordinary, consult your veterinarian. After any country walks, examine your dog's feet and body for cuts, abrasions, ticks, and fleas. If anything is judged to be serious, consult the veterinarian.

Left: *Chewing on chews, hard biscuits, and bones will help to clean your dog's teeth and keep them strong and healthy.*

Below: *You can clean your dog's teeth with a special toothbrush and dog toothpaste. Start doing this when he is still a young puppy.*

Dental care

A puppy's baby teeth will fall out during the first few months but in some toy breeds the baby teeth will persist and the second teeth will not dislodge them. If this happens, veterinary treatment is necessary to remove the first teeth and in order to allow sufficient room for the adult teeth to come through.

Like humans, all dogs produce tartar and plaque. It is thought that this is because of our modern feeding regimes. Should these substances be allowed to build up, they will trap pockets of bacteria that cause gum disease, tooth decay, and bad breath in the dog. It may become necessary for your veterinarian to remove the deposits under a general anesthetic.

If you start when your dog is young enough, it is relatively easy to train him to have his teeth cleaned; it just needs patience and kindness at the beginning. There are toothpastes that are specially formulated for use with dogs, and brushes that are designed for a dog's mouth. Never use your own human toothpaste, which is formulated specifically for our use; dogs find these toothpastes distasteful.

Hard biscuits are good for a dog's teeth, and there are plenty of chews that are designed for cleaning teeth that are now available from most pet shops. Chewing on a bone is a classic remedy but you should give your dog only big raw marrow bones – never cooked chicken or lamb bones or little bones of any description as they can splinter and pierce the dog's stomach lining, causing death.

If you do give your dog bones, make sure you teach him to give them up to you when requested to do so; otherwise, he may become possessive and aggressive.

Caring for eyes

The eyes of some breeds, such as Pugs, protrude slightly and are set forward in the skull. This makes them very vulnerable to scratches from playing in the bushes and running through the undergrowth.

When grooming your dog,

examine him carefully for marks on the eyes themselves. Check if there is any excess tearstaining of the coat or any deposits in the corner of the eyes. If there are any scratches, ulcers, or infection, such as conjunctivitis, go immediately to the veterinarian. Even if there is no evidence of injury, there may be particles of dust in the eye. If so, bathe the eye gently with a clear, warm, damp cloth. Tearstaining on a white coat can be removed with special products available from pet shops.

Feet and nails

Should your dog develop a limp when out walking, examine his feet. If there is any damage, then pressure bandages should be applied immediately if the cut is deep, and any significant cut should receive urgent veterinary

WORMING

Both dogs and bitches should be wormed regularly with a proper veterinary vermifuge. Not to do so can seriously affect the dog's health, resulting in depression, weight loss, hair loss, and, in extreme cases, even death. Ask your veterinarian for advice on worming. Note that the feces should always be disposed of hygienically to protect humans from infection. Remember also to pick up a dog's mess should he defecate in a public place.

▦ **Below:** *It is a good idea to trim the long hair growing between the pads of some dogs, especially if it gets matted. Use an ordinary pair of scissors.*

treatment. Check your dog's feet regularly, trimming the hair if necessary. Leave some between the pads but keep it clean. Grass seeds can embed themselves into the pad and migrate up the dog's leg, so always check for these in the summer months.

Nails should be kept short. Great care should be taken when cutting nails as there is a sensitive part containing a vein and to cut into this causes great pain and a lot of blood. Before undertaking this task, watch an expert – a groomer, dog breeder, or veterinarian and ask them to show you how to trim them.

Ear hygiene

Some breeds are more prone to ear infections than others, and dogs with erect ears suffer less than those with floppy ears, the reason being that erect ears allow the circulation of air. Floppy ears trap warm, moist air that is ideal for bacterial and fungal growth. The first indication of infection is when the dog persistently shakes his head and scratches an ear

deeply and slowly. When this happens, you are probably already too late to apply home remedies and a visit to the veterinarian is indicated.

The veterinarian will probably prescribe ear drops that should clear up the ear condition fairly quickly. Failure to do so will certainly result in a dog becoming so irritated that his general health will deteriorate.

You can keep your dog's ears clean by wiping them once a week with an ear-cleansing liquid available from pet shops or the veterinarian. The excess hair inside the ears of some breeds can harbor mites, so it should be plucked out with your fingers. Do not cut it or the hairs will fall into the dog's ear. Long ears should always be cleaned and combed after exercise, and these dogs should be fed in a tall, narrow dish so the ears are not immersed in their food.

▦ **Left:** *You can clean your dog's ears with a specially formulated cleanser. Just aim into the ear canal and squeeze the container gently.*

▦ **Left:** *Massage the ear gently with your hand. If you wish, use some cotton balls soaked in cleanser to clean the accessible parts of the ear.*

FEEDING YOUR DOG

Feeding, walks, and play are the highlights of your dog's day. As he has no control over what he is given to eat, it is important to give the most nutritious food you can afford. Canines are among the most remarkable of animals as far as food is concerned: they can live on the most unlikely foods or, rather, they can subsist on them, but incorrect or bad feeding will inevitably result in some health problems, such as skin disorders, anxiety, obesity, wasting of the muscles, and a shortening of life.

Below: *A quick test to assess if your dog is overweight is to run your hands down his flanks; if his ribs are not easy to feel or he has no visible waistline, he may be overweight.*

Food requirements are different for every breed and for individual dogs within a breed. They are based on size and energy output, and thus a hound or a gundog working in the field needs more food, calories, and protein than a sedentary dog of the same breed.

Equipment

Before the advent of complete diets and store-bought frozen foods, kennels needed a great deal of equipment to provide suitable food. Convenience foods of today obviate a need for any equipment except refrigerators and can openers. Most kennels of any size feed a manufactured complete diet or canned foods. If you feed your dog one of the complete diets, remember to store it in mouse-proof containers.

The type of feeding dish has some importance: dogs with long ears, such as Cocker Spaniels and Basset Hounds, should be fed from a tall, narrow dish so that when feeding, the dog's ears fall outside the dish, keeping them clean and free from potential infection and making it easier to groom them. The very big breeds, such as Great Danes and Irish Wolfhounds, are quite often fed from elevated bowls. The bowl is fitted inside a metal frame that lifts it about 2 feet (60 cm) above the ground. This is thought to ease digestive problems.

Types of dog food

There is a bewildering array of dog food available today, each one claiming to be the ultimate nutritious food for feeding to your pet. However, for the novice dog owner, it is probably best to take advice from either your

Right: *It is very important to feed a dog correctly from puppyhood on if he is to be truly fit and healthy.*

veterinarian or the breeder of your puppy or dog.

◆ **Complete dry food:** One of the most popular convenience foods, it is mostly composed of cereals and their by-products, meat from various sources, soya, and vegetables, vitamins, oils, fats, and minerals; there may also be artificial coloring and preservatives. They can be marketed as biscuits, pellets, meal, or extruded products.

◆ **Semimoist foods:** These contain up to twenty-five percent moisture and, to avoid refrigeration, some preservatives. The composition is similar to that of most other commercial dog foods.

◆ **Canned foods:** These are often more than seventy-five percent moisture but the best of them are nutritionally complete with similar ingredients to the other dog foods. Unless otherwise stated, most of these foods contain artificial coloring and additives. Canned food is mainly made up of meat, organ meat, and animal by-products, which are augmented by vitamins and minerals.

Feeding your dog

The argument as to whether it's better to feed once or twice a day has raged for centuries. Modern thinking is that if a dog has food in his stomach he is more likely to be calm and content, and therefore the advice is twice a day. It gives the dog two high points in his day. Most people divide the food into three parts: one part is given in the morning, and two parts in the evening. Unlimited fresh water should be available at all times, whatever type of food is served.

Table scraps are not considered suitable food, although there is no reason why meat and vegetable scraps (except onion) should not be added to a dog's food providing it is not extra to his normal amount.

Some people like to prepare their dog's food themselves. Meat can be served either parboiled or lightly cooked and accompanied by some vegetables, rice, or even pasta. The amounts fed will vary but, as a rule of thumb, a 22-pound (10-kg) dog should have 10 ounces (300 g) of meat, 3 ounces (75 g) of rice, and a similar amount of vegetables, plus some vegetable oil and brewer's yeast. The problem is that there may be a deficiency of some minerals and vitamins and it may be necessary to add a high-quality supplement. However, seek veterinary advice because oversupplementation may cause health problems.

Most dogs will eat all that is placed in front of them but they should not be allowed to put on excessive weight. Ideally a smooth-haired dog's ribs should be just visible. His calorific input should not exceed his output. Printed

PRENATAL AND POSTNATAL FEEDING

A good-quality, balanced diet is of prime importance for a pregnant or postnatal bitch. You should gradually increase her food by about twenty percent in the last three weeks of the pregnancy and feed four meals. As the pups grow inside her, her womb presses on the stomach so several small meals are essential. After the birth, increase the food slowly to about three times the norm, depending on the number of puppies she needs to feed. However, if she has only one or two, she won't need much additional food to produce the milk. After the beginning of the weaning process the amount of food she consumes should be progressively reduced.

quite clearly on all commercially prepared food packaging are the approximate amounts to be given but bear in mind that each dog is different. Forty percent of pet dogs are overweight; obese dogs need special attention as extra weight can shorten their life. Your veterinarian will recommend a special diet and proper exercise. It is best not to give a dog of any age cookies, candy, or cake. Chocolate should not be fed to your pet because it contains a substance, theobromine, that is toxic to all dogs. Give only the treats that are specially formulated for dogs, which are available at your pet shop.

Caring for elderly dogs

Some elderly dogs behave with the vigor of much younger dogs, in which case the usual feeding regime can be followed. However, when the day comes that the dog is not so eager go to for a walk or will run after a ball only a few times before lying down, then it is time to consider his requirements.

Take him to the veterinarian to find out the reason for his deterioration. It may be a failure of his kidneys, in which case the veterinarian will advise you to reduce the protein and calorific content of your dog's food. He will also recommend some appropriate supplements. Every effort should be made to stimulate the old dog's mind and make him feel wanted.

He should be gently persuaded to take some exercise; it stands to reason that his intake of food will lessen as his activity becomes less. Give him the food you know he likes, make an extra fuss over him, and don't be angry with him if he makes a mistake.

Above: *Scrambled eggs are an ideal food for an elderly dog or one recovering from a stomach upset.*

Left: *This elderly Cocker Spaniel has a raised bowl so that he does not have to bend right down to the ground to eat. This is thought to aid digestion.*

GROOMING

There are several good reasons why you should groom your dog regularly. The act of gentle grooming, the passage of a comb pulled through the hair, and the brushing give a pleasurable feeling to the dog and assist in the bonding process. It also gives the groomer the opportunity to examine his pet – to look for any skin conditions, cuts, abrasions, or discharges. For good hygiene reasons, you must be prepared to pay special attention to the rear ends and muzzles of Old English Sheepdogs and other hairy breeds.

Some coats tangle and mat easily. They are uncomfortable to the dog and hotbeds of infection, an ideal place for bacteria and fungi to grow, which will irritate the dog. Some shedding dogs suffer from matting unless the dead hair is removed; in severe cases this is very painful for an affected dog.

Some breeds require a daily grooming session, whereas others need weekly attention. Smooth-coated dogs require only a twice-weekly brush and polish. Regular grooming, particularly at the time of shedding, will prevent hairs from covering rugs and furniture.

Pet grooming and advanced preparation for dog shows can be learned by anyone. The breed clubs have grooming charts and will give you advice, and most breed books contain chapters on show preparation and the tools required.

Grooming equipment

Above: *Shaggy, long-haired dogs will need more grooming than smooth-haired breeds. If your dog has a thick, long coat, be prepared to put aside time every week for a long grooming session.*

The amount of equipment you require is in direct proportion to the number of dogs and type of coats. The owner of one or two Poodles, for instance, would need hairdresser's scissors, good-quality clippers and several blades, a hair dryer, and the proper brushes and combs. Such specialized equipment would be enough to maintain a good-looking coat even to show standard. Show people should have a grooming table, a restraint to stop the dog from leaping off, and a grooming cart to carry the gear.

Owners of dogs with wire coats should have the same equipment in addition to stripping knives of various types and sizes, special palm brushes with very short

TOOLS OF THE TRADE

The basic grooming tools are designed for different coat types and the ones you buy will depend on the breed of dog that you own.

I Wide and fine-toothed combs
2 Soft pin brush
3 Bristle brush
4 Stripping comb

5 Thinning scissors
6 Pointed-end scissors
7 Nail clippers
8 Brush

teeth and even a rake for controlling the dog's undercoat.

People who keep many dogs and show them may use a drying cabinet, which is a special box with a wire front in which there are air ducts allowing the hot air to circulate. This speeds up the drying process considerably after bathing a dog for showing. They might also invest in a special bath that makes life easier by having a built-in movable shower head, recirculating water, and a side opening. The dog does not have to be lifted in – he just steps in.

Coat types

Strictly speaking, there are as many coat types as there are dog breeds and there are different types within the breeds. The first division has three types:
◆ Short-haired (Doberman).
◆ Medium-length (German Shepherd Dog)
◆ Long-haired (Yorkshire Terrier).
These divisions can then be subdivided into smooth, rough, wire, and curly. A further division is soft, medium, and harsh. In order to groom all the different types correctly, they all demand special treatment and handling.

With a few exceptions, they all have an undercoat of various textures, thicknesses, and colors.

Some dogs are born with the color that stays all their life; others change. The Kerry Blue Terrier starts black and finishes blue/gray. Yorkshire Terriers start black and tan and finish blue/gray and golden tan. Puppy hair is fluffy and bears no relationship to the adult hair. Although it can be removed, it's best to wait for it to drop out naturally with brushing.

Short-haired dogs

The hair on short-haired dogs is invariably smooth and relatively thin and usually has a very fine undercoat. It is the easiest coat to care for, needing only a brush to remove any dead hairs and a

Above: *If you own a Doberman with its distinctive glossy, short-haired coat, grooming your dog will be minimal.*

polish with a grooming mitt or a chamois leather that distributes the coat oils and gives it a shine.

Although to the touch these short coats appear to be silky, a closer examination will show that the hair is really quite harsh. The fact that it lies flat and close gives the impression of silkiness but stroke it in the opposite direction to the way in which it lies and it is quite spiky. The short coat of a Bullmastiff is said to be hard. The coat of the Shar Pei is described as short and bristly. Most of these coats are self-cleaning: they do not absorb water and when they dry, any mud or dirt falls off. The smooth-coated Collie has a medium-length smooth coat that, although dense, is harsh to the touch. It is waterproof by virtue of the thick undercoat.

Medium-haired dogs

Dogs with medium-length hair will require more grooming than short-haired dogs but less than long-haired breeds. Most dogs in this category will need only brushing and combing two or three times a week to keep their coats in good condition and to remove mud and tangles.

Long-haired dogs

Long coats are some of the most time-consuming ones to keep in good condition. The softer they are, the more they tangle and the more dirt and debris they pick up. It is not really feasible to keep a long-haired dog in full coat as an ordinary pet. The flowing white coat of the Maltese, the floor-length

Below: *A long-haired Shetland Sheepdog will need regular grooming on a daily basis to keep his coat healthy, free from tangles, and in good condition.*

coat of the Yorkshire Terrier, the sweeping locks of the Shih Tzu present problems that can be solved only by the special attention given by breed fanciers.

Most pet owners will keep their long-haired dogs in a short cut, known in some breeds as a "puppy cut." It is quite simple to train the dog to stand on a table and, using a pair of good sharp scissors, give him the rough shape of the breed. Dogs prefer to have short hair than to have knotted long coats. Once a year perhaps, they can go to a professional groomer to be shaped properly. Old English Sheepdogs are difficult to maintain and the coats mat very easily. Therefore they are often taken to a groomer to have all the hair shorn off in the manner of a sheep.

Rough-haired dogs

This type of coat consists of harsh, stand-off outer guard hairs and a soft undercoat, whose thickness will vary according to the breed. The Spitz-type dog, such as a Chow Chow, has a very thick undercoat, whereas the Rough Collie has much less. All these breeds should be groomed regularly. Dirt and dust gather in

the undercoat, which should be deep combed.

The area surrounding the anus can become unhygienic and the underneath of the male dogs can be stained with urine. These dogs shed copious amounts of hair that, if left, can get knotted and cause irritation to the dog.

Poodles and wire-haired breeds

Poodles and wire-haired breeds do not shed. If a Poodle's hair were left to grow, it would become corded. Most people keep Poodles in a "puppy cut" – it is scissored all over to a length of about 2 inches (5 cm) with the face, feet, and rear end trimmed close to the skin. With practice, most owners can manage this but those who cannot should take the dog to a groomer every eight weeks. For maintenance, the dog should be brushed and combed every day.

Wire-haired breeds need special attention. If the hair is cut it tends to lose its texture and the color will gradually fade. The proper treatment of the coat is to hand-strip or pluck it. This is an art that can be achieved only with practice and an understanding of the coat growth. For example, the hair on the body of a Welsh Terrier should be just over 1 inch (2.5 cm) in length, the neck hair thicker, the head hair very short, and the furnishings on the legs profuse. To achieve this, stand the dog on a table. Hold the skin where the hair is to be removed

■ **Left:** *This Jack Russell Terrier has the rough coat that is typical of many terriers. It is water-resistant.*

with one hand and, with a stripping knife in the other hand, trap a few of the longest hairs between your thumb and the stripping knife. Pull the hairs out evenly and smoothly without any jerking. Slowly, over several weeks, the required shape appears. Most owners do not go to this trouble; instead they take their dog to a groomer every three months and they clip it into shape.

■ **Above:** *To keep a Poodle in good condition, you will have to trim him regularly or visit a groomer.*

■ **Above:** *The adult Yorkshire Terrier has a silky long-haired coat that will need regular grooming even if you don't show your pet dog.*

■ **Right:** *It is easy to hand-strip a terrier. Just take a few hairs between your thumb and forefinger and pull them out gently. This will not hurt your terrier.*

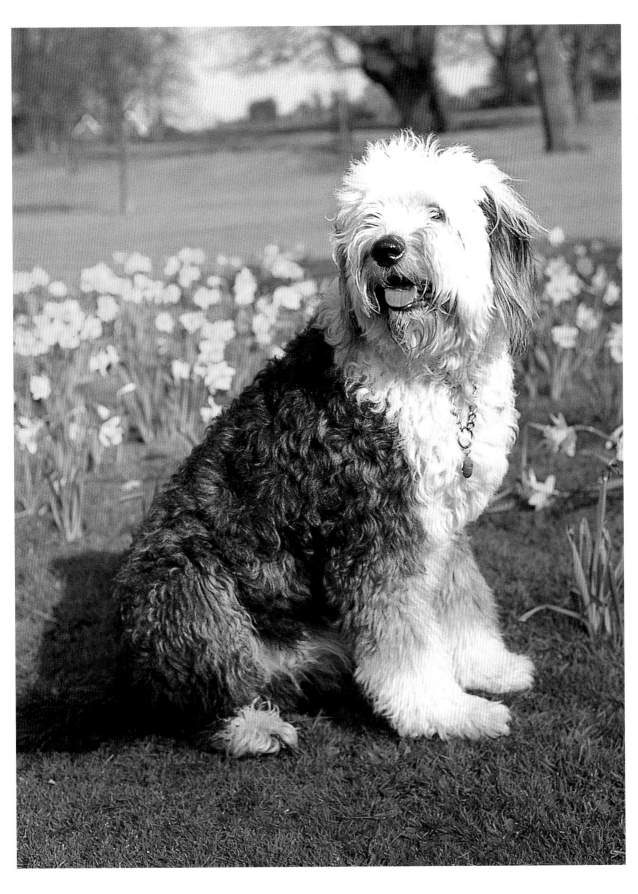

■ **Left:** *Sometimes with very heavily coated breeds, such as this Old English Sheepdog, the coat can be shorn off to varying lengths, depending on how much time you want to spend grooming your dog after a walk in the country!*

Grooming your dog

Grooming your dog should be a pleasurable experience for both of you. Develop a grooming routine when your dog is still a puppy and he will soon come to accept and enjoy this time you spend together. Depending on the breed, you can groom him on your lap, the floor, or up on a table.

■ **Right:** *To groom a Poodle's head, brush or comb upward from the root of the hair. Be careful not to hurt the dog.*

Brushing out tangles

To remove really matted tangles, it is sometimes a good idea to tease them out with your fingers before gently pulling a brush or comb through them.

Brushing long ears

Dogs with long ears should have them brushed every day and also checked for tangles and foreign objects, especially after a walk. First tease out any thick tangles at the end of the earflap with your fingers before you start. Then start at the top of the ears, slowly but smoothly brushing down to the ends. A hand placed under the earflap at the base of the ear will help avoid pulling on the sensitive skin around the ear opening.

Keep the inside of the ears, especially folded ears, clean with a veterinary product. Excess hair is best plucked out with your fingers as scissoring may allow hairs to fall into the ear.

■ **Above:** *Use a comb to ease out any matted hair and tangles on the ear feathering of spaniels.*

■ **Left:** *Use a brush to groom the long hair on a Poodle's ears and then tease out tangles with a wide-toothed comb.*

STRIPPING KNIVES

These are often used on breeds such as spaniels. It's best to watch a professional at work before attempting it yourself.

Tails

There are many different styles of dogs' tails, many of which do not require much attention. Very hairy hanging tails the need most grooming. With sharp scissors, preferably those with a slight curve, carefully cut the hair away from where it touches the dog's anus. Otherwise, give the area a routine brushing and combing. Keep the folds of skin clean on very short tails, such as the Bulldog's. Wire-haired breeds should have the underside of the tail kept short.

■ **Above:** *When grooming feathering on a tail, use a wide-toothed comb. Don't be rough – always be gentle.*

Rears

Virtually every medium- and long-haired dog needs to have his or her rear end kept clear of excessive hair for obvious reasons. Great care must be taken as the area is most delicate. Curved scissors prevent accidental "digging in." Bitches can suffer staining of the hair on the hind legs, which is known as "skirts." Excessive hair growth on the male's penis sheath should be cut very carefully for hygiene purposes.

▦ **Above:** *After grooming the dog's tail, check his rear as the hair may need trimming to keep it short.*

Using a slicker

To groom short-haired hounds and terriers, you will need to use a slicker or grooming mitt. Made of rubber, it glides through the coat and massages the skin underneath.

▦ **Left:** *You can use a rubber slicker with a handle or a hound grooming mitt that fits snugly over your hand for grooming terriers and hounds.*

Bathing

It is rarely necessary to bathe sporting dogs, hounds, or terriers. If they get covered in mud, wait for it to dry and simply brush it off. It is not recommended that you wash dogs very often as bathing will remove the oils and other skin secretions that keep a dog's skin and coat healthy. If you do need to bathe your dog, follow these simple guidelines.

Bathing your dog

1 Sit a small dog in a bowl or sink and splash with tepid water or pour it over him with a pitcher. Protect his ears to prevent any

▦ **Left:** *After rinsing thoroughly, wrap the dog in a towel and rub him dry. If he does not mind, dry him off with an electric hair dryer.*

water from getting inside them. Use a bath for larger dogs.
2 Use an emollient or special dog shampoo to lather the coat, protecting the dog's eyes and ears.
3 Rinse all the shampoo out of the coat, especially around the dog's rear and under his legs.
4 Gently rub your dog dry with a towel and then dry with a hair dryer if he will accept it – some dogs are frightened of the noise that they make.
5 Make sure that your dog is thoroughly dry and don't let him lie in a draft until he is dry.

▦ **Left:** *Another way to dry your dog is to put him inside a clean zip-up terrycloth bag after towel-drying him. This will keep him snug and warm until he is thoroughly dry all over.*

EXERCISE

Dogs are running animals and they do need some regular free running for their physical and mental well-being. The amount needed depends on their size, conformation, breed, and age. When exercising your dog, you need to follow a few basic rules, which are as follows:

◆ Always keep your dog on the leash in public places; it is illegal to allow a dog to be out of control.

◆ Use an extension leash; this allows you to control your dog and, at the same time, gives the dog some freedom.

◆ Never let a dog loose near traffic, no matter how light the traffic and how obedient the dog. However well trained he is, he should be on a leash, not just walking at your side.

◆ Always have a reflective strip on the dog's leash at night so that it will show up in car headlights.

◆ Never allow a dog to run loose near sheep or other livestock; farmers are likely, and may be legally entitled in some states, to

◼ **Above:** *If your pet dog has been properly socialized, he can "work out."*

shoot the dog.

◆ Make sure that your dog obeys the commands "*Come*" and "*Sit*"; they can save a dog's life.

How much exercise?

Hounds, Sporting dogs, Working dogs, and Herding dogs generally require a great deal of exercise. They are built to move over great distances and thus a stroll around the block twice a day is unlikely to keep these breeds in their optimum condition. It follows that they are best kept in the country where there is plenty of space for them to run. Swimming is also great fun for most dogs; Sporting dogs, in particular, enjoy water. Dogs kept alone do not have the motivation for running around unless they hunt, and it is up to you, the owner, to provide the motivation. Most dogs can take as much exercise as their owner can give, but if you live in a congested urban area, two good walks a day and a run on the weekends are the very minimum that you should give your dog.

Don't forget that yards are also good for exercising dogs, and thirty minutes' playing with a ball or a Frisbee is good exercise for your dog's mind and body.

Terriers, Non-sporting, and Toy dogs

Dogs from the Terrier Group and also some from the Non-sporting and Toy Groups are busy dogs that like exploring yards and gardens,

◼ **Right:** *Springer Spaniels need lots of exercise but take care that you don't overexercise young puppies while their bones are growing.*

sniffing around in the bushes and trees, play-hunting, looking for mice or rats, and trying to catch birds. However, they will still enjoy taking walks – seeing new things and smelling new smells. A walk twice a day, and a long run in your local fields or woods and a swim on the weekend do the dog and his owner a great deal of good. These types of dogs are usually very playful up to old age; an hour spent with the children in the yard playing "Catch" or "hide-and-seek," as well as exercising them, occupies their mind and keeps them out of mischief, especially the Terrier breeds.

Tiny breeds, such as Pekingeses, Chihuahuas, and Pomeranians, will need very little in the way of formal exercise – just their normal activities plus some playing in the yard are sufficient. However, they love to go out on excursions, even if it means carrying them.

What surface is best?

There is an ongoing discussion as to which surface is best for dogs: exercise on hard surfaces, such as roads, or soft ground, such as grass. Generally speaking, softer ground is much better because it cushions the impact of the feet and is obviously less stressful on the muscles; it also smells better and there is no chance of being poisoned by exhaust fumes.

However, there are some good reasons for exercising a dog on hard surfaces. For one thing, the nails tend to overgrow if the dog runs only on grass; by walking on sidewalks the friction against the abrasive surface helps keep the nails short. Long nails force the dog's foot back, causing strain on

Left: Jack Russells have a well-deserved reputation for being very energetic. They can leap high up into the air from a standing start. Make sure your fences are high enough!

the joints of the foot; eventually, the pain can cause the dog to limp and he may even be unwilling to go out. Country dwellers would do well to check their pets' nails regularly and either have them trimmed by their veterinarian or do it themselves, providing they have the necessary expertise.

Good movement

The correct movement of a dog is important to dog exhibitors and there are exercises to improve it. The speed at which a human being walks is not the natural pace for

most dogs, and they have to learn to walk in a way that is foreign to their conformation. Controlled walking on a leash on hard surfaces will achieve this aim, and it will also harden the leg muscles and strengthen the joint sinews. Dogs generally should have tight feet but, unfortunately, this is not always the case. To tighten the feet, show-dog owners will walk their dog on a gravel surface so that the dog will have to clench his toes to stop small pieces of gravel from getting into the tender part of the foot. Eventually, the muscles develop and the foot stays tight.

GOING AWAY

It would be an act of cruelty to leave a dog alone in the house, even with sufficient food and water, while the owners go away on vacation. Almost certainly it would attract the attention of the neighbors and animal control authorities and might lead to court action. There is no reason why a pet dog should ever be left at home; he can either be taken along or left in a boarding kennel.

What is needed is more research. There are hotels and guesthouses that will accept dogs. The tourist information services in towns are always pleased to help and many issue a booklet containing the names of any establishments that will welcome dogs.

Some tourist towns prohibit dogs on their beaches at certain times of the year; the tourist information services will advise. There are many beaches a little way from the fashionable ones where a dog can run and swim as he pleases. Keep your dog under control in public places and always have enough plastic bags

■ **Above:** *Many dogs enjoy car travel and happily accompany their owners on vacation. Many hotels welcome dogs.*

handy to pick up after the dog – some authorities are extremely hard on owners who fail to do so.

Traveling

Buses and trains will accept dogs only at the company's discretion. Fares vary according to the combined volume and weight of the dog and its travel crate. Many airlines allow very small dogs to travel in the cabin if their travel crate can fit under the seat in front of the passenger. If the dog is too large to travel in the cabin, it can travel in the hold of the plane, in a safe area that is heated and pressurized just like the cabin. If the dog travels on the same flight as its owner, the fee for the dog is usually the same as that for one piece of excess luggage.

In a car it is always best to put a dog in a travel crate, which is safer for both the dog and driver. Get the dog used to the crate by feeding him in it with the door open at first. After a day or so, close the door. Soon the dog will accept and enjoy being in his own crate. Follow the same procedure in the car and then drive the car slowly for a couple of hundred yards a day for a week. Go somewhere the dog connects with pleasure: the park, the beach, or open ground where he runs. If the dog is car sick after this training, consult the veterinarian, but do not use human remedies.

Feeding the traveling dog

Do not change the dog's food on vacation; he may suffer an upset

■ **Right:** *Rather than travel alone in the back of the car, your dog can be put in a travel crate with a front wire grill on the front seat. For safety's sake, the seat belt can be wrapped around the crate and secured.*

BOARDING KENNELS

If you decide to place your dog in a boarding kennel, you should visit the kennel and inspect it first. If the proprietor is not willing to permit you to do this, then find another kennel. Look for cleanliness, lack of odors, and neatly dressed staff. Make sure they exercise the dogs regularly and feed them properly. Check which veterinarian visits regularly and phone him if you're uncertain. Put in writing any special diet or medication your dog may require and make sure that he is fully vaccinated, especially against kennel cough.

stomach. If ordinary and easily available complete diet or canned food is the norm for a dog, there is no need to take food with you. If he needs special food – for instance, he may be elderly with a kidney dysfunction – you would

be wise to take the right food with you. For a day out, there are food carriers that are specially designed to hold a day's food and water, keeping them hygienic and cool. Frequent stops to allow the dog to stretch and relieve himself should be made; if the day is hot, offer him water regularly.

Hot days

All dogs suffer badly from heat, especially thick-coated, short-nosed, and black ones, so on hot days take ice packs or bags of frozen peas to place on the heads of overheated dogs. Never, under any circumstances, leave a dog in a car in the sun. Even with the windows open, he can be "cooked" to death in a short time. If a dog shows heat distress, his tongue will hang fully out, he will pant deeply and be unwilling to move. Pack him with ice, immerse him fully in cold water, then get him to a veterinarian immediately.

Left: *With a dark thick coat and short nose, this Lhasa Apso will have to be watched carefully on hot days when you are traveling.*

Elderly dogs

Unless an old dog is full of vigor, it would not be fair to take him on a long trip. It's no problem if he is used to particular boarding kennel and you are satisfied with the service and treatment. If not, he can be placed in the home and care of a trusted friend whom he knows and who will feed and exercise him properly. Alternatively, you can engage the services of a dog sitter. Dog fancy magazines advertise for people who make a living by staying in dog owners' homes and looking after their animals.

PET TRAVEL TIPS

◆ Before you travel, train your dog to become accustomed to his travel crate by giving him special treats in the crate, taking him on short trips in the car, and letting him sleep overnight in the crate. Make sure he feels comfortable in his crate before you take your trip.
◆ Make an appointment for your dog to visit the veterinarian at least one week before you leave, to be sure your dog is healthy and capable of making the trip.
◆ Remember to ask your veterinarian for an official health certificate for your dog within one week of travel.

◆ If your pet has a tendency to be carsick or airsick, ask your veterinarian for preventive medication.
◆ If you are traveling to an area in which exposure to heartworm disease is a risk, be sure to start your dog on heartworm preventive medication at least thirty days before you travel.
◆ Make sure your dog is up to date on all of his vaccinations, especially rabies immunization, which is required before your veterinarian can issue an official health certificate for travel.
◆ Order an identification tag or collar for your pet, and add a family member's phone number to it in the

event you lose your dog and cannot be reached immediately.
◆ Ask your veterinarian to microchip and/or tattoo your dog so that you will have a permanent form of identification in case he is lost.
◆ Check in advance which hotels accept dogs and make your reservations as early as possible.
◆ If you are traveling out of the country, contact the consulate of the country for specific information regarding importation requirements.
◆ Take your dog's usual food with you and whenever possible, take a break so your pet can relieve himself.

Chapter Seven

HEALTH CARE

The arts of medicine and surgery that relate to the dog, whether he's a champion or a rescued foundling, are now very highly sophisticated veterinary specialities. The actual health problems that can afflict the species are being intensively researched and much is known both about how similar and how different dogs are compared to other animals or to humans when they are ill or in trouble.

An intricate machine needs a skilled mechanic, so do not be tempted to tinker with your dog. Our aim in this section of the book will be to explain certain symptoms and what you should do about them, and to give you some simple, useful first aid with an emphasis on the "first." It is very important that you seek veterinary help for all but the mildest and briefest conditions. The basic principles behind the more common diseases of dogs are outlined, together with the ways in which the veterinarian combats these problems.

However, in all of your pet's ailments, whether they are mild or serious, you will normally have to be prepared to do something, usually acting as a nurse, and there are some essential nursing techniques to be learned. These are explained later in this chapter (see page 126) so that you are armed with the knowledge and also the basic skills to look after a sick dog with loving care.

Left: *The specialist terminology for the dog's anatomy is shown here.*

Stop — Skull — Occiput — Muzzle — Cheek — Neck — Withers — Back — Croup — Set-on of tail — Shoulder blade — Upper arm — Thigh — Loin — Stifle (knee) — Lower thigh — Chest — Brisket — Hock or tarsus — Forearm — Metatarsus — Pastern

What to look for

As already advised, it is a good idea to examine your dog regularly and to check for any warning signs of potential health problems. If you know what to look for, this is a good way of preventing ill health or identifying telltale symptoms early enough to treat them effectively before they become more serious. Check your dog over once a week – when you are grooming him is usually a good time to do this. If you handle him in this way from an early age, he won't mind you opening his mouth and peering into his ears and eyes when he grows older and bigger.

A healthy dog should always look healthy, be bright-eyed and full of energy, and always ready for a walk or a game. He should not be too fat or too thin and should have a healthy appetite. Any changes in his normal appearance, temperament, and behavior should be analyzed carefully as they may be clues to present or future health problems. Watch out especially for persistent scratching and licking, which may be caused by parasites, allergies, injuries, or skin inflammation.

WARNING SIGNS

Here are some of the signs of poor health that you should look for. If you think your dog is not well, contact your veterinarian.

◆ Loss of appetite
◆ Asking for food but not eating
◆ Eating more without weight gain
◆ Sudden weight loss
◆ Increased or excessive thirst
◆ Reluctance to exercise
◆ Limping and holding up a paw
◆ Decreased agility
◆ Pain on movement
◆ Discharge from eyes and nose
◆ Persistent cough
◆ Bad breath
◆ Yellowish brown, cracked, or missing teeth
◆ Bleeding, swollen, or sore gums
◆ Persistent scratching
◆ Obsessive licking
◆ Skin inflammation
◆ Skin abscesses
◆ Dull coat
◆ Bloated abdomen
◆ Dragging the hindquarters
◆ Diarrhea
◆ Vomiting
◆ Constipation

Anal region

This should be clean without any feces clinging to the fur. The dog should not lick this area excessively or drag his rear along the ground.

Nails

The nails should end level with the pad and not be too long. Look out for broken or damaged nails or dewclaws (if they have not been removed), and grass awns embedded in the pads.

Ears

They should be responsive to any sound. The insides should be pale pink with no visible wax or unpleasant odor. Your dog should not shake his head excessively or scratch his ears too often.

Eyes

The eyes should be bright, alert, and without any signs of discharge, swelling, or tearstains. A tiny amount of mucus in the inner corners is quite normal.

Nose

The nose of a healthy dog should be cold and damp without any discharge. Occasionally there may be a little clear fluid.

Teeth

Healthy teeth are white and smooth, not yellow, which is a sign of plaque and tartar formation. The breath should not smell unpleasant and there should be no loose or missing teeth or inflamed or bleeding gums.

Body

The dog's body should be firm and well muscled. He should not carry excess weight or be so thin that his ribs stick out.

Coat

The coat should be in good condition and should smell pleasantly "doggy." It should be glossy and pleasant to touch. When you part the hairs, there should be no signs of flea droppings or sore or bare patches.

CHECKING YOUR DOGS'S WEIGHT

Feel your dog along the flanks. You should be able to just feel his ribs under his skin. However, they should not be visible.

HEREDITARY DISEASES

There is a wide variety of diseases in dogs, as in humans, that can be inherited, and these may occur in both purebred and crossbred animals. Caused by genetic faults or aberrations, they may appear to a lesser or greater degree in any individual of a particular breeding line, or they may even be absent altogether in some litter members or whole generations.

The genetic background of this type of ailment can be highly complicated and it is the concern of the professional dog breeders, veterinarians, and geneticists. Screening tests are available for tendencies to some hereditary diseases, and potential owners of dogs, particularly purebreds, should discuss the lineage and history of the parents concerned

and of the specific breeding kennel involved with the breeder and their veterinarian before purchasing a puppy. Although some hereditary diseases are treatable, the underlying genetic faults cannot be eliminated.

Here are some of the best known hereditary diseases with the breeds most commonly affected. This list is not exhaustive.

HIP DYSPLASIA

Hip dysplasia is one of the most common inherited diseases and affects many breeds. In a normal, healthy dog the hip is a ball and socket joint and allows a wide range of movement. The rounded end at the top of the femur fits tightly into the cup-shaped socket (acetabulum) in the pelvis. In hip dysplasia a shallow acetabulum develops with an irregular, distorted femur head and slack joint ligaments. There can be excessive movement between the femur and pelvis, leading to a malfunctioning joint that will gradually become arthritic.

◆ Early symptoms
If a puppy develops severe hip dysplasia he may have difficulty walking. Getting up from a sitting position may be painful and he will cry out. When he runs, he may use both hind legs together in a "bunny hop" or look as though he's swaying. These symptoms may be identifiable from five months on. Mildly affected puppies may show no signs at all of hip dysplasia at this age, but they will begin to develop arthritis at about eight years of age.

◆ OFA
The Dysplasia Control Registry of the Orthopedic Foundation for Animals (OFA) is a voluntary program established to evaluate radiographs of purebred dogs and to identify X-ray films showing no radiographic evidence of canine hip dysplasia or other orthopedic problems. A panel of qualified veterinary radiologists reviews the radiographs and a report is sent to the dog's owner and the referring veterinarian. Only dogs that are twenty-four months of age or older at the time of radiography, with no radiographic evidence of hip

dysplasia, are assigned a breed OFA number. The OFA does offer a consultation service for dogs under twenty-four months of age. OFA hip evaluations are sent to the AKC and the hip ratings-certified parents appear on the registration and pedigree papers of their offspring.

◆ Treatment
Mild hip dysplasia can be managed in a growing puppy with limited exercise and proper diet and he will often grow into a healthy adult. However, you may have to restrict his exercise later on.

Hip dysplasia

Severe hip dysplasia

Flattened head

Shallow socket

Neck

Enlarged joint space

Thickened neck

Normal hip joint

Head of femur

Acetabulum

Femur

Pelvis

COMMON HEREDITARY DISEASES

Disease name	Nature of disease	Breeds most commonly affected
Bone/skeletal diseases		
Hip dysplasia	Deformation of hip joint	Labrador, other Retrievers, German Shepherd Dog
Elbow dysplasia	Deformation of elbow joint	German Shepherd Dog, Afghan Hound
Osteochondrosis dessicans	Disease of joint surfaces, particularly shoulder	Larger breeds, including Border Collie, Golden Retriever, Great Dane, Labrador Retriever
Wobbler syndrome	Malformation of neck bones	Great Dane, Doberman Pinscher
Eye diseases		
Entropion	Inversion of the eyelids	Many breeds, but particularly Shar Pei
Ectropion	Eversion of the eyelids	Clumber Spaniel, Saint Bernard
Cherry eye	Enlargement of gland in third eyelid	American Cocker Spaniel
Progressive retinal atrophy (PRA)	Degeneration of retina with progressive loss of sight	Irish Setter, Springer Spaniel
Collie eye	Degeneration of the choroids	Collie, Shetland Sheepdog
Glaucoma	Increased pressure within the eye	American Cocker Spaniel, Poodle
Cataract	Cloudiness of lens in the eye	Poodle, Labrador Retriever, Golden Retriever, American Cocker Spaniel, Beagle
Cardiovascular diseases		
Subaortic stenosis	Narrowing of the aorta with effects on heart	Boxer, German Shepherd Dog, German Short-haired Pointer, Newfoundland
Pulmonary stenosis	Narrowing of pulmonary artery with effects on heart	Beagle
Ventricular septal defect	Hole in the wall separating heart chambers	Bulldog
Patent ductus arteriosus	Heart defect	Poodle, German Shepherd Dog, Collie, Shetland Sheepdog, Pomeranian
Bleeding disorders		
Hemophilia	Clotting defects	Many breeds
Von Willebrand's disease	A special form of hemophilia	Golden Retriever, German Shepherd Dog, Doberman Pinscher, Scottish Terrier
Neurological diseases		
Cerebellar atrophy	Degeneration of the cerebellum in brain	Many breeds, including Rough Collie, Kerry Blue, Gordon Setter
Deafness	Associated with color in some breeds	Border Collie, Boston Terrier, Bull Terrier, Collie, Dalmatian, English Setter, Old English Sheepdog
Hydrocephalus and epilepsy; seizures	Fluid accumulation in the brain Seizures of varying causes	Can occur in many breeds; suspected of having a genetic cause
Hormonal diseases		
Hypothyroidism	Underactive thyroid gland	Beagle, Doberman Pinscher, Golden Retriever
Cushing's Disease	Overactive adrenal glands	Poodle

PREVENTING HEALTH PROBLEMS

Let us begin at the beginning and look at the mouth of the dog and then wander from head to tail through the various systems of the canine body.

Remember that many common diseases and health problems can be avoided if your dog is looked after properly and receives regular exercise and a high-quality diet. By checking your dog regularly for telltale signs of illness or poor health, you can prevent many from occurring or treat them at an early stage before they become serious. You should also make sure that your dog is vaccinated against canine distemper, canine parvovirus, leptospirosis, and infectious canine hepatitis.

The mouth

Common symptoms

- Salivating (drooling)
- Pawing at the mouth
- Exaggerated chewing motions
- Tentative chewing as if dealing with a hot potato
- Bad breath

What you can do

This important end of the animal should be inspected from time to time to see that all is well. Cleaning of the teeth once or twice weekly with cotton balls or a soft toothbrush dipped in salt water (or dog toothpaste from a tube kept specially for your pet) will stop the buildup of troublesome tartar.

Special dog toothpaste, in various flavors that appeal to the animals, is now available. Giving chewable things like "bones" and chews made of processed hide (available from the pet shop) and the occasional meal of coarsely cut, raw butcher's meat will also help. Providing bones of any kind does not keep tartar down.

The teeth and jaws

Function of teeth

Incisors: Cut and nibble food, biting, and grooming

Canines: Hold and tear food

Premolars: Cutting, shearing, and holding food

Molars: Chewing and grinding

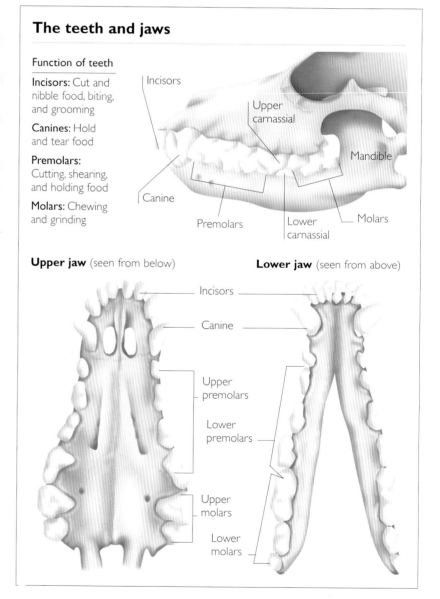

Upper jaw (seen from below)   **Lower jaw** (seen from above)

Tooth anatomy

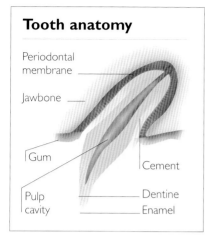

Periodontal membrane

Jawbone

Gum

Cement

Pulp cavity

Dentine

Enamel

Tartar

When tartar, a yellowish-brown, cementlike substance, accumulates, it does not produce holes in the teeth that need filling. Instead, it damages the gum edge, lets bacteria in to infect the tooth sockets, and thus loosens the teeth. Tartar always causes some gum inflammation (gingivitis) and frequently bad breath.

If your pet displays any of the symptoms described, open his mouth and look for a foreign body stuck between his teeth. This may be a sliver of wood or bone stuck between two adjacent molars at the back of the mouth or, quite commonly, a bigger object jammed across the upper teeth against the hard palate. With patience, you can usually flick such foreign bodies out with a teaspoon handle or a similar instrument.

Gingivitis

Bright red edging to the gums where they meet the teeth, together with ready bleeding on even gentle pressure, are the prime signs of gingivitis. Tap each tooth with your finger or a pencil. If there are any signs of looseness or tenderness,

wash the mouth with some warm water and salt, and contact your veterinarian.

Broken tooth

Sometimes Fido breaks one of his teeth, perhaps by fighting or by chewing stones (a bad habit that some dogs get into). The large "fang" teeth (canines) are most often the ones damaged. These injuries do not usually produce any signs of toothache, root infection, or death of the tooth. Treatments used in human dentistry, such as fillings, root treatments, or crowning, may be necessary and are all possible.

Ulcers and tumors

Mouth ulcers, tumors (juvenile warts are common in young dogs), and tonsillitis need veterinary diagnosis and treatment where they are the cause of some of the symptoms listed above.

At the veterinarian's

Canine dentistry is easily tackled by the veterinarian. Using

The teeth and jaws

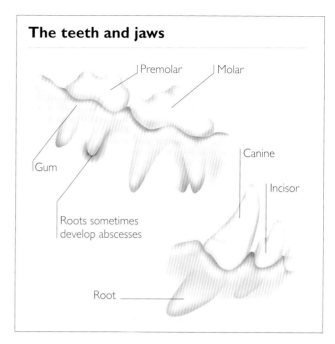

Premolar

Molar

Gum

Canine

Incisor

Roots sometimes develop abscesses

Root

tranquilizers or short-acting general anesthetics, your veterinarian can remove tartar from a dog's teeth with special scrapers or the modern, ultrasonic scaling machines. Antibacterial drugs may also be prescribed if encroaching tartar has provoked secondary gum infection.

Bad teeth must be taken out to prevent root abscesses and socket infection from causing problems, such as septicemia, sinusitis, or even kidney disease, elsewhere in the dog's body.

▨ **Left:** *Periodically check the lip pouch on soft-mouthed dogs, such as Cocker Spaniels, as they may contain leftover food that can cause bad breath and lead to infection.*

The eyes

Common symptoms

▓ Sore, runny, or inflamed eyes
▓ Blue or white film over the eye
▓ Partially or totally closed eye or eyes

What you can do

If only one eye is involved and the only symptom is tearing or a sticky discharge without marked irritation, you can try washing the eye with boric acid eyewash once every few hours, followed by the introduction of an appropriate ointment (obtainable from your veterinarian) onto the eyeball. If any symptoms in or around the eyes last for more than a day, consult your veterinarian.

Distemper

Particularly in young dogs, eyes with a pus discharge may indicate distemper (see page 109).

Eye conditions

Persistent watering of one or both eyes can be due to very slight

The eye

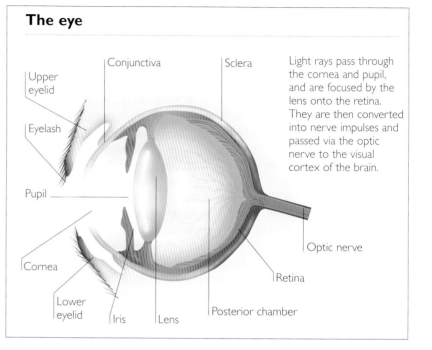

Upper eyelid

Eyelash

Pupil

Cornea

Lower eyelid

Iris

Lens

Conjunctiva

Sclera

Optic nerve

Retina

Posterior chamber

Light rays pass through the cornea and pupil, and are focused by the lens onto the retina. They are then converted into nerve impulses and passed via the optic nerve to the visual cortex of the brain.

inversion (entropion) of the eyelid, or blocked tear ducts. A blue or white film over one or both eyes is normally a sign of keratitis (inflammation of the cornea); this is not a cataract but requires immediate veterinary attention. Opacity of the lens (cataract) is a blue or white film much deeper in the eye. It usually occurs in older animals but may be seen in young pups (congenital cataract) and at other ages (diabetic cataract).

Inflammations of the eye

These are treated by the veterinarian in various ways. Antibiotic injections, drops, and ointments are available, plus other drugs to reduce inflammation and surgical methods of tackling ulcerated eyes under local anesthesia. Problems due to deformities or inversion of the eyelids, foreign bodies embedded in the eyeball, and even some cataracts can be treated surgically today.

GIVING EYE OINTMENTS

There is an important technique in applying ointments to animals' eyes.

1 Hold the tube parallel to the eyeball and pull the lower eyelid down slightly. Let ½ inch (1 cm) of the ointment fall onto the eyeball or inside the lower lid.

2 Now hold both lids closed for five seconds to allow the ointment to melt and begin dispersing.

The nose

Common symptoms

▓ Discharge from the nostrils
▓ The appearance of having the human common cold
▓ A cracked, sore, dry nose tip
▓ A dog "with a cold," particularly if both eyes and nose have a discharge, may have distemper

What you can do

Don't let the nostrils get caked and clogged up. Bathe them thoroughly with warm water and apply cold cream to the nose pad. If there is the "common cold" symptom, seek veterinary advice at once. Old dogs with cracked, dry nose pads need regular attention to keep their nostrils free and to deal with bleeding from the cracks. Bathe the nose frequently, apply vegetable oil or Vaseline twice or three times daily and work it in well. Give any medications prescribed by the veterinarian, who may use corticosteroid preparations on tough cases of sore noses.

Rhinitis and sinusitis

Sneezing, a purulent discharge from the nostrils, head shaking, and, perhaps, nosebleed may indicate rhinitis (inflammation of the nasal passages) or sinusitis (inflammation within one or more of the sinus chambers in the skull). Bacterial, viral, or fungal germs, foreign bodies, growths, tooth abscesses, or eye disease can be the cause, and treatment again depends on precise diagnosis.

SINUSITIS

Like humans, dogs possess air-filled spaces in the bones of their skulls (sinuses) that can become diseased. Infections or tumors can occur in these cavities. Sometimes an infection can spread into them from a bad tooth root nearby. The signs include sneezing, persistent nasal discharge that may be purulent or blood-tinged, and head shaking.

The veterinarian can X-ray the head to investigate the problem and treatment can involve antibacterial or antifungal drugs, surgical drainage, or dental work as appropriate.

The ears

Common symptoms

▓ Shaking the head, scratching the ear
▓ Pain on touching the ear, bad smell, discharge from the ear
▓ Tilting the head to one side
▓ Ballooning of the earflap

What you can do

Where the symptoms suddenly appear, an effective emergency treatment is to carefully pour a little warmed (not hot) mineral oil into the ear – but do this outside in the yard. Acute inflammation will be greatly soothed by the oil. Don't stuff proprietary liquids into an ear; you don't know what you may be treating. Most of all, avoid those so-called canker powders as the powder bases of these products can cause added irritation by forming annoying accumulations that act as foreign bodies.

Prevention

Clean your dog's ears once a week. If it is a breed with hair growing in the ear canal (such as a Poodle or a Kerry Blue), pluck the hair out between finger and thumb. Don't cut it. Using cotton-tipped applicators or cotton balls moistened in warm mineral oil, clean the ear with a twisting action to remove excess brown earwax. See the veterinarian with any ear trouble. Chronic ear complaints can be very difficult to eradicate.

▓ **Left:** *Check your dog's inner earflap once a week and carefully pluck out any unwanted hair.*

Anatomy of the ear

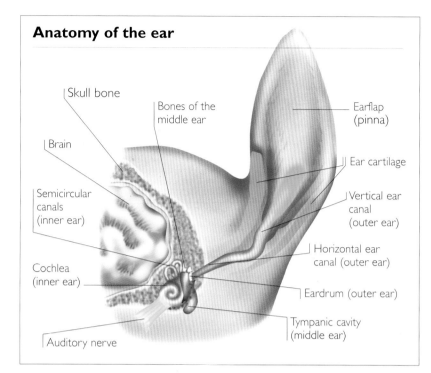

Skull bone

Bones of the middle ear

Brain

Semicircular canals (inner ear)

Cochlea (inner ear)

Auditory nerve

Earflap (pinna)

Ear cartilage

Vertical ear canal (outer ear)

Horizontal ear canal (outer ear)

Eardrum (outer ear)

Tympanic cavity (middle ear)

Grass seed in the ear

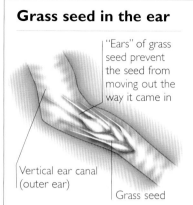

"Ears" of grass seed prevent the seed from moving out the way it came in

Vertical ear canal (outer ear)

Grass seed

Ear problems

Below: *To remove surface wax from a dog's ear, gently use some twisted absorbent cotton. If the dog is holding his head to one side, you may suspect a foreign body in the ear. Seek your veterinarian's help.*

These may be due to various things that find their way into the ear canal. A grass awn may need professional removal. Small, barely visible white mange mites that live in dogs' ears cause itching and allow bacteria to set up secondary infections. Sweaty, dirty conditions, particularly in the badly ventilated ears of breeds such as spaniels, provide an ideal opportunity for germs to multiply. The veterinarian will decide whether mites, bacteria, fungi, or other causes are the main source of inflammation, and will use antiparasitic, antibiotic, or anti-fungal drugs as drops or injec-tions. Where chronically inflamed ears are in need of drainage, sophisticated plastic surgery under general anesthetic is often performed.

Middle ear disease

Although tilting of the head may be due simply to severe irritation on one side, it can indicate that the middle ear, the deeper part beyond the eardrum, is involved. Middle ear disease does not necessarily result from outer ear infection but may arise from trouble in the Eustachian tube that links the middle ear to the throat. It always requires some rigorous veterinary attention with the use of antiflammatory drugs, antibiotics, and, more rarely, deep drainage operations.

Ballooning of an earflap

This looks dramatic and serious but isn't. It is really a big blood blister, caused by the rupture of a blood vessel in the earflap. It generally follows either vigorous head shaking, scratching where ear irritation exists, or a bite from another dog. It is treated surgically by the veterinarian, who may drain it with a syringe or open it, and then stitch the earflap in a special way to prevent further trouble.

Aural hematoma

Normal earflap (side view)

Aural hematoma

Cartilage

Blood clot

The chest

Common symptoms

- Coughing
- Wheezing
- Labored breathing

Dogs can suffer from bronchitis, pleurisy, pneumonia, heart disease, and other chest conditions. Coughing and sneezing, the signs of a "head cold," possibly together with a discharge from the eyes, diarrhea, and listlessness, may indicate the serious viral disease, distemper.

Distemper

Although more common in younger animals, it can occur at any age and shows a variety of symptom combinations. Dogs with distemper can recover although the outlook is serious if there are symptoms such as seizures, chorea (uncontrollable limb twitching), or paralysis, which suggest that the disease has affected the nervous system. These may not appear until many weeks after the virus first invades the body, and can be the only visible symptoms.

What you can do

Make sure you have your dog vaccinated against distemper at the first opportunity and keep up the annual boosters. At the first signs of generalized illness, perhaps resembling flu or a cold, contact the veterinarian. Keep the animal warm, give him plenty of liquids, and provide some easily digestible nourishing food.

The veterinarian, using clinical methods of examination, can confirm or deny the presence of distemper. Since it is caused by a virus, the disease is very difficult to treat. Antibiotics and other drugs are used to suppress any dangerous secondary bacterial infections. Vitamin injections strengthen the body's defenses. The debilitating effects of coughing, diarrhea, and vomiting are countered by drugs that reduce these symptoms.

Other types of chest disease can be investigated by the veterinarian using a stethoscope, X-rays, laboratory tests, and electrocardiographs.

Coughs

Where troublesome coughs occur in the older dog, contact your veterinarian for an appropriate cough suppressant.

Heart disease

It is common in senior canines and often responds well to treatment. Modern drugs can, under careful veterinary supervision, give a new lease on life to dogs suffering from heart disease.

It is important in cases of heart trouble and indeed, in all older dogs, to feed a reduced salt diet and be sure your dog has plenty of fresh water at all times.

Bronchitis

Inflammation of the tubes that conduct air throughout the lungs (the bronchi) can be caused by a variety of bacteria and viruses, parasitic lungworms, allergy, inhalation of dust, smoke, or foreign bodies, or by too much barking. Specific therapy is

The respiratory system

The larynx, trachea, lungs, and bronchi, together with the nose, make up the dog's respiratory system. Air is inhaled through the nose, filtered, and passed through the larynx into the trachea. It enters the lungs through the bronchi, which subdivide into bronchioles and end in alveoli, or air sacs. Oxygen and carbon dioxide are exchanged in the alveoli.

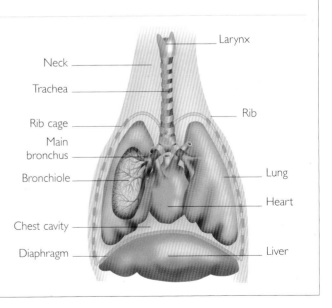

Neck — Trachea — Rib cage — Main bronchus — Bronchiole — Chest cavity — Diaphragm — Larynx — Rib — Lung — Heart — Liver

applied by the veterinarian after making a diagnosis and sometimes, in the case of foreign bodies, surgery or the use of a fiber-optic bronchoscope is necessary under general anesthetic.

Kennel cough

This condition is caused by a bacterium (Bordetella) or viruses (canine parainfluenza virus, canine herpes virus, canine adenovirus) or a mixture of these. The signs are a dry cough, often with sneezing and a moderate eye and nostril discharge. Laboratory tests are available for confirmation of the diagnosis and dogs can be protected by kennel cough vaccines administered by injection or, in some cases, as nasal drops, after four to six weeks of age.

Pneumonia

There are numerous causes of pneumonia in dogs, the most common being infections by microorganisms such as viruses or bacteria. Migrating parasitic worm larvae and inhalation of foreign bodies are less frequent causes. The signs are faster and/or more labored breathing, coughing, a raised temperature, and, sometimes, nasal discharge. Using the stethoscope and tapping the chest, the veterinarian can quickly make a diagnosis and begin treatment with antibiotics, corticosteroids, cough medicines, and other medication aimed at relieving symptoms. Pneumonia, whenever diagnosed, or even suspected, always demands immediate professional attention.

The heart and circulatory system

As with human beings, dogs can suffer from heart ailments; these can either be congenital (the animal is born with a defect such as a hole in the heart or an unwanted extra blood vessel, most commonly in the form of a patent ductus arteriosus) or be acquired (developing during life as a result of infection, trauma, or the animal's advancing years).

Signs of heart and circulatory problems can include easy tiring when the dog is exercised, fast or labored breathing, a rapid pulse, swelling of the abdomen (due to an accumulation of ascitic fluid or enlargement of the liver), cough, particularly during the night, pale or unusually brightly colored gums, and weight loss.

The veterinarian will use a stethoscope to detect any heart murmurs, as well as blood tests, an electrocardiograph, X-rays, and perhaps other specialized medical equipment in order to arrive at a diagnosis.

Treatment again depends on precise diagnosis, and dog owners should seek professional advice early on. Heart stimulant drugs, diuretics to dispel any fluid accumulations, and preparations that dilate the breathing tubes and stimulate respiration are widely used. A good low-salt diet and, where necessary, weight reduction in the patient may play an important role in the handling of such cases.

How the heart works

The dog's heart consists of two pairs of chambers: the atria and ventricles. Deoxygenated blood enters the right atrium and is then pumped out through the right ventricle to the lungs, where it is oxygenated. This blood flows into the left atrium and from there through the left ventricle to the body's organs.

The circulatory system
▬▬ Oxygenated blood
▬▬ Deoxygenated blood

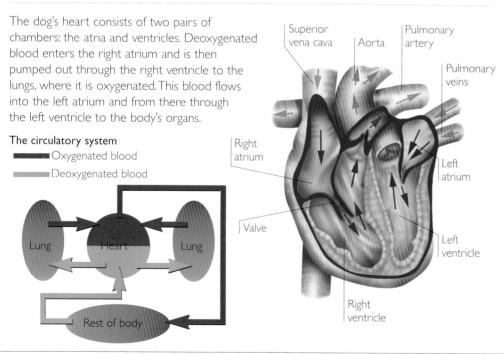

Lung   Heart   Lung

Rest of body

Superior vena cava | Aorta | Pulmonary artery

Pulmonary veins

Right atrium

Left atrium

Valve

Left ventricle

Right ventricle

The stomach and intestine

Common symptoms

■ Vomiting, diarrhea, constipation
■ Blood in the droppings

There are numerous causes for any of the symptoms listed above and sometimes more than one symptom will be observed at the same time. We will deal only with the most common symptoms and not attempt to describe all the diseases that can involve the abdominal organs.

Note: Any symptom persisting longer than twelve hours despite sensible first aid treatment needs urgent veterinary attention.

Vomiting

Vomiting may be simple and transient due to a mild infection (gastritis) of the stomach or to simple food poisoning. If severe, persistent, or accompanied by other major signs, it can indicate the presence of serious conditions, such as distemper, infectious canine hepatitis, leptospirosis, a heavy worm infestation, or an obstruction of the intestine.

Diarrhea

This may be nothing more than the result of a gastric irritation or a mild bowel infection. It may be more serious and profuse where important bacteria are present, in certain types of poisoning, and in some allergies.

Constipation

This can be due to age, to a faulty diet including bone particles, or to intestinal obstruction.

Blood in the stool

This can arise from a variety of minor and major causes: from nothing more than a bone splinter scraping the rectal lining to the dangerous leptospiral infection.

What you can do

By all means, try to alleviate the symptoms, but if they persist you must contact the veterinarian no later than the following day.

With both vomiting and diarrhea, it is important to replace liquids lost by the body. Cut out solid food, milk, and fatty things. Give a little fluid, glucose and water, or weak bouillon cube broth – and often. Ice cubes can be supplied for licking. Keep the animal warm and indoors. For vomiting, administer 1–3 teaspoons of Milk of Magnesia, depending on the dog's size, every three hours.

Don't use castor oil on constipated animals. Give mineral oil ($1/2$–2 tablespoons). Where an animal is otherwise well but you know it to be constipated from something like bone that, after being chewed, sets like cement in the bowels, get a baby enema from the pharmacy. This disposable, small, ready-loaded enema is very easy to use; just take off the top and insert the nozzle into the animal's rectum. Then squeeze, using half the contents for a toy breed and the full enema for all other sizes.

Abdominal conditions in general will need veterinary attention. Diseases such as contagious canine hepatitis and

The digestive system

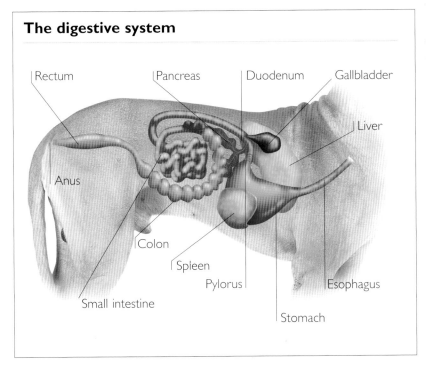

Rectum
Pancreas
Duodenum
Gallbladder
Liver
Anus
Colon
Spleen
Pylorus
Esophagus
Small intestine
Stomach

Above: *If your dog refuses to take his medicine, you may have to give it to him through a syringe (needleless). If he resists, you can make a temporary muzzle and then administer the fluid into the cheek pouch behind it.*

leptospirosis require intensive medical treatment with antibiotics, transfusion to replace fluids, vitamins, and minerals.

Acute abdomen

The sudden onset of severe pain, vomiting with or without diarrhea, and the collapse of the dog into shock is a major emergency that necessitates immediate veterinary attention. The cause may be a powerful, rapidly developing infection, obstruction of the intestine by a foreign body or a twist of the bowel itself, torsion (twisting)

of the stomach, acute kidney, liver, or uterine disease, or poisoning. Successful treatment depends mainly on quick diagnosis.

Flatulence

"Gassy" dogs may be the product of a faulty or changed diet. Often, flatulence is associated with food that is too low in fiber although, paradoxically, too much fiber can cause a similar effect.

What you can do

Generally, adjusting the diet to one of high digestibility and low residue will do the trick. Helpful medications available from the pharmacy are bulking agents such as psyllium seed powder. Adding bran to the dog's food will alleviate many cases.

Malabsorption

Some dogs with chronic diarrhea (often rather fatty looking), associated with a strong appetite but loss of weight are not able to digest or absorb their food normally. The causes may be due to enzyme deficiency (liver or

pancreas problems) or disease of the bowel walls.

The veterinarian will use a variety of tests to establish the cause and will then prescribe the appropriate therapy. Animals deficient in pancreatic enzymes can be given pancreatic extract supplements with their food.

Polydipsia and polyphagia

Polydipsia (drinking more than normal) and polyphagia (eating more than normal) can be associated with diabetes, disease of the adrenal glands, kidney disease, and other conditions. Careful examination of the patient together with laboratory tests on blood and/or urine samples are necessary to pinpoint the cause and lead to the correct treatment.

Salmonella infection

The newspapers are full of salmonella scares. Salmonella is a type of bacterium that occurs in a wide variety of strains (serotypes) that may cause disease in, or be carried symptomlessly by, almost any species of animal. Sometimes,

PARVOVIRUS INFECTION

Only recognized for the past twenty-two years, this viral disease is spread via the feces (droppings). It only affects the Canid family that includes dogs, wolves, and foxes (although the latter are fairly resistant to it). The incubation period is five to ten days and the symptoms vary from sudden death in young pups, through severe vomiting, foul-smelling diarrhea (often bloody), absence of appetite, and depression to mild, transient bouts of diarrhea.

The veterinarian can confirm a diagnosis of parvovirus by means of a laboratory test of the feces.

Professional treatment includes the use of fluid replacement, antivomiting and antidiarrhea drugs (such as the ever-useful kaolin), and antibiotics to combat secondary infections.

Puppies can be vaccinated against parvovirus from twelve weeks of age (older dogs and pups over twelve weeks of age) or six to nine weeks (young pups under twelve and twenty weeks; these will need revaccinating at twelve weeks). Combined vaccines that give "all-in-one" protection against distemper, kennel cough, infectious canine hepatitis, and parvovirus are available.

salmonella can be found in the droppings of apparently normal healthy dogs. Dogs can contract salmonellosis with signs of diarrhea (sometimes bloody), vomiting, stomach pain, and collapse, sometimes ending in

death, by eating infected food (meat, eggs, etc.), or by coming into contact with rodents or their droppings or other infected dogs or, more rarely, reptiles or birds.

Diagnosis is made by the veterinarian sending away

samples for bacteriological culture and identification. Treatment is by specific antibiotics, fluid replacement, and other methods. It is worth remembering that salmonella infection in animals may be transmissible to humans.

Anal glands

Common symptoms

■ Rubbing the bottom along the floor or suddenly chasing the rear end as if stung by a bee

Two little glands, one on each side just within the anus, cause a lot of trouble for dogs. Worms are usually blamed as the cause but

they rarely are. The anal glands are at the root of the problem, since they tend to get blocked up and impacted. By rubbing his rear end on the floor, the dog will often clear the glands and relieve his irritation. However, if the glands become infected, anal abscesses can result, which may mean antibiotic therapy and, in chronic cases, surgical removal of the glands.

What you can do

Exercise the glands by making sure the dog produces bulky stools. Add fibrous foods, such as vegetables, to the diet. Mix a teaspoonful or two of bran or psyllium seed powder with meals once a day for bulk. Learn how to clean out the anal glands by squeezing them with cotton balls.

The liver

The liver is the largest organ in the dog's body and one performing dozens of varied functions essential for life. It can be the site of a number of distinct diseases.

Hepatitis

Hepatitis, or inflammation of the liver, comes in two main forms: acute and chronic.

Signs of acute hepatitis can include vomiting, loss of appetite, abdominal pain, and sometimes, but not invariably, jaundice.

Chronic hepatitis is more subtle with a more gradual onset and longer duration. Signs can include weight loss, a swollen abdomen due to fluid accumulation, jaundice, poor appetite, and sluggishness.

The causes of both kinds of hepatitis are, once again, many

and varied and include viruses, bacteria, and certain poisons. The veterinarian will use urine and blood tests, X-rays, ultrasound, and sometimes a procedure called needle biopsy to investigate a faulty liver. Treatment will depend on the cause.

What you can do

Apart from specific therapy which is prescribed by your veterinarian, it is important to support undamaged liver cells and encourage their multiplication by giving a proper diet. This normally should contain high-quality protein and plenty of carbohydrates including sugars.

Vitamin supplementation may be helpful as recommended by your veterinarian. (Sometimes, vitamin supplementation, especially if excessive, can do more harm than good.)

Chronic liver disease

Characterized by jaundice, loss of weight, fluid accumulation in the abdominal cavity, and sometimes neurological symptoms, chronic disease of the liver can follow hepatitis, hormonal disease, tumor development, or cirrhosis.

The veterinarian will diagnose and treat this condition as in chronic hepatitis.

Infectious canine hepatitis

This condition, which is caused by a virus, is also known as canine adenovirus 1(CAV-1).It is a serious disease that can present the symptoms mentioned above in acute hepatitis as well as a blue-white "film" of the corneas in the later phases as a dog recovers.

Treatment is as for acute hepatitis (see page 113) in general. As always, prevention is better than cure and all puppies should be vaccinated against the disease.

This can be done by means of a vaccine that also protects against other important diseases such as canine distemper and parvovirus. The age of vaccination depends on the individual animal, risk of exposure, and veterinary advice, but will, in any case, need repeating. Booster vaccinations should be given annually to maintain protection.

Leptospirosis

There are two main types of leptospiral infection that affect dogs. One of these, Leptospira icterohemmorhagiae, attacks principally the liver and the other, Leptospira canicola, is associated with interstitial nephritis of the kidneys. Both are bacteria. Symptoms of the two forms can sometimes resemble one another.

The liver form, often picked up from contact with rat droppings or urine and with an incubation period of five to seven days, produces fever, vomiting, thirst, painful abdomen, diarrhea (often bloody), increased red and bloody gums, and jaundice. Treatment, which must be given quickly, includes specific antibiotics, antiserum, fluid therapy, and drugs to suppress vomiting and diarrhea.

Again, vaccination will give excellent protection against this serious ailment. Leptospira icterohemmorhagiae can infect humans so care and good hygiene are absolutely essential when you are handling canine Leptospira patients.

Jaundice

Yellow gums, mouth lining, and eye membranes often indicate a significant liver problem but there are other possible causes including certain blood disorders, poisons that destroy red blood cells, and disease of the pancreas.

Jaundice always requires immediate veterinary attention.

Above: *Make sure you have your dog vaccinated at the correct age and thereafter have a booster injection anually.*

Urinary system

Common symptoms

- Difficulty passing urine
- Frequent urination
- Blood in urine
- Perhaps increased thirst

What you can do

Although kidney disease is a major area of canine medicine, it is outside the scope of normal owner treatment. Whenever you notice that there is something wrong with the dog's urinary system, you must see the veterinarian. Inflammation of the bladder (cystitis), stones in the bladder or associated tubes, and kidney disease are common and need immediate professional advice. Whatever you do, don't withhold drinking water from an animal with urinary problems.

Leptospira

One of the most important diseases of the dog's kidneys is infection by Leptospira canicola, a bacterium. As with the liver form of Leptospirosis, the infection of human beings by contact with dogs suffering from the disease is possible.

Dogs contract Leptospiral nephritis mainly through contact with some infected urine. The incubation period is four to twelve days. Symptoms can be acute with loss of appetite, depression, pain in the kidney (lumbar) area of the back, vomiting, thirst, foul breath, and mouth ulcers, or more chronic with thirst, loss of weight, frequent urination, and, sometimes, hind leg weakness.

The veterinarian will confirm a diagnosis by means of blood and urine tests. The treatment involves specific antibiotics and supportive measures. Protect against this disease by vaccination from six weeks with annual booster shots.

Kidney disease needs careful management and supervision of diet. Chronic kidney disease patients can live to a ripe old age if the water, protein, and mineral content of the diet are regulated, bacterial infection controlled, protein loss minimized, and stress of any sort avoided. Prescription diets for chronic kidney cases are available from veterinarians and pet shops.

Cystitis

This inflammation of the bladder generally responds well to treatment with antibiotics, such as ampicillin, perhaps together with medicines that alter the acidity of the urine and urinary sedatives.

Calculi

A diagnosis of stones (calculi) in the urinary system can be confirmed by X-ray or by ultrasound and, in most cases, the stones are easily removed surgically under general anesthetic.

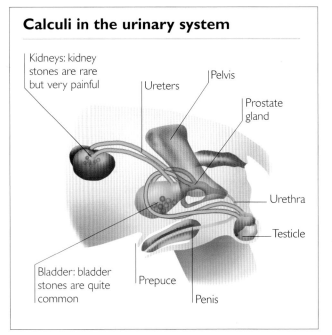

Calculi in the urinary system

Kidneys: kidney stones are rare but very painful

Ureters

Pelvis

Prostate gland

Urethra

Testicle

Bladder: bladder stones are quite common

Prepuce

Penis

Brain and nervous system

Via the intricate network of nerves that extends throughout the body the brain monitors and controls the myriad functions that make up life. But this amazing communications system, like the infinitely cruder man-made Internet, can break down. As with humans, canine neurological disorders form a complex and frustratingly difficult field of medicine.

Inflammation of the brain (encephalitis)

Common symptoms

■ Seizures
■ Changes in personality
■ Depression/dementia
■ A range of nervous signs or failures of nervous function
■ Head pressing and pawing (usually indicating pain)

What you can do

Seek professional attention at the earliest opportunity. Give older dogs a diet of high-quality protein that contains plenty of vitamins and minerals, and have a medical check on them annually. The possible causes of encephalitis are numerous. They include viral infections, such as distemper or rabies, bacterial infections, tumors, and so-called "old dog encephalitis," which may be the distemper virus raising its ugly head in later life.

Other things that don't actually inflame the brain but can produce similar symptoms by affecting the nervous system in general are poisons, such as lead, strychnine, and car antifreeze, and advanced liver disease that produces high levels of toxic ammonia in the affected animal's blood.

The veterinarian will make a diagnosis that is based on a

careful clinical examination together, as required, with X-rays, electroencephalography, and analysis of cerebrospinal fluid. Treatment depends on cause and will usually mean a combination of specific drugs, such as antibiotics, and symptomatic drugs, such as corticosteroids and diuretics to reduce brain swelling. Special methods and antidotes can be employed where the poisons are producing encephalitis-like symptoms in the dog.

Epilepsy

Epileptic seizures are caused by electrical discharges, which could be described as "shorts" in the "wiring" of the brain's cells (nerves) and connections.

Symptoms include convulsions, loss of consciousness, and collapse, occurring usually when the dog is asleep or at least relaxed. They can last a few seconds or several minutes. Animals very rarely die while they are having a seizure. Before and after an epileptic episode the dog may be depressed, badly behaved, or confused.

Causes are canine distemper (late stage), encephalitis, brain tumor, tetanus, severe kidney or liver failure, or, in postparturient bitches, eclampsia (see page 150). Some epileptic cases are of totally unknown origin.

What you can do

When an epileptic episode begins, remove all stimuli from the dog's surroundings. Dim the lights, turn off the radio or TV, and do not touch, pet, or generally fuss with the patient. He is not in pain although it may be upsetting to watch. Do not try to administer medications. When the animal comes out of the seizure, contact your veterinarian to arrange an appointment.

Veterinary treatment will be targeted at the cause of the epilepsy if this can be determined. In most cases, anti-epileptic drugs will be prescribed, which may have to be administered for a long period,

The nervous system

Brain
Cerebrum
Sacral region
Thoracic spinal cord
Brain stem
Cerebellum
Cervical spinal cord
Peripheral nerves
Major nerves
Major nerves

perhaps for life, but they are very effective and, often, inexpensive.

Paralysis

Dogs can lose the use of parts of their body suddenly or gradually. The reasons are many and varied. Hind leg or hind end paralysis is one of the more common and most alarming forms of paralysis. The dog literally can't use his

back legs. This may be associated with pain in the back (lumbar) region or absence of sensation anywhere in that part of the body.

The causes include prolapsed intervertebral disk ("slipped disk"), particularly in long-backed breeds such as Dachshunds, spinal injury or inflammation, poisoning, distemper, eclampsia (see page 150), and pyometra (see page 119).

Medical treatment or surgical intervention will be indicated depending on the diagnosis. In my opinion paralytic conditions that do not begin to improve within three weeks of onset generally have a poor prognosis. If they do begin to improve, many months may pass before total or maximum possible recovery.

What you can do

Paralyzed limbs are liable to be damaged by trauma, abrasion or, in bilateral hindleg paralysis, scalding by urine. Bedsore-type ulcers may

OVEREXCITABILITY

Some dogs of certain breeds, bloodline, upbringing, or personal character show a tendency to marked excitability, to being a bit hyperactive. Careful selection when acquiring a dog and the services of a training class or animal behaviorist may help to avoid or correct such individuals.

But overexcitability, hyperexcitability, nervousness, call it what you will, can be abnormally excessive. Causes include psychological aberration (a behaviorist's help is essential), hypersexuality, and poisoning (snakebite, strychnine, lead, and certain insecticides). The veterinarian will try to pinpoint the precise cause and give specific treatment. In general, sedatives and tranquilizers will also be prescribed.

appear. Protective dressings, silicone-based barrier creams, and extra-soft bedding can be useful during the healing phase. Severely paralyzed animals can get into all sorts of trouble and be an embarrassment to themselves. Sometimes, owners will go to great lengths to construct devices such as wheeled trolleys to enable their paralyzed pets to live contented lives, but in many cases where more than one limb is out of action for many weeks, euthanasia is the kindest solution.

Skeletal problems

Arthritis and associated conditions

Common symptoms

- Lameness
- Difficulty rising
- Stiff, slow, or unusual gait
- Painful places on bones or joints

What you can do

Most importantly, slim down an overweight dog by modifying his diet (reducing the carbohydrates and fats), feeding special canned weight-reduction foods, not giving sweets, chocolates, and other treats, and gradually increasing his exercise.

If you are too soft-hearted, ask about your veterinarian's pet weight-reduction plan. Expert guidance will be provided and your dog's progress monitored by regular weighing. Avoid taking the dog out in very cold or wet weather and consider getting him a snug coat for outdoor use.

Arthritis is a result of an imbalanced diet, congenital weakness of certain joints, excessive wear, injury, and, in some cases, infections. Obviously it is more common in elderly canines. Similar symptoms can, on occasion, be caused by fractures, abscesses, tumors, or poisons, such as warfarin.

Your veterinarian can investigate by clinical examination, X-rays, and, if appropriate, drawing off a little joint fluid for laboratory analysis including bacteriology.

Treatment

Treatment by medication is similar to that in humans: corticosteroids, nonsteroidal antiinflammatory drugs and various analgesics, and, if indicated, sedatives.

Massages, perhaps using certain anti-inflammatory gels or creams under the supervision of your veterinarian, homoeopathic remedies, and acupuncture have also afforded relief and improved mobility in some cases. Whenever you are considering trying out alternative medical treatments for pets, consult your veterinarian first.

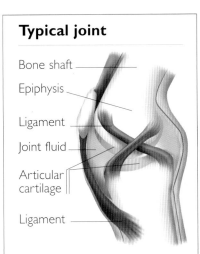

Typical joint

Bone shaft

Epiphysis

Ligament

Joint fluid

Articular cartilage

Ligament

Prolapsed intervertebral disk

This condition is also known as disk protrusion or "herniated

■ **Left:** *"Slipped disk" is more common in long-backed breeds such as the Dachshund.*

disk." The adjacent spinal vertebrae are separated by disks that act as shock absorbers when functioning correctly. With the passing of time, as dogs grow older, the disks lose their elasticity and become more brittle, less compressible, and degenerated. Then a sudden movement or trauma can cause a disk to "burst" with the discharge of crunchy material that piles up against the spinal cord or a nerve root with consequent rapid onset of symptoms. The disk itself does not actually "slip" out of line with the spine. Certain dog breeds, particularly ones with relatively long backs for their size and short legs, such as

The skeleton

The skeleton is the framework for the body. All the dog's ligaments, muscles, and tendons are attached to the bones – 319 in total. By a process called ossification, cartilage template is calcified to produce bone. Bones are living tissue and respond to the stresses and strains placed upon them. To build and maintain healthy bones, dogs need a nutritionally balanced diet that contains the appropriate ratio of calcium, vitamin D, and phosphorus.

Typical long bone

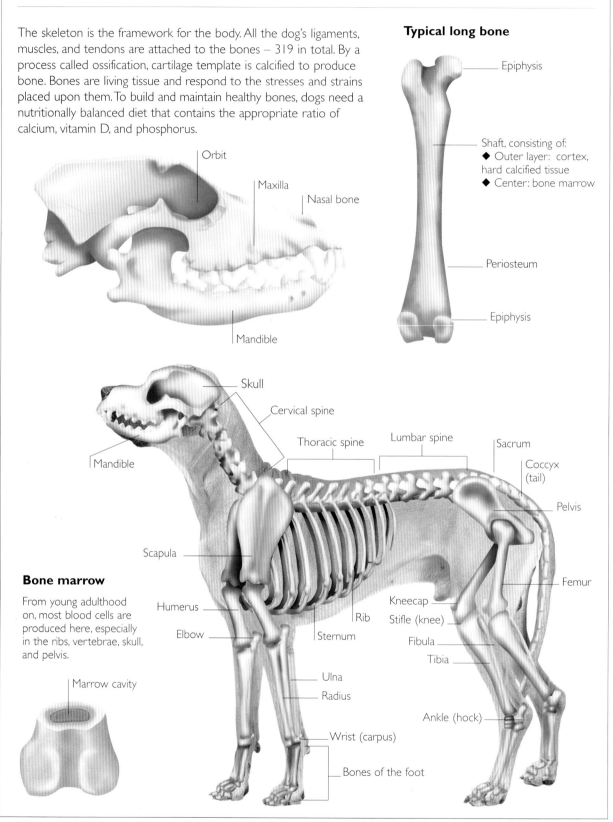

Epiphysis

Shaft, consisting of:
◆ Outer layer: cortex, hard calcified tissue
◆ Center: bone marrow

Periosteum

Epiphysis

Orbit

Maxilla

Nasal bone

Mandible

Skull

Cervical spine

Mandible

Thoracic spine

Lumbar spine

Sacrum

Coccyx (tail)

Pelvis

Scapula

Bone marrow

From young adulthood on, most blood cells are produced here, especially in the ribs, vertebrae, skull, and pelvis.

Marrow cavity

Humerus

Elbow

Rib

Sternum

Ulna

Radius

Wrist (carpus)

Bones of the foot

Femur

Kneecap

Stifle (knee)

Fibula

Tibia

Ankle (hock)

Dachshunds, Basset Hounds, and Pekingeses, are more likely to suffer from disk prolapse.

Symptoms include sudden onset of neck or back pain, paralysis or weakness of the limbs, loss of sensation, limb spasms, and loss of control of the bladder.

Accurate diagnosis is aided by X-rays, sometimes with contrast myelography. Treatment is by means of medication (analgesics, sedatives, anti-inflammatory drugs, anabolic hormones) and, in some instances, surgery to relieve the pressure on nervous tissues.

Good nursing by the owner of the dog along with veterinary advice is essential for the animal's

The spinal cord with prolapsed disk

Vertebral spine

Spinal cord

Vertebral canal

Vertebral body

Movement of Vertebral body

Fibrous band enclosing disk

Normal intervertebral disk

Material from collapsed disk presses on spinal cord

recovery. However, some dogs with severe spinal cord damage do not, unfortunately, improve significantly and may require euthanasia, which may be the kindest thing to do.

Reproductive problems

Mismating

This is when a bitch in heat is accidentally "caught" by an opportunist dog. If you think your female dog has been accidentally bred, but you are not certain, write down the date the breeding may have occurred and contact your veterinarian, who can ultrasound your pet and detect whether or not she is pregnant as early as thirty days after the breeding. If she is pregnant, your veterinarian can administer prostaglandin hormones to terminate the unwanted pregnancy, if you desire. Prostaglandins have side effects, however, and should be used only if really necessary.

Postponement of estrus and contraception

Heat (estrus) can be suppressed when symptoms of it first appear,

postponed temporarily to a more convenient time, or permanently postponed. You should discuss your requirements with the veterinarian, who will have a range of hormonal medications that may be administered by injection or as tablets by mouth. If your dog has irregular estrus cycles, or acts as though she is always in estrus, your veterinarian may recommend an ovarohysterectomy ("spay" or "neuter") as the best treatment.

Common symptoms

- Loss of appetite
- Thirst
- Swelling of abdomen
- Vomiting
- Lethargy
- In "open cases" discharge of white, yellow, or pinkish pus from the vulva

Pyometra

Literally meaning "pus in the womb," pyometra is a uterine disease that is caused by an imbalance in the sex hormones in the body, resulting in an accumulation of substances in the uterus and, often, bacterial growth and uterine infection.

What you can do
If you do not intend to breed your bitch, then you should arrange for an ovarohysterectomy while she is still young to decrease her chances of later developing mammary cancer.

Treatment
Although the veterinarian may treat secondarily infected pyometra cases with antibiotics and give supportive medication, surgery – ovarohysterectomy – is usually the treatment of choice. It is a serious operation, more risky than normal spaying, but it may be lifesaving.

The reproductive system

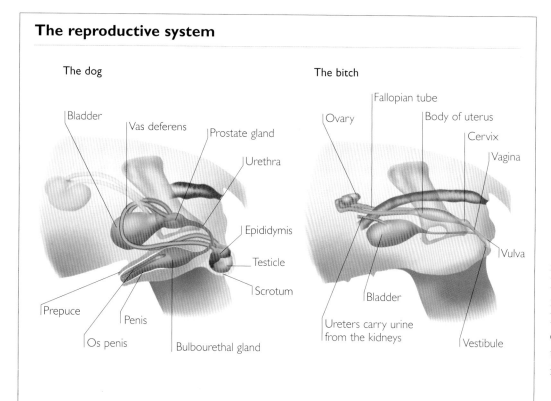

The dog

Bladder
Vas deferens
Prostate gland
Urethra
Epididymis
Testicle
Scrotum
Prepuce
Penis
Os penis
Bulbourethal gland

The bitch

Fallopian tube
Ovary
Body of uterus
Cervix
Vagina
Vulva
Bladder
Ureters carry urine from the kidneys
Vestibule

False pregnancy (pseudopregnancy)

This is a curious phenomenon where a bitch, frequently one who has not been anywhere near a dog, shows all the pregnancy signs, including an increased appetite, distended abdomen, making a bed for the expected litter, producing milk, and trying to "suckle" objects such as slippers or children's toys. It is actually quite common.

Signs like these occur three to nine weeks after the bitch was in heat (in estrus), but they do not indicate that she "craves" puppies. False pregnancies are caused by elevated progesterone levels and usually resolve without veterinary intervention.

Prostate problems

Only male animals possess prostate glands. They are situated in the pelvic cavity close to the urethra (the tube carrying urine from the bladder to the outside), and also to the rectum (the terminal end of the bowel).

The prostate can be the seat of important disease conditions. There are three kinds of possible prostate disease:
◆ Inflammation (prostatitis)
◆ Prostate cancer
◆ Prostate hyperplasia (a noncancerous enlargement).

Common symptoms

The symptoms of prostate enlargement/cancer can include:
▪ Constipation
▪ Straining to pass stool/urine
▪ Blood in the urine

Prostatis may involve similar symptoms plus fever, dullness, lack of appetite, arching of the back, and vomiting. Pain in passing urine and feces may be noted in chronic cases.

What you can do

Seek veterinary attention quickly. The veterinarian will make a clinical examination, probably including rectal palpation, X-ray, ultrasound, blood tests, and urine tests.

Treatment
The recommended treatment of choice for prostate problems is usually castration.

When a dog is constipated due to prostatic enlargement, a high-fiber, bulky diet can assist the passing of stool.

Enlarged prostate

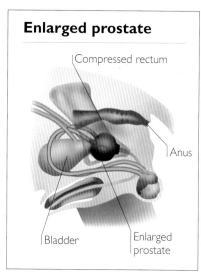

Compressed rectum
Anus
Bladder
Enlarged prostate

Skin diseases

There are many kinds of skin diseases in dogs. Diagnosis needs examination and often sample analysis by the veterinarian.

Common symptoms

■ Thin or bald patches in the coat
■ Scratching; wet, dry, or crusty sores

Mange, caused by a microscopic mite, can cause crusty, hairless sores. **Fleas, lice, and ticks** can cause damage to the coat. **Dietary deficiencies,** e.g., a shortage of certain fatty acids, can cause a poor coat.

Lumps and bumps on the skin may be abscesses, cysts, or tumors, which may need surgical attention if they persist and grow larger. The earlier a growing lump is attended to (consult your veterinarian by the time it reaches cherry size), the easier it is to eradicate.

What you can do

If you see or suspect the presence

Left: *West Highland White Terriers often suffer from skin problems. Ask your veterinarian if your dog has any particular problem relating to its breed.*

of any of the skin parasites – mange mites, fleas, ticks, or lice (see page 122) – ask your veterinarian for a prescription parasiticide. Powders are of little use against mange; products in bath or aerosol form can be helpful. Difficult forms of mange, such as demodectic mange, may be treated by the veterinarian using a combination of pills, topical medication, and injections. As there are different types of mange, let the veterinarian advise you on the best method of treating your particular case.

Ringworm, a fungal infection, may need diagnosis by ultraviolet light examination or fungus culture from a hair specimen. Special drugs given by mouth or applied to the skin are used for ringworm; care must be taken to see that humans don't pick up the disease from pets.

With all treatment of skin diseases, follow the instructions on the label of the preparation being used.

Sudden sore, wet "hot spots" that develop in summer or fall may be caused by an allergy to plant pollen and other substances. Use scissors to clip the hair over and around the affected area to a level with the skin, and apply mineral oil liberally. Such cases will need veterinary attention, perhaps involving antihistamine or corticosteroid creams, injections, or tablets. Though dramatic, they are quickly cured by treatment.

Below: *Certain flea preparations have to be applied directly to the skin, but they should be used in conjunction with parasiticides to treat the carpets, yard, and the dog's sleeping area.*

HEALTH TIPS

◆ Careful attention to providing a balanced diet will avoid most dietary skin diseases.
◆ Never apply creams, powders, or ointments to skin diseases without trimming back the hair. Don't encourage matting. Let oxygen get to the inflamed area.
◆ Groom your pet regularly; it keeps the skin and coat healthy as well as neat.

PARASITES

Dogs can play host to two different sorts of very unwelcome parasites, and these are as follows: external parasites (ectoparasites), which live on the surface of the dog's body (lice, fleas, mites, ticks, and ringworm); and internal parasites (endoparasites), which exist inside the dog's body (roundworms, hookworms, whipworms, and tapeworms).

External parasites

External parasites

(Not to scale)

Flea

Louse

Sarcoptic mange mite

Tick

Fleas

Dogs are usually infested by their own, and the cat's, species of flea but sometimes carry the rabbit fleas. The infestations are more likely to be worse in warm weather, but fleas thrive all year round, particularly where there is central heating. Sometimes it is very difficult to find any fleas on the dog. Only one flea can cause an allergic

Common symptoms

- Scratching
- Tiny reddish scabs or papules on the skin, particularly on the dog's back
- Flea droppings that look like pepper in the coat

reaction when piercing a dog's skin and injecting its saliva.

Such a reaction can result in widespread irritation, skin sores, and rashes. Flea eggs do not stick to the dog's hair like those of lice, but, being dry, drop off onto carpets and furniture.

What you can do

Use flea sprays, shampoos, or powders, obtainable from the veterinarian or pet shop, at regular intervals throughout the summer. Also treat the floors and furniture, especially your pet's favorite sleeping places, crate, and kennel with a specially formulated aerosol product every seven months. Today's modern flea products, available from your veterinarian, prevent flea eggs from hatching.

Lice

Common symptoms

- Scratching
- Lice and nits visible to the naked eye when the dog's coat is carefully searched

There are two kinds of lice:
- Biting lice that feed on skin scales
- Sucking lice that draw tissue fluids from the skin

Above: *When using flea spray, remove and spray the dog's collar, and then spray the dog, making sure you protect his eyes and mouth*

The latter cause more irritation to the dog than the former.

Lice are grayish-white in color and about $\frac{1}{8}$ inch (2 mm) in length. Their eggs (nits) are white and are cemented to the dog's hairs. The dog louse does not infest humans or cats.

What you can do

Sprays, powders, or baths are available from the veterinarian or pet shop. There are several modern products available (in oral, topical, and injectable form) that are effective in killing lice.

Mites

Let your veterinarian advise on treatment, as there are several types of mange.

Ticks

More often seen on country dogs than city dogs, ticks suck blood, their abdomen swelling up as they do so. Ticks cling to the dog's hair, generally on the legs, head, or underbelly, and pierce the skin with their mouthparts. In doing so, they can transmit an organism called Borrelia, the cause of Lyme disease. This is characterized by lameness and heart disease and requires diagnosis by means of blood tests, and then treatment using specific antibiotics and anti-inflammatory drugs.

What you can do

Remove a tick by dabbing it with some alcohol, waiting a few minutes for its head to relax, and then grasping it near the mouthparts with fine tweezers and dislodging by gently pulling straight out. Do *not* ever pull it off without applying the alcohol first as the mouthparts left in the skin may cause an abscess to form.

Another method is to spray the tick with flea spray and then to remove it the following day.

I would recommend regular application of a flea spray or fitting a tick collar during the summer months in order to control tick infestation.

Ringworm

Another occasional skin parasite of dogs is the ringworm fungus (see page 121).

Tick tweezers

Special tick tweezers are useful in removing these nasty little beasts. Avoid squashing the tick and releasing its fluids or leaving any part of the head in the skin as both may cause infection. Afterward, use disinfectant on the affected area.

Internal parasites (endoparasites)

Several kinds of parasitic worms can infest dogs and, in some cases, these parasites can spread to human beings.

Roundworms

These live, when adult, in the dog's intestines but their immature forms migrate through their host's body damaging such organs as the liver and lungs, particularly those of puppies.

Roundworms cause the most trouble for dogs, particularly puppies. Symptoms can include bowel upsets, emaciation, seizures, and chest and liver problems.

It is very important to teach children to wash their hands very well after handling puppies and dogs. Roundworms can be transmitted to humans and have the potential to cause serious problems (including larval migration in the brain and eye damage), especially in children. Good hygiene and a regular canine worming program are important and easy preventive measures you can take.

Hookworms and whipworms

These blood-sucking parasites can cause severe anemia.

Tapeworms

The most common dog tapeworm, Dipylidium, is spread by fleas, in which its larvae develop. You can see segments of this tapeworm like wriggling white grains of rice in droppings or stuck to the hair around the dog's anus.

Tapeworms may cause dogs to drag their rear ends ("scoot") along the floor, due to itching.

What you can do

Give anti-tapeworm medication as needed or when any worm segments are seen in the dog's droppings or on the hair near and around the anus. Flea control will also help to combat tapeworms.

Some treatments are effective for all types of endoparasites (consult your veterinarian).

Internal parasites   (Not to scale)

Hookworm (up to 1.2 in [3 cm])

Echinococcus (.4 in [9 mm])

Whipworm (up to 2 in [5 cm])

Dipylidium (tapeworm) (12–16 in [30–40 cm]); usually single sections seen stuck around dog's anus

MISCELLANEOUS AILMENTS

Diabetes

There are two separate types of diabetes: diabetes mellitus ("sugar diabetes"), which is common, and diabetes insipidus ("water diabetes").

Below: Always monitor your dog's eating and drinking habits. Increased thirst is sometimes a symptom of diabetes.

Diabetes mellitus

Diabetes mellitus is a disease of, or damage to, parts of the pancreas, but there are other less well understood factors, too. Basically, there is a drop in the body production of the hormone insulin, which controls the blood sugar levels. However, some patients are not insulin-dependent. The veterinarian will confirm a diagnosis of diabetes mellitus through urine and blood tests.

Common symptoms

- Excessive drinking, eating, and urination
- Weight loss or weight gain
- Rapid development of cataracts in the lenses of the eyes
- Sometimes vomiting and lethargy

Treatment

Treatment is by daily injection of a long-acting form of insulin – the veterinarian will show you how to do this and advise on the proper dosage. It is very easy and your pet quickly gets accustomed to his "shots." Unfortunately, the oral antidiabetic drugs sometimes used in humans instead of insulin injections seldom work in dogs.

What you can do

Discuss a diabetic diet with the veterinarian. It is important to time feeding correctly and to give a steady, consistent diet without changes. High-fiber, high-quality protein, low-carbohydrate diets may reduce or even eliminate the need for insulin injections.

Diabetes insipidus

This complex disease is associated with problems in the pituitary gland and/or the kidneys.

Common symptoms

- Excessive drinking and urination
- Blood and urine tests will differentiate this condition from diabetes mellitus

Treatment

This is by the use of pituitary hormone injections and, in some cases, paradoxically, certain diuretic drugs.

Eclampsia (lactation tetany)

Common symptoms

- Panting
- Stiffness
- Muscle spasms
- Excitability
- Fast breathing
- Collapse

This condition can occur in some females just before or, more often, just after giving birth. The cause is a drop in blood calcium levels.

The veterinarian will rule out other possible causes of these symptoms and give an injection of a calcium compound. Recovery is swift – within minutes.

What you can do

Do not delay getting professional help – eclampsia can be fatal. Seek veterinary advice as to whether calcium supplementation is necessary during pregnancy and lactation.

Lymphosarcoma

Common symptoms

- Enlarged lymph nodes
- Enlarged tonsils and some abdominal organs
- Poor appetite and weight loss
- Digestive and bowel upsets

Your veterinarian will use clinical examination, blood tests, and, perhaps, biopsies to confirm diagnosis. This serious form of cancer of the lymphatic system is not uncommon in dogs. However, it has not yet been proven that it is caused, as in cats, by a virus.

Treatment
Treating lymphosarcoma is very difficult and often not advisable. However, some dogs have had their lives prolonged by means of specialized corticosteroid and chemotherapeutic treatment.

Toxoplasmosis

Common symptoms

- Loss of condition and weight
- Fever
- Diarrhea
- Pneumonia
- Eye and nose discharge
- Nervous signs

Toxoplasmosis symptoms can resemble those of distemper or infectious canine hepatitis. It can lead to abortion or the death of newborn puppies. Infection by Toxoplasma gondii, a microorganism, can produce a range of subtle symptoms in a dog or even nothing at all.

Treatment
Diagnosis can be confirmed by blood tests. Treatment is by means of sulphonomides or antibiotics. **Note:** Toxoplasmosis can spread to humans, and pregnant women should avoid contact with dogs known to have symptoms or be carrying the microorganism.

Mastitis (inflammation of the breasts)

Common symptoms

- Inflamed, hard breasts when producing milk may indicate the onset of mastitis

Once a month, roll your bitch over and run your hands along her underside. If you feel any hard lumps in the substance of the breast tissue, within the teats or just under the skin, see the veterinarian at once. Breast tumors spread quickly to other parts of the body once established. Caught early, they can be removed surgically.

This condition is more common in breeds such as Boxers, especially where there is a small litter or if the bitch loses her pups.

Treatment
Treat with antiflammatory and antibacterial drugs.

RABIES

Rabies is a fatal disease that affects all mammals. In North America, wildlife (such as bats, raccoons, and skunks) serve as a reservoir for this fatal viral disease.

Symptoms and diagnosis
After an incubation period of 10–120 days, the signs can include change of temperature, restlessness, high excitability, salivation, abnormal appetite, difficulty in swallowing, paralysis, and coma. Treatment is never indicated. Confirmation of diagnosis is by laboratory examination of the brain postmortem.

Protecting your dog
Dogs can be protected from rabies by vaccination. If your dog is bitten by an unvaccinated dog or wildlife, or if you suspect it has been bitten, contact your animal regulatory authorities for information on how to proceed. Regulations vary by state but in most cases, if your dog has been vaccinated, a short quarantine period in your home is all that is required.

NURSING A SICK DOG

In all your pet's ailments, mild or serious, you will normally have to be prepared to do something, usually acting in the capacity of nurse. There are some essential nursing techniques to be learned. You should also know how to handle and restrain your dog when you treat him at home.

Taking your dog's temperature

You can't rely on the state of a dog's nose as an effective indicator of temperature, good health, or sickness. Being able to take your pet's temperature with a thermometer can help you to decide whether to call the veterinarian and can help the veterinarian diagnose and treat what is wrong with the animal.

You should use a digital thermometer (oral or rectal).

Lubricate a rectal thermometer with a little mineral oil or petroeum jelly and insert it about 1 inch (2.5 cm) into the rectum. Once it is in place, hold the thermometer against the rectal wall for good contact until the thermometer beeps to signal the temperature reading is completed. Remove and read the thermometer.

A dog's normal temperature is 101–101.6°F (38–38.6°C). Taking into account a slight rise for nervousness or excitement in some dogs, expect under such conditions to read up to 101.8°F (38.7°C) or even 102°F (38.8°C). Higher than that is abnormal. Clean and disinfect the thermometer.

Administering medicine

Try to avoid putting medicine into food or drinks; it can be very imprecise. Tablets, pills, or capsules should always be dropped into the V-groove at the back of the dog's mouth while holding it open as illustrated, with one thumb pressed firmly against the hard roof of the dog's mouth.

Liquids should be given slowly, a little at a time, by the same method or directly into the lip pouch with the mouth held closed. If you wish, they can be squirted through a syringe.

Pill gun

An alternative method of giving pills is using a water-filled pill gun that "shoots" the pill from a syringe with a dose of water to aid swallowing.

1 When giving a pill, hold the dog's mouth open and drop into V-groove at the back of his mouth.

2 After giving a pill, whether by hand or applicator, massage the throat to help the pill on its way.

▓ **Above:** *Liquids can be poured into the mouth or syringed directly into the lip pouch, thereby ensuring that all of the medication is administered.*

Handling and restraining a dog

Making a makeshift muzzle

This is essential when nervous, possessive, aggressive, or sensitive (in pain) animals have to be handled or examined. Use a length of bandage, string, panty hose, or even a tie. By carefully positioning the muzzle not too far back, liquid medicine can be administered to such a disarmed dog by pouring it into the gap between the lips behind the encircling band.

1 Tie a knot in the bandage and wrap it around the dog's muzzle.

2 Cross the ends of the bandage at the bottom under the jaw.

3 Bring the ends around to the back of the dog's head and tie firmly.

Restraining a large dog

It is important to make sure you know how to adequately restrain your dog, epecially at the veterinarian's where many dogs can be nervous and panicking. Very large dogs will usually be looked at on the floor, whereas the veterinarian will examine small to medium-sized dogs on the examination table.

■ **Above:** *To restrain a large dog, place one arm firmly around his neck and the other around his body. Hold him tightly and speak reassuringly to him.*

Lifting a dog

To avoid injury to not only your dog but also your back, always bend your knees when picking up a large dog. Make sure that you support the dog's body properly.

1 If lifting a medium-sized dog, place one hand under his rear and the other around his chest.

2 Hold the dog securely while you rise to your feet, bringing him up to chest height.

■ **Above:** *To lift a small dog, support him under the rear and at the front with one hand on his chest between the front legs and the other taking most of his weight at the rear.*

FIRST AID

First aid is the emergency care given to a dog suffering injury or illness of sudden onset.

AIMS OF FIRST AID

1 Keep the dog alive. 2 Prevent unnecessary suffering. 3 Prevent further injury.

RULES OF FIRST AID

1 Always stay calm. If you panic, you will be unable to effectively help the dog.

2 Contact a veterinarian as soon as possible. Advice given over the telephone may be lifesaving.

3 Avoid injury to yourself. A distressed or injured animal may bite so use a muzzle if necessary (see page 127 on how to make one).

4 Control hemorrhaging. Excessive blood loss can lead to severe shock and death (see stopping bleeding on page 132).

5 Maintain an open airway. Failure to breathe or obtain adequate oxygen can lead to brain damage or loss of life within five minutes (see opposite).

COMMON ACCIDENTS AND EMERGENCIES

Common accidents and emergencies will all require first aid. In an emergency, your priorities are to keep the dog alive and comfortable until he can be examined by a veterinarian. However, in many cases, there is important action that you can take yourself immediately to help preserve your dog's health and life.

Burns

Burns can be caused by very hot liquids or by contact with an electrical current or various types of caustic, acid, or irritant liquid.

Chemical burns

Below: *To treat chemical burns, wash the affected area of the coat with a lot of warm soapy water.*

Recommended action

Wash the affected area of the coat with a lot of warm soapy water and then seek veterinary advice.

Scalding with a liquid

Hot water or oil spills most commonly occur in the kitchen. Although the dog's coat affords him some insulating protection, the skin beneath may be damaged, with visible signs emerging only after several hours have passed in many cases.

Recommended action

Apply cold water immediately to the affected area and follow this with an ice pack – a bag of frozen peas from the freezer is ideal. Then gently coat the burned area with mineral oil and seek veterinary advice.

Electrical burns

Most electrical burns are the result of a dog chewing a live electrical cord or wire. Such wires should be hidden, particularly

Above: *Apply lots of cold water and follow this with an ice pack.*

from puppies, and electrical devices should be unplugged after use. Biting live wires can cause burns to the inside of the lips and the gums but may, in the worst cases, result in shock and death.

Recommended action

First, switch off the electricity before you handle the patient. Examine the insides of the mouth and apply cold water to any burned areas. If the gums are whiter than normal or blue-tinged, shock may be present. Seek veterinary advice.

RESUSCITATING A DOG

Checking the heart rate

If the dog is unconscious, check his breathing and heart rate with one or more of the following techniques:

Feel for his pulse on the inside of a hind leg.

Press the palm of your hand against the chest just behind the elbow.

Place your ear on the chest to listen for heartbeats. Normal respiration rate is 20–30 breaths per minute. Normal heart rate ranges from about 50 beats per minute in large breeds to 150 beats per minute in very small breeds.

No heartbeat: cardiac massage

If the dog's heart is not beating, try cardiac massage by:
◆ Placing the animal on his right side and then placing the heel of your left hand on the left side of his chest just behind the elbow.
◆ Putting your other hand on top and then pressing down and forward very firmly and sharply.
◆ Do this about ten times at regular one-second intervals.

No breathing: mouth-to-nose resuscitation

Assuming that the dog is also not breathing, you should now give mouth-to-nose resuscitation (CPR).
◆ Maintain an open airway. Clear any saliva or obstruction from the mouth and pull the tongue forward, allowing it to flop to one side.
◆ Keep the head and neck straight and then, cupping the nose with your hands, exhale strongly into the nostrils for two–three seconds. The chest should expand as the lungs fill with air.
◆ **If the heart is still not beating, return to cardiac massage another ten times** and then go back again to artificial respiration.
◆ Continue alternating the massage and the mouth-to-nose until you get a response. It is worth trying for up to a quarter of an hour to restart the heart, and CPR should continue indefinitely where a faint heartbeat can be detected. While all this is going on, make sure that veterinary assistance is urgently being sought.

▓ **Left:** *Put one hand on top of the other and then press down and forward very firmly and sharply. Remember that you are pushing down on the rib cage so be careful not to exert too much force!*

▓ **Left:** *Keep the head and neck straight and then, cupping the dog's nose with your hands, exhale strongly.*

Poisoning

The house, the yard, and the world outside contain a multitude of substances, both natural and artificial, that can poison a dog. If poisoning is suspected, contact your veterinarian without delay. Frequently some symptoms, such as vomiting, blood in the dog's stools, or collapse, which owners may imagine to be the result of poisoning, are caused by other kinds of illness.

Poisonous chemicals may come in contact with a dog through ingestion or by the animal licking its coat when contaminated by a noxious substance. Canine inquisitiveness and the tendency to scavenge can lead dogs to eat or drink some strange materials and sometimes owners negligently give dangerous substances to their pets. Occasionally poisonous gases or vapors are inhaled by animals.

POISONOUS PLANTS

Dangerous plants include the bulbs of many spring flowers, holly and mistletoe berries, leaves and flowers of rhododendrons and hydrangeas, leaves of yew, box, and laurels, sweetpea, wisteria and bluebell seeds, and all parts of the columbine, hemlock, lily of the valley, and ivy. Some mushrooms are as poisonous to dogs as they are to humans, as are the blue-green algae that sometimes bloom on ponds in hot weather.

Among the thousands of highly poisonous compounds to be found in everyday life are weed killers, pesticides (rat and insect killers), fungicides, disinfectants, car antifreeze, lead compounds, caustic cleaning fluids, paint thinners, creosote, and excessive amounts of patent medicines, such as aspirin.

Poisoning can also be caused by certain plants, insect stings, and the venom of snakes and toads.

Common symptoms

- Digestive upsets (vomiting and diarrhea)
- Difficulty breathing
- Convulsions
- Uncoordinated movements
- Coma

Recommended action

Determining which chemical is involved can be difficult if you don't know what the dog has come into contact with. Professional diagnostic methods at the earliest opportunity are vital.

First aid in poisoning cases

Corrosive poisons

Look for evidence of burning or blistering in the mouth. Flush out the mouth carefully with warm

Right: *Flush out the mouth carefully with warm water. Let the dog drink some water or milk if he will take it.*

POISONS

Here are some poisons and their common sources:

◆ **Alphachloralose:** Mouse and rat killer
◆ **Barbiturates:** Sleeping pills
◆ **Carbon monoxide gas:** Faulty heater, car exhausts
◆ **Chlorates:** Weed killer
◆ **Corrosive chemicals:** Acids, alkalis bleach, carbolic acid and phenols, creosote, petroleum products
◆ **Ethylene glycol:** Antifreeze
◆ **Lead:** Paint, solders, putty, fishing weights
◆ **Metaldehyde:** Slug or snail pellets
◆ **Organochlorines, organophosphates, and carbamates:** Insecticides, rodenticides, herbicides
◆ **Paraquat:** Weed killers
◆ **Strychnine:** Gopher killers, illegal bird baits
◆ **Warfarin:** Rodenticides
◆ **Zinc phosphide:** Rodenticides

water. Let the animal drink water or milk if he will.

Other poisons

If your pet has been poisoned, contact your veterinarian immediately. If the poison came in a container (e.g., antifreeze or rodent poison), read the container label and follow the emergency treatment instructions. If you need to induce vomiting, you may accomplish this by administering 1/2 ml per pound of body weight syrup of ipecac or 1/2 teaspoon of hydrogen peroxide 3% for every ten pounds of your dog's body weight.

Corrosive substances

Clean the contaminated area with rags or paper towels and cut off congealed masses of hair with scissors. Cooking oil or petroleum jelly will help soften paint and tar. Wash thoroughly with dog or baby shampoo and rinse well. Don't use solvents, paint thinners, concentrated washing detergents, or turpentine on a dog's coat.

Snakebites

There are four venomous snakes in North America: the rattlesnake, the coral snake, the copperhead, and the cottonmouth. Rattlesnake bites occur most frequently in dogs, particularly in the West and Southwest where rattlesnakes are common. The snake's bite will produce two painful, slitlike puncture wounds that will swell.

Common symptoms

- Trembling and agitation
- Salivation
- Vomiting and staggering
- Swelling, pain, and tissue necrosis
- Shock
- Depression
- Collapse and even death

Recommended action

Urgent veterinary attention is necessary, and may require antivenom and antibiotic treatments. If the bite is left untreated, the dog's skin and underlying tissue may turn dark and slough off (rot). If a venomous snake bites your dog, contact your veterinarian immediately.

Bee- and wasp stings

Painful, but usually single and with no serious general effects, insect stings require little more than removal of the stinger itself in the case of beestings (wasps and hornets do not leave their stingers behind) by means of tweezers and the application of antihistamine cream. Rarely, death can ensue if a dog is subject to a large number, perhaps hundreds, of stings. Stings can

Common symptoms

- Swelling blocking the throat or, if the dog is allergic to the insect venom, he will go into severe shock

also be serious if the tongue or mouth is involved.

Recommended action

Medical anti-shock therapy, such as intravenous fluids, adrenalin, and antihistamine injections. Keep shocked animals warm. Make sure their breathing is unimpeded. Obtain veterinary attention.

Toad venom poisoning

Toads secrete a venom from their skin, particularly when upset. Dogs that lick this secretion when investigating a toad they may come across in their own yard or when out

Common symptoms

- Irritation and redness of the mouth with a lot of saliva, cardiac arrhythmias, seizures

on a country walk quickly develop symptoms.

Recommended action

Fortunately, toad venom poisoning is rarely serious, and such occurrences can be simply treated by washing out the dog's mouth with some warm water, preferably containing a little baking soda powder (sodium bicarbonate).

Bleeding

The appearance of blood anywhere on the dog's body necessitates immediate close inspection. A variety of accidents and some diseases may produce blood from the nostrils, eyes, or ears, or in the droppings or in vomited material. None of the above types of hemorrhage are usually suitable for first aid by the owner. All need veterinary attention although the causes may often be trivial and ephemeral.

Bleeding from the body surface through wounds inflicted during fights, traffic accidents, or other traumatic incidents can be heavy and this does require prompt first aid.

Recommended action

The most important thing is to apply pressure to the wound. Hand or finger pressure is always invaluable until a pad of gauze or cotton can be found. This should be soaked in cold water, placed on the wound, and kept in place by constant firm pressure or, better, a bandage. Take the dog to a veterinary clinic as quickly as possible. Do not waste any time applying antiseptic ointments or powders to a significantly bleeding wound.

Right: *Soak the bandage in cold water before applying it to the wound, then seek veterinary treatment as soon as possible if the bleeding does not stop.*

Heatstroke

Every summer one reads in the newspapers of cases of dogs dying from heatstroke as a result of the gross thoughtlessness of their owners. Animals that are left in hot, poorly ventilated places, particularly cars, and sometimes without water, overheat. They lose the ability to control their internal body temperature. As the latter rises, the dog will become distressed, pant rapidly, and will quickly weaken. The mouth will appear much redder than normal. Collapse, coma, and even death can follow in a reasonably short space of time.

Recommended action

Cooling the body, particularly the head, with cold water baths, hosing, and ice packs is essential. If the temperature-regulating mechanism in the brain has already been seriously damaged, a fatal outcome may still ensue. Veterinary attention must be obtained at once. Of course, prevention of such emergencies by owner forethought is imperative.

Below: *A dog with suspected heatstroke should be hosed down with plenty of cold water immediately. You may also need to use ice packs.*

Foreign bodies

In the eye

Foreign bodies in the eye are very painful and cause the dog to rub his head on the ground and paw at his eye.

Recommended action

Rinse the eye with saline eyedrops or olive oil to wash out the foreign body. Do not use tweezers close to the eyeball.

In the ear

Plant seeds and grass awns are particularly likely to get into a dog's ears during summer walks. Their presence causes itching and irritation. The dog shakes his head and paws at his ears.

Recommended action

Pour some warm olive oil or other vegetable oil into the ear, filling it. The object may well float to the surface where it can be picked up by tweezers. Deeper, embedded foreign bodies will always require veterinary attention.

In the mouth

Sometimes, pieces of bone or splinters of wood can become lodged in a dog's mouth. Often, the offending object is jammed between the left and right upper molars at the back of the mouth or in the space between two adjacent teeth. Less commonly, an object, such as a small ball, will become stuck in the dog's throat. In all cases the animal will show symptoms of distress, including pawing at the mouth, gagging, trying to retch, or shaking his head.

Recommended action

While someone holds the dog firmly, you should open the mouth and try to dislodge the foreign body with a spoon or kitchen tongs. If the dog is having difficulty breathing and literally choking, try holding him upside down by the hind legs, massaging the throat and slapping his back. If you cannot remove the object, seek veterinary help at once.

In the paws

Splinters of glass, thorns, particles of metal, and fragments of stone can penetrate the pads on a dog's paws or lodge in the skin between the toes. As a result, the dog limps and usually licks the affected paw.

Recommended action

Remove the object with tweezers, if visible. If not, because of being embedded, bathe the foot two to three times daily in warm water and salt (a teaspoon to a cupful) until the foreign body emerges from the softened skin. If lameness persists for more than a day or two, seek veterinary attention; infection may have set in.

■ **Left:** *A grass awn between the pads can be very painful. Use some tweezers to pull it out. Check that the awn is still whole.*

■ **Left:** *After removing a foreign object from a paw, bathe it in warm salty water. Do the same if you can't remove it right away as this may help the object to appear.*

Advanced dog activities

Many pet dog owners will want to get involved in advanced activities with their dogs, including showing, Obedience competitions, Agility and Flyball, and working trials. These are enjoyable occasions for both you and your dog. You will make new friends and broaden your social life as you discover the joy and sense of achievement that can come from participating in dog shows. Many dogs enjoy the experience of the show ring and like to perform. They are stimulated physically and mentally by trials and competitions. You may even consider breeding your dog and want to start a strain of your own. Showing and breeding are both enjoyable hobbies but they carry certain responsibilities.

Chapter Eight

SHOWING YOUR DOG

Showing your dog can be an absorbing and even addictive hobby. Competitive people who like a difficult challenge find the ever-present possibility of breeding, exhibiting, and winning with a really great dog is both exciting and stimulating, often to the extent of changing their lifestyle. From simple beginnings, with one pet dog, many people have gone on to make their living from dogs, to become famous judges of dogs and even world authorities.

Below: Showing dogs successfully is a skillful pastime. A dog must learn to stand properly to show him at his best.

Registering your dog

When you first contemplate showing your dog or indulging in any of the recognized activities with dogs, your priority must be to make sure that the dog is properly registered with the AKC and has been transferred into the owner's name. Most dog shows in the United States are held under the AKC's rules and regulations and if the dog is not registered, entries to the show will not be accepted. Although dog breeders register their puppies, it is usually the responsibility of the new owners to transfer the dog into their name. Sometimes the breeder will have already registered an official name for the dog, but in some cases the owner may be allowed to name it.

Finding out about showing

You are walking down the street with your dog when somebody stops you to admire him. You are told that he is a very good-looking dog and well worth showing. What do you do? You know nothing about dog showing. Well, go to your local bookstore and buy one of the dog fancy magazines that specialize in the purebred dog, its exhibition, and breeding. Within a few weeks, you will learn practically everything that you need to know, especially where the shows are being held, the type of show, and the address of the secretary, who will send you the show schedule. This is the first key document, which contains all the information pertaining to that show. It will also contain the entry form; it is essential to complete this with the utmost care as even the smallest mistakes can lead to disqualification.

Learning about showmanship

The next step is probably the most essential; you must find the nearest canine club or society teaching the required showing skills. The AKC recognizes literally hundreds of breed and obedience clubs involved in different aspects of dog training, showmanship, Obedience, Agility, Flyball, Herding dog tests, and Sporting dog trials. In the latter two, there are special clubs that deal with the needs of specific

Opposite: Labradors love taking part in Sporting dog trials. They are tested on their finding and retrieving abilities.

breeds. A quick telephone call will elicit the secretary's details of any club or society.

To exhibit a dog successfully you must realize that there are rules, both written and unwritten, with which you must familiarize yourself as a competitor; the breed club is the ideal place at which to learn them. There will be instructors and experienced exhibitors who will be delighted to share their expertise, and if you have a relatively common breed, the likelihood is that there will be skilled competitors in the breed who will undoubtedly help in the presentation of your dog.

Grooming and show presentation

In some breeds trimming is of the essence: it would be pointless to take a scruffy, unclipped Poodle into a show

ring as he would not win a placement; and an overgrown Welsh Terrier, looking like a doormat, would also be ignored. However, when novices observe the perfection of the grooming of their chosen breed, inevitably they will wonder how it is achieved.

All the hairy breeds have their own style of trimming; some are scissored and clipped, whereas others are hand-stripped into the traditional shape. The tools with which to do this are many and varied and the job is made easier with the use of the correct tools. They can be bought from special vendors who will not only sell you the grooming equipment, but also will give you some invaluable advice.

However, there are professional groomers who, for a price, will prepare a dog for the show ring, but this is likely to be expensive and will not reflect the owner's natural pride in his dog. Most exhibitors find that one of the pleasures of their hobby is in the preparation and they develop the arts of trimming, grooming, and presentation to perfection themselves. All it takes is application,

▦ **Right:** *Even Springer Spaniels may need some special grooming techniques. This dog is receiving some last-minute attention.*

▦ **Above:** *The long fur on the Lhasa Apso's head can be tied back with bands until he is ready to show.*

study, and, above all, practice.

There are professional dog handlers who combine the skills of grooming and presentation of the dog and who will sell their expertise to owners who either cannot do it themselves or are too busy. Cases in point are some elderly owners of German Shepherd Dogs – the breed is customarily shown trotting fairly fast around the ring several times, which may require a younger and more energetic handler. The formally trimmed terriers, such as

▦ **Above:** *A Poodle in puppy trim. It takes a lot of time and care to show some breeds successfully. Poodles, in particular, have to be trimmed and groomed with great precision and skill.*

■ **Above:** *To prepare Yorkies for show, special paper "crackers" are used.*

■ **Above:** *The crackers keep the show coat straight and in first-class condition.*

Airedales, Wire-haired Fox Terriers, and Lakeland Terriers, are often prepared and then handled by professionals because of the difficulty of trimming their coat and the time involved. The cost has to be negotiated with each individual handler. Most of these handlers prefer to keep the dog on their premises so the cost of feeding as well as trimming has to be considered. On the other hand, travel costs are likely to be less because the handler may be taking several dogs to a show.

Presenting your dog

Every breed is shown differently. For instance, a Fox Terrier can be shown "stacked," which means placing the dog in a certain position and holding him there, whereas a German Shepherd Dog is always posed in a particularly formal fashion. An English Setter is held in a natural standing position, except his tail, which is stretched out horizontally. There are as many ways of presenting a dog to the judge as there are dog breeds, and if, in a competition, you don't show your dog in the traditional manner, you lessen your chances of winning.

Your dog also has to learn his role. He will learn to be handled by strangers – the judge may pass his hands over the dog's entire body and, most difficult, the dog will have to tolerate having his mouth opened and his teeth looked at. With practice, he will succeed in walking or trotting at the correct speed and style and will be at ease with all the bustle and noise of a big show.

Some dogs learn quickly; others take time. Terriers learn quickly but because of their independent characters will often deliberately do something surprising, such as shaking your pants leg in front of the judge. To persuade a dog to behave correctly the club training should be reinforced at home – five to ten minutes a day will suffice. Dogs get bored very quickly so do not pressure a puppy too much. Just let him settle down in his own time; his spirit must not be broken. Firmness with kindness is the best way forward. A loss of patience resulting in shouting or, worse, smacking will be counterproductive, and a puppy trained like

CLUB MATCHES

To give you the feel of actual competition, most clubs hold monthly matches: an elimination contest between the members of the club and sometimes against their neighboring clubs. Both owners and their dogs benefit greatly from these contests, the owner repeatedly going through the same routine as he would at the big championship shows, and the dog getting used to being handled and mixing with other dogs.

this will never give his best.

Set up a little show ring in your backyard and go through the same motions as you did at the training class. Use neighbors, friends, or your family to play the part of the judge. Some trainers advocate getting the puppy accustomed to applause by asking the onlookers to clap their hands; they will also bang trash can lids to accustom the puppy to unusual noises.

Small dogs are known as "table dogs," and this means that they will be placed on a table for the judge to examine. The act of placing a dog on a table should be practiced as he must be lifted gently and calmly and should not be handled by his tail. Take care not to hurt or drop him, otherwise he will lose confidence and this will reflect in his performance.

■ **Below:** *Some breeds, such as this Curly-coated Retriever, can be shown either stacked or free-standing. This dog is prepared by wetting the coat and combing gently through the curls.*

Dog shows

There are several different types of dog shows and although the novice exhibitor is fully entitled to compete at any of them, it is wise not to rush into things and is therefore best to start at the bottom.

The members of the breed club will be pleased to guide you through the labyrinth of class definitions for dogs at the various types of dog shows. Entries to the appropriate shows must be sent in with the correct fee before the appointed date. Any failure to pay will result in your disqualification. Puppies under six months of age cannot be shown, except in fun matches.

Match shows

Match shows are hosted by AKC-approved dog clubs and conducted according to AKC rules. Only AKC-registered purebred dogs or dogs eligible for registration may be entered. Wins at matches do not count toward a championship and dogs that have won championship points do not compete. Judges may be AKC-approved or experienced breeders or handlers invited by the host club. These shows are training grounds for young dogs, new exhibitors, and aspiring judges. They are perfect for you and your puppy to get used to all the excitement of a dog show, from traveling to grooming to exhibiting and, hopefully, to winning.

Specialty shows

Under AKC rules, there are three types of conformation shows: specialty shows, limited shows, and all-breed shows. A specialty show is limited to one breed; for example, the American Boxer Club holds shows for Boxers only. A limited show may be for all the breeds in one group, i.e. Toys, or it may be for several specific breeds, i.e. Setters. All shows are held under AKC rules.

Each AKC-recognized breed

AGE-LINKED DEFINITIONS

◆ **Puppy**: Six to twelve months old
◆ **Minor Puppy**: Six to nine months old
◆ **Junior**: Six to eighteen months old

has a national parent club. There are also many local specialty clubs throughout the United States. The parent clubs are responsible for maintaining the official standards of their respective breeds.

Dogs are judged according to their breed standard, and by a process of elimination, one dog is selected as Best of Breed.

All-breed shows

All-breed shows, as the name indicates, are for evey breed. Judging is conducted according to AKC rules. In addition to Best of Breed winners, these shows offer the title of Best in Group (for dogs considered to be the best

▐ **Right:** *Many people get hooked on showing when they first attend a local match show. These shows are great fun for owners and dogs.*

Left: *Everyone's dream is to win a Best in Show. The 2000 winner at Cruft's, the Kerry Blue Terrier, Ch. Torum's Scarf Michael, is shown here.*

representative of their group) and Best in Show (for the dog selected as the best representative of its breed and group, compared to all other dogs of other breeds and groups).

Most dogs competing in specialty or all-breed shows are competing for points toward their championship. A dog can earn from one to five points at a show. The number of points available depends upon the number of entries present. Wins of three, four, or five points are called "majors."

There are six different classes in which a dog can compete for championship points and the classes are divided by sex:
◆ Puppy class (divided into 6–9 months of age and 9–12 months of age)
◆ 12–18 months of age
◆ Novice
◆ Bred-by-Exhibitor
◆ American-Bred
◆ Open

Male dogs are judged first in this order: Puppy, 12–18, Novice,

Bred-by-Exhibitor, American-Bred, and Open. The first-place winners in each class return to the show ring to compete against each other in the Winners Class. The dog selected as the best male in the Winners Class is the Winners Dog. This is the dog that will win the championship points in the show. The same procedure

is then followed, in the same order, for the females, and the Winners Bitch (who also wins championship points) and Reserve Winners Bitch are selected.

The Winners Dog and Winners Bitch then join a class called the Best of Breed where entered males and females have already won their championship titles. The judge first selects a Best of Breed winner from all dogs present, then chooses either Winners Dog or Winners Bitch to be Best of Winners. Finally, a Best of Opposite Sex is chosen from those dogs eligible.

At an all-breed show, judging takes place for each breed, then each Best of Breed winner competes in its breed group.

The first-place winners of each group then compete for the coveted title of "Best in Show."

Left: *The judge will want to examine your dog. Small dogs, such as this Bichon Frise, are usually lifted onto a table.*

OTHER ADVANCED ACTIVITIES

There are many other interesting canine activities that can be enjoyed by enthusiasts. Many clubs and societies specialize in teaching both dogs and owners. Details are available from the AKC or your local breed club. Dogs must be registered with the AKC to compete in Obedience, Tracking, Field and Hunting, Herding, Lure Coursing, or Junior Showmanship. The events are advertised and schedules are available from the show secretary. All disciplines are designed around teamwork and rapport between the owner and dog. Anyone can join in.

Obedience

In Obedience competitions, the dogs are taught a series of formal exercises based on walking to heel on the leash, without the leash, *recall*, *sit/stay*, and *down/stay*. There are three levels that increase in difficulty: Novice – Companion Dog (CD), Open – Companion Dog Excellent (CDX), and Utility – Utility Dog (UD).

To earn a CD title, the dog must be able to perform six exercises: heel on leash, stand for examination, heel free, recall, long sit, and long down. To earn a CDX title, the dog must be able to heel free, drop on recall, retrieve on flat, retrieve over the high jump, broad jump, long sit, and long down. To earn a UD, the dog must be able to respond to signal exercises, scent discrimination tests, directed retrieve, directed jumping, and group examination.

■ **Above:** *This dog has learned to scale a 6-foot (2-m) jump from a standstill.*

Agility and Flyball

These are the fastest growing canine sports; the action is very fast and is exciting for both the participants and audiences.

◆ In Agility the idea is for the dog to negotiate obstacles built to strict criteria against the clock; smaller obstacles are erected for small dogs. Agility tests are structured so that the competitor can compete against other dogs that are at approximately the same level of expertise.

◆ Flyball is furious, fast, and fun for all. Teams of dogs compete against each other in relay. The object is to run a straight course of 12-inch (30-cm) high hurdles, activate a pedal on a box that flings a ball into the air, catch the ball, and return to base. The next dog is released on the return of the previous dog.

■ **Above:** *Most dogs enjoy competing in Agility tests. They derive mental stimulation as well as physical exercise and a better rapport with their owners.*

Herding Trials

The Herding program is divided into two parts: Testing and Trial. In the Herding Testing division, a dog can earn the title of Herding Tested Dog (HT) and Pre-Trial Tested Dog (PT). The HT title is earned by demonstrating an inherent herding ability and trainability to herding. The PT title is awarded to dogs that have had some training in herding and herd a small group of livestock through a simple course.

Herding trials offer four titles: Herding Started (HS), Herding Intermediate (HI), Herding Excellent (HX), and (after earning the HX title, accumulating fifteen championship points) Herding Championship (HCH). A dog with an HCH title can herd difficult livestock in a variety of situations.

Herding trials are conducted on three distinct courses differing in physical appearance.

Field Trials

Field trials are held separately for pointing breeds, retrievers, and spaniels.

Any dog that competes should be a purebred and properly registered with the AKC. The Trial secretary will send schedules to members together with the entry form that must be accurately completed.

Hunting has been man's preoccupation for thousands of years and breeds of dogs have been developed to help him in his quest for food. Field Trials exist to test the ability of Sporting dogs

TYPES OF HERDING TRIALS

◆ **Matches and Rallies**
Competition between club members or two or more clubs, this is the ideal competition for Herding trial beginners.
◆ **Members' Herding Trials**
These are limited to members of the organizing club.
◆ **Open Herding Trials**
Open to everyone; very fierce

to do their specific work in situations resembling, as closely as possible, a day's shooting in the field.

Anyone wishing to compete should become a member of an appropriate club that will help in the training of the dog and advise on the regulations and traditional behavior. Because of the use of shotguns, safety is of the essence and full instructions are given at the morning's briefing at the venue. There are several eliminating faults, such as whining or running out, and it is considered bad form to leave the Trial early even if a dog is eliminated on his first run. Most people take food and drinks to enjoy a day in the country.

Hunting Tests

The same rules and procedure apply as with Field Trials. They are restricted to dogs registered with the AKC. Hunting tests allow the owners to obtain an evaluation of the dog's hunting ability and skills. The dog's performance is evaluated at three

competition attracting entries from all over the country. The best dogs in the country take part because competitors can compete for the Herding Trials Certificate, which, when won, will entitle the dog to be known as a Herding Trials Champion.

levels and each succeeding level is more difficult. Upon successful completion of the first level, a dog earns the title of Junior Hunter. Completion of the second level wins the dog the title of Senior Hunter. Finally, once the dog has mastered the third level, it is awarded the title of Master Hunter.

There are three types of tests:
◆ **Retrievers:** These are tested on finding ability, quick pickups, quickness and directness of retrieve, natural nose, marking ability, quietness, drive, and style.
◆ **Spaniels:** As above but also the ability to quarter the ground, finding and flushing game within range of the handler.
◆ **Hunt, point, and retrieve breeds:** The tests are roughly the same as for both retrievers and spaniels.

Please note: Every effort should be made to arrive on time because if the competitor is late he may lose his place to the reserve. Care should always be taken of the dog.

Chapter Nine

BREEDING

It is no longer considered socially acceptable to have a litter of puppies without an understanding of the implications. It is too easy to fall in love with an entrancing puppy, not realizing that without careful training he will be chewing the carpets, being dirty in the house, and annoying the neighbors by barking. If it's a bitch, she is also likely to have unwanted puppies unless she is carefully controlled. Many male dogs are still thrown out of homes to become one of the thousands of stray healthy dogs that walk the streets and need rehoming or are even put down but not before impregnating another stray bitch and adding to the problem.

Most communities have regulations regarding dog ownership, the number of dogs a person can keep in a specified neighborhood, rabies vaccination requirements, and licensing laws. Many communities are considering laws limiting the number of litters or puppies a dog breeder can produce each year. To discourage dog breeding, many animal regulatory authorities allow a significant discount in animal licensing fees if the animal is neutered. Dog owners are held responsible for their dog's actions, including property damage and bodily injury. Basically, to avoid any trouble, all dogs must be kept under control in a public place, any feces should always be picked up, and dogs must not cause a nuisance. If it is the intention to breed on a regular basis, the breeder should contact the local authorities to check the regulations regarding licenses.

Spaying and castration

Unless it is an owner's intention to breed the bitch, the right thing to do is to have her spayed before her first estrous cycle. Ask your veterinarian for advice. The operation consists of surgically removing the bitch's reproductive organs – by today's standards, a routine surgical procedure. The cost of the operation varies considerably depending on where you live, but some organizations offer financial assistance. Apart from negating the risk of crossbred puppies, spaying will stop neighborhood male dogs from haunting your street and yard when your bitch is in season.

It would be an act of real social responsibility to have a male dog castrated if there is no intention of using him as a stud dog. The surgical removal of the testicles will usually stop him from wandering in search of a bitch and adding to the stray problem. The dog will recover remarkably quickly and there will be no change to his basic character.

Below: *Some breeds have small litters. For instance, Pomeranians usually have only one or two puppies and they therefore tend to be expensive. In this basket are three generations of dogs.*

Backyard breeding is one of the major causes of canine overpopulation. In recent years, the price of purebred puppies has shot up and this accounts for the main motivation for casual breeding – to earn extra undeclared income to go on vacation, or help pay various expenses. However, there are traps for the unwary and unless you know what you are doing, you are likely to have a litter of ten puppies of a popular breed, such as a Golden Retriever, reaching twelve weeks of age and not a buyer in sight; that is very heavy on the pocket. After this age the worth of

a puppy becomes progressively less, and the end result will probably mean a financial loss.

Be well informed

If your motivation for breeding your dog is based on a love of dogs and the desire to breed excellent animals in optimum circumstances, go ahead. If you are a novice, you must seek detailed information and obviously an excellent source will be breed books, the best of which will contain detailed information of different lines that will be invaluable when selecting the dog.

Next, consult the breeders of your bitch. If they are well-known breeders/exhibitors, they will be interested in improving their own strain and will offer all the help necessary. If you adopted the proper procedure when buying your puppy, the breeder selected will be someone who has all the breeding stock tested for whatever genetic anomalies may exist in the breed. The bitch should be of a calm temperament, not given to nervousness, and she should be subjected to all available and applicable genetic tests. If she's within normal parameters, a stud dog can then be selected.

Right: *The stud dog should be healthy with no family history of hereditary diseases. He should have a good temperament and be a fine example of the chosen breed.*

The stud dog

The choice of a stud dog is of ultimate importance and cannot be left to chance. The bitch must be studied objectively and her faults and strengths assessed; the dog you select should be strong in the areas in which your bitch is weak. For instance, if the bitch's head is not correctly shaped as required by the breed standard, the dog selected should have the correct head shape. The aim is that the influence of the dog on the puppies will correct this type of fault but, at the same time, maintain the good qualities of the bitch.

It is a good idea for the bitch's owner to visit the stud dog – be sure to telephone in advance to arrange a mutually convenient time. Take a good look at the dog. He should be fit, healthy, and muscular with a good, friendly disposition. The fee, which will vary according to the breed, will be agreed on, and as the bitch's owner, you must satisfy

yourself that the stud dog is properly registered with the AKC and the terms of the mating have been discussed and agreed upon.

It should be noted that the stud fee is for the service of the dog and does not depend on whether puppies are conceived.

ONE OR TWO MATINGS?

Traditionally, a breeder will allow two matings with twenty-four hours separating them, but this is not mandatory and is entirely up to the stud dog's owner. Opinions vary; some hold that only one mating is necessary, but the author is of the opinion that because the timing of conception can be critical, it is possible to miss the moment and therefore he has always advocated two matings. The main reason for bitches missing is because the mating is not properly timed.

The bitch

If you intend to breed your bitch, you must make sure that she is healthy and has no hereditary conditions. It is best to mate her in her third season when she is a mature adult and fully developed.

The season (estrus)

It is popularly thought that a bitch comes into season (estrus) every six months from the age of six months, but there is no hard-and-fast rule about this and it does vary. It is not considered correct practice to take a litter from a bitch under the age of one year or from her first season. There is no need to worry if the first season is delayed; after the first time the likelihood is that she will come into season roughly three times every two years.

Watch carefully for the onset of the season; the first physical indication is a blood-colored discharge from the vulva. When

Right: Some breeds need more specialzed knowledge to breed them successfully. Pugs are notoriously difficult and may have either an easy pregnancy or serious problems.

you see the first signs, contact the owners of the selected stud dog, explain what is happening, and then be guided by their experience.

The color of the discharge will gradually change to a light straw color and by the eleventh day will be virtually colorless – normally this is the time to mate the bitch. Again, the timing is flexible, and twenty-four hours either way is not unusual. A good test is to stand the bitch on her four legs squarely and press your hand firmly on her back by the tail root. If the tail switches from left to right exaggeratedly over the back, she is ready for mating.

Litter restrictions

The value of puppies is enhanced by AKC registration but by paying for and accepting a registration, a breeder accepts the rules and regulations regarding that litter. Puppies born of a mother under the age of eight months will not be accepted for registration, and neither will puppies born of a mother over the age of twelve years. No dog or litter out of a sire under seven months or over twelve years of age at the time of mating will be registered unless the application for registration is accompanied by an affidavit or evidence that will prove the fact to the satisfaction of the AKC.

Left: Some breeds, such as Golden Retrievers and Irish Wolfhounds, have very large litters.

Mating

It is traditional for the bitch to be taken to the dog. On arrival at the stud dog's home, she should be allowed time by herself to get over the trip and to relieve herself. From now on it is better that the bitch is not fussed over – what will happen is natural and therefore too much interference from well-meaning owners may be counterproductive. It is better that an experienced dog is used for a first-time bitch and novice owners would be well advised to be guided by the stud dog's owner. During the mating there may be snarling that the novice may think is aggression but it is extremely unusual for

Right: The happy couple should be allowed to get to know each other before mating.

dogs to bite bitches and vice versa during foreplay or the mating.

The two animals are introduced and may play together a little. The dog should be interested if the bitch is ready and he will try to mount her. At this point the stud dog owner will probably ask you to hold the bitch's head. The stud will probably enter the bitch now and, if not, will be assisted by the owner. The amount of assistance varies from a great deal to none, depending on the dog. The seminal fluid is passed in the first few seconds of the mating.

The "tie"

A "tie" usually takes place and this is when the dog's penis is swollen and cannot leave the vaginal vault. During this time, the bitch's vaginal muscles constrict and the two animals are joined. This varies in time and can last from five minutes to an hour. The reason for this tie has been postulated as a method for ensuring that sperm succeeds in reaching the oviduct.

Conception does not rely upon a tie as sometimes there is no tie at all and yet puppies are still conceived, but breeders are happier when it has been achieved.

Above: *Dogs may play fight before mating but it is rare for them to bite each other. Give them time to play together and don't hurry them.*

Post-mating

After the mating the bitch should be given a drink of water and be allowed to rest, either in the travel crate or in the car.

WHAT NEXT?

Now is the time for business. The agreed fee should be given to the stud dog's owner, who must give you a receipt and the AKC form confirming the mating and noting the date and the registered names of both the dog and bitch. The AKC Litter Registration Application Form, indicating the parents, their AKC numbers, the date of litter birth, and the number of surviving males and females in the litter, will have to be completed and signed by the owners of the parent dogs to register the litter.

PREGNANCY AND BIRTH

As soon as possible, notify your veterinarian of the probable date of birth. The period of gestation averages sixty-three days, but a few days either way is not unusual. For the first six weeks there is nothing much for you to do except feed the bitch normally with high-quality food, exercise her to make sure that she stays in good condition, gradually phasing it down until the day of the birth.

Signs of pregnancy

There are indications that the bitch is pregnant:
◆ Her demeanor will change
◆ She will fill out and gain weight.
It is not easy to determine the number of puppies she will have so it is probably best to leave her alone and then be pleasantly surprised. Some bitches will have a colorless discharge after three weeks but there is no need to worry.

Preparing for the litter

Decide now where to put the bitch for the birth and for the first eight weeks of the puppies' lives. She will need a small, quiet room in which the temperature can be maintained at about 70°F (20°C). Ideally, she should have a whelping box that should be big enough for her to stand up in and to lie down at full length. There should also be sufficient room for her to lie aw~ from her puppies. Around ~' inside of the box will b~

enough for a puppy to get under to avoid being accidentally squashed by the mother. Train the bitch to go gently into the box, so there'll be no surprises.

Prenatal feeding

Your bitch should be fed high-quality dog food – sweets, cakes, and cookies should be avoided. At about six weeks into the pregnancy, begin to increase the amount of food by about ten percent and feed her three times a day. As the puppies grow inside her, the stomach capacity will be less and she will need smaller, more frequent meals. Gradually increase the overall amount of food per day but serve it four times daily. Always put down unlimited amounts of fresh water that is

THINGS YOU WILL NEED

Be prepared for the birth and make sure that you have the following items:
◆ Whelping box
◆ Book on puppy birth
◆ Several pieces of man-made fur fabric bedding (available from pet shops)
◆ Several pieces of clean towel, 18 inch (45 cm) square
◆ Surgical scissors
◆ Gentle baby antise~
◆ Canine milk ~
◆ Glucose~ dr~

■ **Left:** *You can buy a ready-made, specially designed whelping box, such as this one, or you can construct your own if you are good at such projects.*

easily available for her. After the puppies are born, the bitch will probably eat up to three times her normal quantity of food as she will have become a milk-producing machine.

Getting ready for the birth

About a week before she is due, introduce the bitch to her new quarters and watch her carefully. Cut away any excess hair from the vulvar area and from around the teats. Twenty-four hours before the birth she may be restless, her temperature will drop, and she'll scratch up her bedding and pant. At this point, put in several layers of newspapers and alert the veterinarian that his or her services might be needed.

The birth

Here is a brief description of the birth process; the trick really is to allow the bitch to give birth naturally but to be there to assist and comfort her if necessary. Some breeds experience difficulties and may need Caesarean sections. Before you start, scrub your hands and cut and smooth your nails. Watch carefully for the first contraction and make sure that the bitch is in her whelping box. A first-time bitch may be confused so you should comfort her with some soft, reassuring words.

The birth process

◆ The first sign is usually a gray membrane protruding from the vulva like a bubble; it may be withdrawn and emerge several times. Be patient and watch the contractions; they'll get quicker.
◆ When the puppy's head appears, she should expel it. If it seems not to be moving, you may have to help out. Grasp the head lightly with a towel and pull gently with the contractions. A green liquid will come out and stain your fingers, but don't worry as this is quite normal.
◆ Clamp, then cut the umbilical cord about 2 inches (5 cm) from the body, being careful not to pull

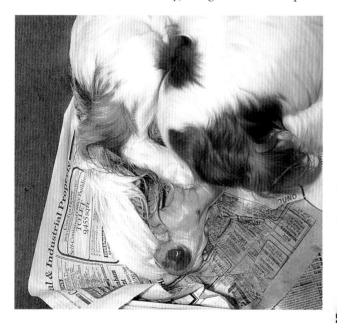

Below: This tiny Cavalier King Charles Spaniel puppy is just emerging into the outside world.

it. Open the mouth and clear out any mucus. Clear away the membrane that may be around the pup's body.
◆ Briskly rub all over the body with the towel. When the puppy is squeaking loudly, open its mouth and place it on a back teat. If it rejects the nipple, keep trying.
◆ The bitch will turn and lick the new arrival, which she must be allowed to do. She may expel the placenta (afterbirth) with the puppy and then may eat it (it looks like a piece of liver). It is wise to allow her to eat only one or two, otherwise her stools will be loose. Try to count the number of placentas – there should be the same number as there are puppies; if not, inform the veterinarian.

Birth problems

If a pup presents itself backwards, it is a breech birth. Breech presentation is normal in dogs but every effort should be made to get it out quickly. However, any attempt by you to help the puppy out must always be in time with the mother's contractions.
~~itch~~ stops contracting

■ *Above: After the birth, the bitch will suckle her puppies. If any are reluctant to suck, place them on a teat.*

during the whelping, contact the veterinarian immediately; she may be suffering from primary inertia. Always have some tepid glucose water available to refresh her. When the bitch is apparently contentedly suckling her new family, take her outside to relieve herself; get someone to remove the soiled newspaper and put in clean soft fabric. This should be changed daily.

IMPORTANT

If the bitch shows signs of acute distress, such as violent trembling, whining, or staggering after the whelping and up to three weeks after the birth, it's an emergency! She may be suffering from eclampsia and will need urgent veterinary treatment immediately; without treatment she may die.

POSTNATAL CARE

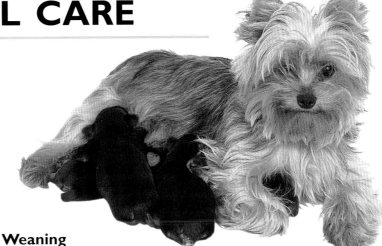

Apart from removing the dewclaws and docking, if required by the breed standard, by a veterinarian on the second day, there is little for you to do until the pups are ready to wean at three to four weeks. Have the veterinarian visit them and check them over to make sure that they and their mother are healthy and the puppies' nails aren't too long.

Don't allow strangers or young children near the bitch; she may be defensive. Children should not handle the pups for a week or so as they can be delicate. Examine and handle the puppies every day; it's important to socialize them even when their eyes aren't open. They open at around fourteen days and what they see and hear will have a profound effect on their lives. Take the bitch out to relieve herself several times a day and start giving her a little exercise.

Weaning

When the puppies are three to four weeks old, scrape a piece of stewing meat with a sharp knife to make a paste. Let the puppies suck it off your fingers, and after two days put some in a dish. The next day, add a little scrambled egg and mix it with some puppy milk replacer (available from your vet). Offer this once a day for two or three days, and then add some cooked minced meat – this should always be good-quality meat, not pet grade, because of the possibility of tiny slivers of bone, or the puppy can be fed a premium commercial canned puppy food. After about a week, offer meat meals twice a day plus two canine milk replacer and egg meals but only in small amounts because of the puppies' small stomachs. Gradually increase the amounts and always provide fresh water in a shallow bowl.

During this time the pups will still take milk from their mother but in smaller amounts, so gradually reduce the amount of food she is getting. By the time the pups are five to six weeks old, her milk supply will dry up and any suckling is for comfort only. If she wants to leave her pups she can, but let her sleep with them at night. Vaccination is advisable at six or seven weeks. If given at six to seven weeks, you will be advised to repeat it at ten weeks because antibodies in the mother's blood may make the first injection ineffective. In any case, seek veterinary advice.

Above: *Always be gentle when handling very young puppies. This Yorkshire Terrier puppy is particularly tiny and fragile and no force can be used.*

SELLING THE PUPPIES

Make preparations for the sale of the puppies a week after birth and sell them after eight weeks of age. Try the bitch's breeder, stud dog's owner, breed club, advertisements in dog fancy publications, and the AKC, which, for a small fee, will put potential buyers in touch with you. The best breeders include the following in the price of a puppy:
◆ One month's insurance
◆ A week's free supply of the puppy's usual food
◆ A diet sheet
◆ Unlimited advice
◆ A buy-back agreement if the puppy is unsuitable

◆ A receipt for all monies you have received and any special terms agreed upon in writing.

Finding good homes
Ask some searching questions of any potential buyers:
◆ Will someone be at home during the day with the puppy?
◆ Do they have young children?
◆ Are they prepared to exercise the puppy?
◆ Do they have other pets?
◆ Do they have a secure yard?
If you aren't satisfied with their answers or feel that something's wrong, don't sell them the puppy.

Popular dog breeds

Some of the world's best-loved breeds of dog are featured in the following pages with detailed information and expert advice on their history and origins, their temperament, working ability, appearance, and suitability as family pets. If you are considering owning one of these dogs, you can check on how much exercise they need as well as their grooming requirements.

Chapter Ten

DOG BREED GUIDE

In the following pages you will find detailed information on many popular dog breeds plus brief descriptions of some other well-loved breeds that make good family pets. The way dogs are classified varies, and different countries and their canine governing bodies still use different systems. However, they are usually classified according to the type of work they perform.

Sporting group

These dogs were specifically bred to work at finding, flushing out, and retrieving game birds.

Hound group

These speedy dogs were developed to hunt, chase, and kill prey. They are divided into scenthounds and sighthounds for locating prey.

Working group

These dogs have been bred over the centuries to perform specific tasks, including guarding, rescue work, and police work.

Terrier group

These dogs were bred to hunt and dig out vermin and small game. Most terriers evolved in the British Isles and they all love to dig.

Toy group

These miniature dogs were first developed and bred to become companions and pets. Their size makes them suitable for city life.

Herding group

These ancient dogs have been used to protect livestock for centuries. They tend to be highly intelligent but need a lot of exercise.

Non-sporting group

This group of popular pet dogs contains all the breeds that do not fit easily into the other categories. Dogs in this group make good pets.

HOW TO USE THE BREED GUIDE

Guarding instinct

Longer bars mean a stronger guarding instinct and denote a good watchdog that will warn of approaching strangers and deter any unwanted intruders.

Temperament

Longer bars mean a good temperament and indicate a breed that is noted for its friendly nature, making it more suitable as an affectionate family pet.

Exercise

Longer bars mean that a breed needs a lot of daily exercise, including free running and playing stimulating games in addition to regular walks on the leash.

Grooming

Longer bars mean that you must be prepared to spend more time grooming and tend to apply to long-haired breeds and those that need clipping or stripping.

Other dogs

Longer bars mean that a breed is friendly and nonaggressive to other dogs, and will socialize well with dogs of most breeds in a range of surroundings.

Summary and height

This sums up the specific breed's main attributes, temperament, and suitability as a family pet, followed by a box related to the height ranges for the breed.

Sporting group

Cocker Spaniel

Guarding instinct

Will warn of any approaching intruders

Temperament

Enjoys adults

Exercise

As much as possible

Grooming

Daily attention to ears and feathering

Other dogs

Friendly and sociable

Summary

Happy-go-lucky, makes a fine family pet

H

Males:
Over 15½ in. (39 cm)

Bitches:
Over 14½ in. (37 cm)

Right: *The friendly Cocker Spaniel loves to join in all family activities.*

This charming spaniel is believed to have originated in pre-fourteenth-century Spain. It evolved through selective breeding from several Sporting breeds, depending on the terrain worked and the prey. Originally, Cockers assisted in falconry and were later used to drive birds into nets. When game bird shooting reached its zenith during the nineteenth century, the Cocker was found to be particularly effective in flushing out woodcock.

Temperament

Today there are more pets than there are workers because Cockers are gentle, intelligent, biddable, and easily trained. A classic companion, Cockers love the fellowship of their human family. Their greatest pleasure is to join in family activities, lying by the fire, shopping with mother, and shooting with father.

Work

A hallmark of this breed is its happiness when working. Indeed, the Cocker's enthusiasm knows

no bounds, underlined by the incessant tail wagging. It hurriedly quarters the ground, freezing as it bolts a bird or rabbit waiting for the shot, and then goes after the next. Remembering where the game lies, the Cocker can easily find and retrieve it unmarked because it has an extraordinarily soft mouth.

Left: *The Cocker is renowned for its long, silky ears and sweet expression.*

General care

To stay happy, the Cocker Spaniel needs all the exercise possible, particularly free running in woods and fields. It is important to comb the ears daily, and you should feed him from a tall narrow dish that keeps the ears out of the food. Comb out any debris after exercise and groom the dog at least once a week.

Appearance

A square dog with a merry nature and a soft expression. It is well muscled with good bone and an easy mover. It has a silky, flat coat, well-feathered forelegs and underparts and above the hocks.

Health problems

Some hip dysplasia (page 102) and kidney problems (page 114). Buy puppies only from eye-tested parents.

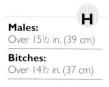

English Springer Spaniel

One of the oldest recorded sporting dogs, the lively Springer Spaniel was first mentioned in literature by the poet Chaucer. The word "Spaniel" may be derived from the Spanish word "Espagnnol." The Springer was developed to become one of the great sporting dogs during the nineteenth century.

Temperament

This is a gentle, loving dog whose natural desire is to please. The Springer is highly intelligent and reacts well to kind training. Being so energetic, these dogs become a nuisance without early training. They need things to do, especially retrieving games and play, and take to Agility and Flyball with enthusiasm. They crave and give affection, hating to be alone, and are very good with children.

Work

Springers are Sporting dogs with boundless energy. Their prime objective is to "spring" game from its hiding place for the shooters but they can also point and retrieve. They will enter the thickest cover fearlessly and leap into freezing water to retrieve a bird. Their extraordinary sense

of smell has recently been used by police and customs agents, who train Springers to sniff out drugs and explosives.

General care

Springers need plenty of free running and play daily. They should be brushed and combed once a week. Trim the feathering with scissors and make sure you keep the ears dry and clean.

▓ **Above:** *Springers like nothing better than to be outside in the open air.*

Appearance

The Springer is taller than the Cocker Spaniel with a weather-resistant coat and feathering on the ears, forelegs, and hindquarters. The coat may be black and white, liver and white, or one of these with tan markings.

▓ **Below:** *This show Springer has a weather-resistant coat.*

Health problems

Some hip dysplasia (page 102). Eye problems include progressive retinal atrophy (page 103). Buy only from tested parents.

Guarding instinct

Will warn but friendly

Temperament

Gentle and kind

Exercise

A great deal daily

Grooming

Weekly brushing, ears daily

Other dogs

No problems

Summary

A loving family pet

H

Males:
Approx 20 in. (50 cm)

Bitches:
Approx 19 in. (48 cm)

Sporting group

Labrador Retriever

Guarding instinct

Will warn but friendly

Temperament

Cool and laid back

Exercise

As much as possible

Grooming

Negligible

Other dogs

No problems

Summary
A wonderful
companion dog

H

Males: 22½–
24½ in. (57–62 cm)

Bitches: 21½–
23½ in. (56–60 cm)

The seventeenth century saw trade between Britain and Newfoundland – slates in exchange for saltwater fish. An all-purpose water dog helped the fishermen to retrieve dropped articles, haul carts, and retrieve game. Called Saint John's Dogs, they were originally brought to England by sailors. The Earl of Malmesbury, recognizing their skills, developed them as gundogs. This is the most popular retriever of all. Almost the perfect Sporting dog, the Labrador has a natural inclination to retrieve on land and water, a desire to please, and the ability to learn easily.

Temperament

An affable breed, the Labrador Retriever is tolerant and easy-going with dogs and human

beings, enjoys the company of children, and will allow them to take liberties. However, it is easily upset by shouting or harsh treatment of any kind.

General care

Puppies are very exuberant but with early and kind domestic training, they fit into the family quickly. Labradors have a voracious appetite and a tendency to become overweight, so monitor your dog's diet carefully. Stimulating them prevents destructive habits from forming; owners should invent search and retrieve games and involve them in all family activities.

Above: *This lineup of sporting dogs shows the range of colors, from black through yellow to liver and cream.*

Health problems

Hip dysplasia (page 102). Some eye conditions: Multifocal retinal dysplasia (MRD), progressive retinal atrophy (PRA), hereditary cataracts, and entropion (see page 103). The best breeders test their breeding dogs.

They have a need for love and understanding. The Labrador is an active, country dog needing plenty of exercise, free running, and play. Grooming is minimal; just clean the ears and brush the coat weekly to rid it of dead hairs.

Appearance

A strongly built dog, the Labrador has a broad, deep chest and a distinctive short, dense coat that can withstand cold and wet weather. Coat colors are chocolate or liver, yellow, or black.

Below: *Labrador puppies may look small and cute but they grow up into large, powerful dogs. Their natural desire to play makes them good family pets.*

Golden Retriever

In 1825 Lord Tweedmouth mated his "Yellow" Retriever to a Tweed Water Spaniel (now extinct). One of the resulting progeny was mated to another Tweed Water Spaniel, the progeny of which was mated back again. It is rumored that a Bloodhound was added together with a Sheepdog from a troupe of performing Russian circus dogs with which his Lordship became enamored and bought. And thus, today's Golden Retriever evolved.

Temperament

A gentle, biddable dog that is highly intelligent and capable of combining the best sporting qualities with those of a near-perfect pet dog. Delightful family pets, Golden Retrievers are happy to be the gundog for the father, an elegant companion for the mother, and a playmate for the children.

■ **Right:** *The handsome Golden Retriever makes a wonderful family pet and sporting dog.*

Work

These excellent retrievers have a soft mouth and a good nose for finding lost game. They are easily trained to be all-purpose Sporting dogs and work with great enthusiasm, braving the thickest cover and the coldest water. Their versatility and intelligence have led them to become great guide dogs for the blind and assistance dogs for the disabled.

■ **Left:** *The eyes are gentle and loving.*

General care

Being mainly a country hunting dog, the Golden Retriever needs frequent exercise and plenty of mental stimulation. It excels at Obedience and Flyball. These dogs should always be brushed and combed twice a week to rid the coat of dead hairs and tangles from the feathering.

Appearance

This medium-sized dog is strongly built and muscular with a gentle, loving expression in the eyes. The coat is dense with good feathering and a water-resistant undercoat. The color varies from a cream to a rich, lustrous gold.

Health problems

Hip dysplasia (page 102), elbow dysplasia (page 103), and some eye problems. Buy from tested stock.

Guarding instinct

Will warn of approach but no aggression

Temperament

A gentle, kindly disposition

Exercise

Can never have enough

Grooming

Twice-weekly brush and comb

Other dogs

Friendly

Summary

A great companion

H

Males: 23–24 in. (58–61 cm)

Bitches: 21½– 22½ in. (55–57 cm)

Hound group

Beagle

Guarding instinct

Will warn but no aggression

Temperament

Easy-going, friendly

Exercise

Plenty

Grooming

Weekly brush and polish

Other dogs

No problems

Summary

A happy, laid-back companion

Ideally: (H)
13–16 in. (30–40 cm)

A small hound dating from Norman times, the Beagle evolved and was developed from the Talbot Hound and the Southern Hound. A further mix with small hounds produced the breed first recorded by name in the "Privy Accounts" of Henry VIII. As the larger hunted animals became scarce, huntsmen developed the Beagle to hunt rabbits, which they do with enthusiasm and skill.

Temperament

An intelligent dog with a peaceful nature, the Beagle can adjust well to city or country life. It readily accepts children as part of its family and likes to feel part of the human pack. Beagles are happy, easygoing, and people-orientated, adapting well to most environments. However, they are not the easiest dogs to train and require a lot of kindness and patience.

Work

As a pack dog, the Beagle has few equals. It is not quarrelsome and is relatively easy to train to be behaved when hunting. Having short legs, it works slower than the Harrier or English Foxhound but hunts cheerfully with its flag (tail) held high and enters dense cover with equanimity. Packs are usually hunted with hunters on foot.

Health problems

Rare hip problems. An eye problem under investigation. Otherwise, a hardy, long-lived companion.

Right: *This dog has the color and conformation of the traditional English-type hound.*

General care

Beagles need plenty of exercise that must be augmented with playing in the yard. They eat well and care should be taken to keep them in athletic form as they have a tendency to become overweight. A weekly brush and a polish with a chamois leather keeps them looking good.

Below: *The build and markings of this Beagle are favored in the United States.*

Appearance

Small to medium in size, in the United States; height cannot exceed 15 inches (38 cm). Tricolors are most popular with a black back, tan sides and top of legs, and a white chest, stomach, and lower legs.

Dachshund

Mystery veils the real origins of this breed. Its German name is *Teckel*, a word that is found at the base of an ancient Egyptian sculpture of familiarly long-bodied, short-legged dogs. "Dachshund" means "badger dog" and it is one of the oldest hunting breeds in Germany, mentioned in records since the fifteenth century. The different sizes and coats have evolved since around 1850 and today the most popular variety is the Miniature Long-haired Dachshund. Few, if

■ **Below:** *The Dachshund is a game little dog that loves hunting.*

any, Dachshunds hunt in the United States, but they have not lost their instincts. A few are still used in Germany and in France, particularly the very small variety known in Germany as the Rabbit Dachshund. They will go underground but are in danger of getting trapped. At one time, the Standards were general hunters of foxes, deer, and even boar.

Temperament

The Dachshund is easy to live with and very affectionate within its human family. Playful and mischievous, it is sometimes stubborn as befits a hunting dog. An adaptable breed, living with equal ease in city or country. Intelligent and easily trained, although house-training can be a challenge! Spirited and humorous, the Long-haireds are more independent than the Wires and Smooths, which are more demonstrative.

General care

All varieties adore activity and need free running and play daily. Each variety has its miniature equivalent. Whereas the Smooths need a soft brush and polish weekly, the Long-haireds need brushing and combing biweekly, and the Wire-haireds should be hand stripped every three months.

Appearance

A long, low dog known as the "sausage dog," it is full of life and always alert. All colors are acceptable but only small white patches on the chest are permitted.

Health problems

All varieties can have back problems and they should not be allowed to run up and down steps or stairs. Buy miniature Dachshunds only from eye-tested parents.

■ **Right:** *The Smooth-haired Dachshund makes a spirited companion and pet.*

Guarding instinct

Distrustful, all sizes will warn off strangers

Temperament

Easygoing, playful, but can be stubborn

Exercise

Needs plenty plus play and hunting in woods

Grooming

Smooths: minimal

Long-haired: biweekly

Wires: weekly

Other dogs

No great problems

Summary
One of these varieties will suit any family

H

Miniatures and Standards:
5–10 in. (13–25 cm)

Working group

Boxer

Guarding instinct

A serious guard

Temperament

Good natured but
boisterous without
aggression

Exercise

Must have plenty

Grooming

Weekly brushing

Other dogs

Easy going

Summary

The right dog for the
right family

H

Males:
22½–25 in. (57–63 cm)

Bitches: 21½–
23½ in. (53–59 cm)

The Boxer is a German
manufactured breed
derived from the ancient
Mastiff-style dog that
accompanied the Roman legions
across Europe. Like several other
big breeds, Boxers have, in their
lineage, the blood of the
Bullenbeiser – dogs bred for the
purpose of bullbaiting. However,
the Boxer did not appear until
around 1890, after bullbaiting
was outlawed.

Temperament

Bred to be a companion, guard
dog, and show dog, the Boxer's
intelligence and brightness of
spirit endear him to most of the
world. It is alert with a booming
voice but never vicious. As a
member of a family, the Boxer is
truly a fun dog, very affectionate
and loyal to the end.

Below: *The boxer's aggressive
appearance belies its soft nature.*

Health problems

Some hip dysplasia (page 102), skin
and immune disorders. Buy from
reputable breeders who test their
stock. Some deafness in white dogs.

Work

Once over the puppy stages,
Boxers are easily trained for all
kinds of security work. The breed
is used in Europe as a police dog,
where its muscular, hard body can
stop a criminal in his tracks.
Armed forces make use of its
determination and confident
attitude. The Boxer's aggressive
appearance often warns off
wrongdoers, but this dog is not
a biter and its formidable looks
belie its soft nature.

Above: *Easily trained and strongly
built, the Boxer is a good guard dog.*

General care

The Boxer can be boisterous and
exuberant and should be trained
not to jump up on children whom
it loves. Natural athletes, Boxers
need plenty of activity, free
running, and play. Minimal
grooming is required: a weekly
brushing will remove dead hairs,
then polish with a chamois leather
or grooming mitt.

Appearance

Typically, in the United States,
Boxers have their ears
cropped.
A superb athletic body
rippling with muscles, of
medium size with a short,
glossy coat in fawn shades
from light to deep red, or
distinct brindle stripes.
White is allowed but not
exceeding one-third of the
base color.

Standard Schnauzer

Above: *Although this dog may look fierce and is very protective of its family, it has a very friendly nature.*

This friendly, muscular dog was almost certainly derived from the ancient Wire-haired Pinscher to which it bears a startling resemblance, as can be seen in a picture by Albrecht Dürer (1492). A fourteenth-century statue of a hunter in Mechlinburg, Germany, has a similar-looking dog crouched at his feet. This old breed was once a general farm dog, killing rats, hunting, and protecting its owners. It was used to accompany stagecoaches in order to defend them against robbers who worked the forests, and thus it became known as the "Carriage Griffon."

Typically, in the United States, Standard Schnauzers have their ears cropped.

Temperament

Absolutely devoted to its family, the Schnauzer is a happy dog that can be trained fairly easily to be obedient. There is no need to worry about your property or children if this fellow lives with you – it is an outstanding watchdog. Courageous and assertive, it is a friendly dog and needs strong but kind handling.

Work

The original Pinscher was an all-around farm dog doing anything that was expected of him. The modern Schnauzer is usually a much-loved family pet and does not generally have work to do, but even so it still retains the will and the ability. In some European countries, these dogs are used as guard dogs – a role they relish.

General care

All Standard Schnauzers require frequent running exercise and play to maintain their athleticism and mental health. They are also the natural friends of horses. The wire coat needs hand-stripping four times a year, and the leg and face furnishings should be combed out twice a week.

Appearance

A chunky, medium-sized muscular dog, the coat is black or pepper and salt (grayish) in color. The outer coat is wiry, harsh to the touch, and the dog is distinguished by a beard and bushy eyebrows; the undercoat is dense.

Health problems

Prone to skin problems.

Guarding instinct

Suspicious, so prowlers beware

Temperament

Affectionate family dog; brave, loyal, and cares deeply

Exercise

Enough to keep muscle tone

Grooming

Needs hand-stripping quarterly

Other dogs

Males can be dominant

Summary

A good all-around family pet

H

Males: 18–20 in. (46–51 cm)

Bitches: 17–19 in. (43–48 cm)

Left: *The dense, wiry coat will need combing through twice every week.*

Working group

Siberian Husky

Guarding instinct

Not a guard dog, too easy-going

Temperament

Kind, gentle, and very affectionate

Exercise

A glutton for running; try cart training

Grooming

Twice-weekly deep grooming required

Other dogs

Generally friendly, good disposition

Summary
An excellent companion for energetic families

H

Males:
21–23½ in. (53–60 cm)

Bitches:
20–22 in. (51–56 cm)

Husky sled dogs were the only means of transport in Alaska during the gold rush of 1900. Dog team drivers developed rivalries and started to stage races. In 1920 a team of

twenty Siberians pulled a sled for 340 miles carrying vaccines to the diphtheria-stricken city of Nome, saving the population. A statue of a sled dog in Central Park, New York, celebrates that achievement. Because the breed lived closely, probably for thousands of years, with the Chukchi nation, they are people-oriented.

■ **Right:** *Huskies are very energetic, friendly dogs.*

Temperament

The Siberian Husky is gentle, friendly and people loving, intelligent, and biddable. Easygoing, easy to train, and anxious to please, the Siberian Husky is a pack dog that understands its family, particularly the children.

Work

In the land of their origin, the Husky is a much-cherished working dog and was used for hauling sleds laden with meat and fish. Their tremendous strength and stamina allow them to make some phenomenally long journeys. When necessary, they also helped with hunting. Today, they are usually companion dogs, although the sport of sled dog racing is growing rapidly.

General care

Without their work, all Huskies will need frequent free running and exercise, and new owners should consider

■ **Below:** *Elegant and athletic, the Siberian Husky does not bark but howls and "talks."*

joining a specialist club that races with wheeled carts. These dogs shed freely and have a double coat that needs grooming with combing at least twice a week; the undercoat can knot.

Appearance

The medium-sized Husky looks very alert and is lithe with grace. It has an abundant weatherproof coat with a thick, soft undercoat. The breed comes in a variety of colors; the facial colors can be contrasting, unusual, and striking.

Health problems

Hip dysplasia (page 102) with a low breed average. There are some eye problems so puppies should come only from eye-tested parents.

Rottweiler

The likely origin is from the Mastiff-style dogs that traveled with Roman armies driving livestock as they swept northward conquering Europe. First used as boar hunters, then as cattle drovers in the German city of Rottweil (a cattle market town in medieval times), they doubled as custodians of traders' money. The Rottweiler is devoted to its family but must be taught its place kindly but persistently. Because of its intensely protective nature, it is not advisable to leave this dog with young children as, like all guarding breeds, it might misinterpret their signals.

Temperament

Highly intelligent, the Rottweiler's strong naturally protective instincts need socialization with firm but kind training. These dogs can be difficult in the wrong hands.

Work

Very few Rottweilers are used for their droving ability today. Instead, their strong protective instincts are now put to use in security work. They are often used to patrol building sites and industrial installations as well as acting as security truck guards. Because of their singular intelligence, some countries train them as customs and police dogs, mountain rescue dogs, and even for sled hauling.

Below: *In spite of its powerful body and formidable appearance, this dog can make a good pet if properly trained.*

General care

Keep these big dogs' muscles hard with walking, free running, and play. If you live in the city, you should take them out for a brisk walk at least twice a day. With their thick, smooth coat, they need to be brushed only once a week with a stiff brush to remove dead hairs.

Appearance

A big, thickset, muscled dog, the Rottweiler should show

Health problems

Occasional hip dysplasia (page 102); Osteochondrosis dessicans (OCD), largely under control (page 103); entropion (page 103).

boldness and confidence, never nervousness or aggressiveness. It has a calm look that indicates a good nature and needs no training as a house guard dog.

Guarding instinct

Great guard dog, intruders beware

Temperament

Good-natured but can be dominant without training

Exercise

Frequent, thrives on plenty of activity

Grooming

Easy care; weekly brush and comb

Other dogs

Take care, as they will not back down

Summary
The time spent training pays dividends

Males:
24–27 in. (61–69 cm)

Bitches:
22–25 in. (56–63 cm)

Left: *A young puppy will need kind but firm training and lots of socialization if it is to grow into a good-natured adult.*

Working group

Doberman Pinscher

Guarding instinct

A powerful guard dog

Temperament

A great family dog needing to be trained

Exercise

An hour a day walking plus free running

Grooming

A weekly brushing

Other dogs

Seldom picks a fight but never backs down

Summary

A family dog for experienced owners

H

Males:
26–28 in. (66–71 cm)

Bitches:
24–26 in. (61–66 cm)

This breed was designed in the 1880s by Herr Louis Dobermann, a German tax collector. At a time when taxes were collected personally, he wanted a fearless, alert dog with stamina to defend him as he traveled the country on horseback. His secondary job, a dogcatcher, gave

Above: *Powerful but elegant, this big dog makes an ideal guard dog and an affectionate pet.*

Left: *If it is well-socialized and trained, a Doberman puppy can adapt really well to family life.*

him the ideal opportunity to study various breeds. The Rottweiler, the old German Pinscher, and also the Manchester Terrier were probably the foundation. Later the breed may have been further refined by adding Pointer and Greyhound blood. Typically, in the United States, dogs of this breed have their ears cropped.

Temperament

A devoted, affectionate house dog, the Doberman is very intelligent and is easily trained, but its power must be kept under control. It is a devout family companion that loves to be part of daily activities. Its guardianship of the family's children is legendary but it must be trained firmly but kindly.

Work

Highly regarded as a guard and security dog, the Doberman is much favored by many security companies moving large sums of money. It was a watchdog soldier and messenger in battles during

Health problems

Low to average hip dysplasia (page 102). Buy from eye-tested parents and test the puppy. Von Willebrand's disease (page 103) is also possible.

Above: *A well-trained Doberman can be a formidable guard dog as well as a loving and loyal family pet.*

World War II, and it is now used by the police in many countries worldwide because of its bravery, intelligence, and alertness, to say nothing of its athletic strength.

General care

An hour or so of walking every day with about ten minutes' free running will suffice. Add fifteen minutes' play in the yard and a Doberman will be happy and fit. Very little grooming is required; a a weekly brush and polish with a grooming mitt will be enough.

Appearance

A big dog, the Doberman is very graceful with a refined outline; a powerhouse athlete. The coat is a glossy black, brown, blue, or fawn (Isabella) with rich tan that must be well defined.

Great Dane

▓ **Above:** *The Great Dane is a majestic-looking dog with its powerful physique and appealing expression.*

There is no doubt that this dog's ancestors were giant war dogs from Asia Minor known as Allens. They probably originated from ancient Egypt. They were used as war dogs by Attila the Hun and fought wild animals in Rome's Colosseum. The modern dog was developed in the 1500s in Germany for hunting wild boar. A pack owned by Earl Philip of Hessen killed 2,572 boar in 1563, and another German aristocrat had a pack of 600 Great Danes. From about 1882, when the Breed Club was formed, the breed changed course and became a pet and guard dog. It

Health problems

Hip dysplasia (see page 102), elbow dysplasia (see page 103), bloat and eye problems, and Wobbler's Syndrome.

has been many years since Great Danes were worked in any form.

Typically, in the United States, dogs of this breed have their ears cropped.

Temperament

It is a courageous, devoted, but sensitive breed that belies its bloodthirsty past. Very family-oriented, Great Danes are easily trained and obedient. Although large, they are not clumsy and don't take up too much space. However, a big house and yard are best. Extremely fond of their family's children, they will defend them if any danger threatens.

General care

These dogs need only some gentle exercise when young, which can be built up gradually over time to develop their muscular, athletic body. A fully grown adult Great Dane will demand plenty of walks and free running. Never play-fight with this breed. A weekly good brushing will keep the dog's coat lustrous; the ears need cleaning at the same time.

Appearance

A majestic dog, the Great Dane has a soft expression and an athletic body with a look of "dash and daring." Colors range from brindle with stripes to fawn-light to dark, blue-light to dark slate, black, or harlequin with black or blue patches that appear torn.

▓ **Below:** *The Great Dane is a gentle giant in spite of its size.*

Guarding instinct

Suspicious nature, will guard owners

Temperament

Friendly, outgoing, favors children

Exercise

Puppies not too much; adults need plenty

Grooming

Minimal: just a weekly brush and polish with a grooming mitt

Other dogs

Gets along with others

Summary

A deeply affectionate big dog, loyal and caring for his family

H

Males:
Min. 30 in. (76 cm)

Bitches:
Min. 28 in. (71 cm)

Terrier group

Jack Russell Terrier

Guarding instinct

A very watchful dog; intruders beware

Temperament

Happy-go-lucky fun dog, very intelligent and trainable

Exercise

Running and playing as much as possible

Grooming

Smooth-haired needs very little grooming; rough-haired needs brushing

Other dogs

Not aggressive but will stand his ground

Summary

Ideal for the dynamic country family

Males:
14 inches (35 cm)

Bitches:
13 inches (33 cm)

Parson Jack Russell was a cleric who was, rather unjustly, more famed for his hunting exploits than for his pastoral work. Born in Devon in 1795, he took a degree at Oxford and was ordained in 1819. As a student he aggravated the college authorities by keeping an illicit small pack of hounds. It was while he was at Oxford that he acquired the terrier bitch who was to be the foundation of the breed that was named after him. While strolling in Magdalen Meadow one day, he met the local milkman and saw, for the first time, the terrier named Trump. He did not move until he had persuaded the milkman to part with her. The parson died at eighty-four, still in the saddle, his breed of dogs a fitting memorial.

Temperament

Highly intelligent, the busy Jack Russell is always doing things and is very affectionate as well as being a good guard – ever alert and watchful. Their wonderful friendly nature blossoms within a happy family and they are very patient with children. This is an easily trained, fun dog that is into everything.

Health problems

A generally healthy breed but buy from eye-tested parents.

Above: *The long-legged Jack Russell loves to be outside hunting.*

Work

This is a working terrier, which is reflected in the breed standard. The Jack Russell must have the conformation to go to earth and to run with hounds. Its job is to either mark the fox underground or

Left: *Ever vigilant, the Jack Russell's keen senses will flush out small prey, such as rats and mice.*

bolt it. This dog has courage without recklessness coupled with stamina. It is also one of the great ratters with razor-sharp reactions.

General care

There are two coats: the smooth variety requires only a weekly brushing; the rough coat needs hand-stripping or trimming every four to five months as well as weekly brushing. Basically, this is a country dog needing plenty of exercise and mental stimulation.

Appearance

A small athletic dog, it is full of vitality, slightly longer than high at the shoulders. The wiry or smooth coat is mostly white with black and/or tan patches. Note that the long-legged Jack Russell should not be confused with the shorter-legged Jack Russell terrier.

West Highland White Terrier

U ntil the mid-1800s the terriers of Scotland were a rough, hard, ill-disciplined, and nondescript mixed lot that kept down the rats and foxes on small farms. As foxhunting became fashionable, gentlemen began taking notice of terriers but did not like white dogs. Some people thought they were not as game as colored dogs. However, a Colonel Edward Malcolm, thinking one of his own brown terriers was a fox as it emerged from an earth, accidentally shot him, and from then on he developed this unmistakable white terrier and was the club's first chairman in 1906. The Westie was used as an all-purpose worker and was kept as a "vermin" killer and was taken out to hunt foxes, otters, and wild cats. It had stamina and courage and was agile enough to clamber over rocks and penetrate the smallest holes where its prey could hide.

▥ **Left:** *Westie puppies are spirited and extremely energetic.*

Temperament

Feisty, stubborn, friendly, playful, and affectionate, the Westie is a bright pet for city or country. Very few pet dogs can replicate this bundle of paradoxes – a fun dog that one minute will be digging up your flowerbeds while hunting nonexistent moles and gophers, and the next minute will be lying on your lap with all the love of a spaniel. A clean and biddable dog.

General care

Twice-daily walks are essential and the Westie needs the freedom to run and play-hunt in a yard with the family. It needs stripping and shaping every three months and combing daily.

▥ **Right:** *The Westie is a fun-loving little dog with a feisty character.*

▥ **Above:** *The head should be slightly domed with very dark eyes.*

Appearance

A short-legged, square dog with a profuse wiry white coat that needs careful attention in order to maintain the typical shape.

Guarding instinct

A good, alert guard dog

Temperament

Playful, mischievous, happy

Exercise

Plenty of play and running

Grooming

Frequent combing to stop tangling; stripping every three months

Other dogs

Seldom picks a quarrel but will defend itself

Summary
A family dog full of zest

H

Males:
11 inches (28 cm)

Bitches:
10 inches (25 cm)

Health problems

Some eye problems are under investigation; a type of eczema and fairly rare Perthe's disease.

Terrier group

Staffordshire Bull Terrier

Guarding instinct

A forceful deterrent

Temperament

Easy-going, happy clown

Exercise

Walking, running, and play essential

Grooming

Very little; use a hound glove to polish

Other dogs

Not confrontational but beware, he will never back down

Summary

For the experienced dog owner only

Ideally:
14–16 inches
(35.5–40.5 cm)
Note: Height is related to weight

▓ **Right:** *Affectionate and loyal, these dogs make good pets.*

As a breed the "Staffie" is a comparative newcomer. However, its antecedents probably go back 6,000 years as it belongs to an exclusive club of Mastiff-style dogs bred game enough to fight against all odds on the bidding of their masters. They fought in battles shoulder to shoulder with the soldiers; they fought wild animals in Roman times; and they fought bulls, bears, rats, and, finally, each other. The Duke of Hamilton, a sporting rake of around 1770, developed a lighter fighter, the big Bulldogs not being fast enough, which is claimed to be the forerunner of the breed today. At the end of the eighteenth century, they were the best fighting dogs. Later on, they also proved themselves in rat pits where a dog, Billy, killed 100 rats in seven minutes, thirty seconds.

▓ **Right:** *Even though it is very muscular, the Staffie is an agile dog.*

However, it was not until the 1930s that a Breed Standard was created and the Staffie became a showdog and companion.

Temperament

The loyal Staffie is fearless, people-friendly, and intelligent but must be disciplined and trained. This dog is relatively easy to train, providing patience is asserted. Despite its bloody history it is, today, one of the most faithful and affectionate, family-loving pets. A Staffie will fiercely guard property and is an outstanding house guard.

General care

Grooming is minimal; all that is needed is a brush and polish weekly to get rid of dead hairs. Staffies need both physical and mental stimulation, with plenty of exercise including free running and play.

▓ **Right:** *The Staffie has a wide, deep chest and straight forelegs.*

Appearance

A chunky, well-muscled, medium-small dog, the Staffordshire Bull Terrier has a wide head, a pump handle tail, and walks with a jaunty air. The smooth coat is red, fawn, white, black, or blue.

Health problems

Generally a healthy breed but buy from eye-tested parents and have your puppy tested.

Cavalier King Charles Spaniel

Toy group

The modern Cavalier King Charles was almost certainly developed from the land spaniels of the fourteenth century that may have come from Spain. The Stuarts adored them and named them "King Charles." Indeed, Charles II shared his bed with several. They went out of fashion when William of Orange reigned but staged a comeback in the nineteenth century when a toy red and white spaniel was bred at Blenheim in Oxfordshire by the Duke of Marlborough. Although the breed started as a gundog and companion, it became a showdog and pet when dog shows started in the mid 1800s. A fashion developed for short-nosed dogs and the original breed began to decline again. An American, Roswell Eldridge, then offered handsome prizes to anyone who could reverse the trend and, gradually, by selective breeding, today's type of longer-nosed Cavalier King Charles evolved, and it has become one of the most popular of the Toy Spaniels.

Temperament

Docile, gentle, and intelligent, the Cavalier King Charles quickly learns the ways of its human family. With its friendly nature, this dog is a joy to own. Confident and gently assertive, it loves to play with children but doesn't like roughness.

Health problems

Some hip dysplasia (page 102); both sexes should be heart tested; and puppies and their parents should undergo eye testing.

General care

Being small, the Cavalier King Charles needs less exercise than the bigger spaniels. However, it loves activity of all kinds, particularly play. The silky coat needs weekly combing; look for any tangles in the feathering and ears after walks.

Appearance

An elegant, refined small dog with a kind expression and outgoing perky character displaying a free action when moving. A silky coat with colors that are vivid and clearly delineated.

Left: *These perky little dogs come in a range of colors, including ruby, the traditional Blenheim, and tricolor, as well as black and tan.*

Guarding instinct

Will warn but with no aggression

Temperament

Kind and gentle

Exercise

Loves frequent free running and play

Grooming

Pay strict weekly attention to ears and feathering

Other dogs

Not aggressive

Summary
An ideal family companion

H

Ideally:
12–13 in. (30–33 cm)

Left: *A five-month-old King Charles looking eager to please.*

Toy group

Pug

Guarding instinct

Not a guard dog but will warn

Temperament

Even-tempered, lively, and humorous

Exercise

Regular exercise, not excessive

Grooming

A light brushing daily

Other dogs

No problems

Summary

A great companion if you don't mind a little snoring

Ideally: **H**
10–11 in. (25–28 cm)

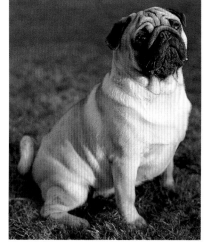

■ **Left:** *The Pug is always an amusing companion.*

The great canine authority Clifford Hubbard believes that the Pug and Pekingese were originally related because of the striking similarity of their muzzles and their body shape. However, they were separate by the 1600s, as shown in Chinese art. Dutch mariners brought them to Holland whereupon they became favorites of royalty after a pet Pug warned William, Prince of Orange, that Spanish soldiers were approaching to capture him at the battle of Hermingny and he escaped. William and Mary introduced the Pug to Britain where it was often decorated with orange ribbons as an honored member of the Royal Household of Orange. There is no evidence that this breed ever worked, although, from an evolutionary point of view, they are Mastiffs. Their "work" has always been to bring solace to human beings, for whom they have an uncanny understanding.

Temperament

Tolerant, easygoing with children, Pugs are very intelligent with an independent comical character. They are guaranteed to bring laughter into any house with their strange facial expressions. They like sitting up high to watch the world go by. They can easily be trained to be clean.

■ **Above:** *The Pug has a distinctive flat face and prominent eyes.*

General care

Pugs do not require excessive walking but enjoy a walk twice a day as they like seeing the world. Grooming is easy; a light brushing daily gives a glow to a Pug's coat. In addition, you should keep the eyes and ears clean.

Appearance

A sturdy, thickset small dog with flat features and a fine, smooth, short coat, which may be colored silver, apricot, fawn, or black with a facial mask.

■ **Left:** *Pugs have forceful characters and are very strong-willed. They make rewarding and entertaining pets.*

Health problems

The Pug enjoys good health generally but sometimes experiences a little difficulty breathing so take care in hot weather.

Chihuahua

E xperts are baffled as to the real origins of this tiny dog. Some Americans discovered the breed in Chihuahua State, Mexico, and they thought it was Mexican, but there is no evidence to support this. Some believe the ancient Toltecs bred them, others that they were sacred dogs of the Aztecs, but, again, there is no evidence. Interestingly, some European breeds resemble them closely, especially the Portuguese Podengo and the Maltese Kelb Ta But (the pocket dog). In 1519 the Spanish Conquistador Cortes conquered the Aztecs. His forces took their war dogs; did little companion dogs go too? In 1530, the Knights of Saint John, including the Spanish and Portuguese, captured Malta; did they take back tiny dogs for their

Health problems

Slipping patella, some heart murmurs. Check with your veterinarian.

ladies? When the Spanish colonized Mexico, would not the ladies have taken their companion dogs?

Temperament

Totally unaware of their truly diminutive size, these dogs believe themselves to be Mastiffs in heavy disguise. Intelligent and easy to live with, their only work was to be amusing companions and furry

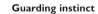 **Left:** *The long-haired Chihuahua will need regular twice-weekly grooming.*

hot-water bottles in the past! Most people keep more than one as they live together easily and will share their home with cats and other household pets. Care must be exercised when children handle them as their bones are very small. Most Chihuahuas adore being fussed over.

General care

The smooth-coated variety needs minimal grooming, but the long-haired variety should be brushed and combed lightly twice weekly. Active and athletic, this little dog loves to walk and to play in the yard. However, it does not need excessive exercise.

Appearance

Tiny, dainty, active, and even feisty, the Chihuahua comes in smooth-coated and long-haired varieties in any color or mixture.

Guarding instinct

Will warn of approach of strangers

Temperament

Very affectionate, active, and a bit feisty

Exercise

A daily walk with plenty of play

Grooming

Brush and comb long coats twice weekly; minimal for short coats

Other dogs

No problems, quite sociable

Summary

Ideal for the elderly, easy to keep

Ideally:
6–9 in. (15–23 cm)

Left: *The smooth-haired Chihuahua is a dainty little dog. Affectionate and bright, it makes the perfect companion.*

Toy group

Pomeranian

Guarding instinct

Will bark a warning

Temperament

A joyful, active, and dynamic dog

Exercise

Running and playing in the yard

Grooming

Essential to brush deeply daily

Other dogs

Being self-confident, big dogs are no worry

Summary

An ideal pet for a busy urban family

Ideally: **H**
8½–11 in. (22–28 cm)

A type of tiny Spitz dog is depicted on some Roman artifacts and there is evidence of this dog's existence throughout Europe ever since. However, almost certainly, the close relations of this miniscule dog are the much larger Nordic Spitz breeds, such as the Samoyed and Keeshond. It went to Great Britain from Pomerania, Germany, around 1870 in the form of the much bigger German Spitz weighing 30 pounds (13.6 kg). The British bred them smaller and gave them their new name, and by 1896 they were much smaller. However, they did not become popular until Queen Victoria exhibited her own dog at the Kennel Club's show, after which the breed's future was assured.

Temperament

A happy and amusing dog that is very fond of its family and given to being noisy unless trained otherwise. Full of vitality and fun, Pomeranians are always anxious to involve themselves in family activities. They are docile with children, who must take care not to be rough as the Pomeranian's bones are very small.

General care

Running and playing in the yard is sufficient exercise for most Pomeranians but they do enjoy an outing. It is also essential to thoroughly brush the coat deeply on a daily basis to prevent knotting and tangles that form due to the plush thickness.

■ **Left:** *Pomeranians have a large, distinctive Spitz-type ruff of fur.*

■ **Left:** *A wide range of colors is permissible for the Pomeranian, including cream, sable, white, brown, red, and orange.*

Appearance

A Lilliputian dog, a tiny round ball of fluff. The adult coat is abundant, thick, and plush. All colors are permissible, including whole colors – white, black, brown, pale blue, or vivid orange – and particolored.

■ **Below:** *Pomeranians look very cute but they are actually good watchdogs and will warn of approaching strangers.*

Health problems

Very healthy but can suffer slipping patella.

Yorkshire Terrier

I n the early nineteenth century, coal mines were riddled with rats, and some miners in northern England developed a terrier small enough to carry in their pockets when they went down into the mines. Starving workers came south from Scotland seeking work and bringing their rough terriers, the Clydesdale and Skye Terriers. These were interbred with the Old English Broken-haired and Manchester Terriers to produce the Yorkshire Terrier. When dog

showing began around 1850, the breeders realized that pretty little companion dogs were worth more money and therefore refined the terrier, producing today's dog.

Health problems

There are rare cases of slipping patella and Perthe's disease. Some eye problems are under investigation.

Temperament

This little dog will give you his unlimited affection, but because he is independent by nature, his early training will need patience and kindness. Under the gentle looks and loving nature lurks some of the feisty nature inherited from his rough ancestry. He will still hunt mice and rats but at home he is full of fun and mischief. Children need to be careful as the Yorkie is very small.

General care

The Yorkshire Terrier makes a perfect house pet, particularly for the elderly as he eats only a tiny amount of food and takes up little space. His acute hearing picks up strangers in the vicinity and, although he's not a yappy dog, he will let you know they're there. He loves going out and will need a long walk or once around the block twice daily. Sniffing around the yard and

play-hunting are an equal joy to him. Because of the length and texture of his coat, it does tangle and mat so a daily gentle combing session is essential. Otherwise, keep the coat cut short.

Appearance

The tiny Yorkshire Terrier is an extremely elegant dog with a spectacular coat, which is long and silky and of a steel blue color with a rich golden tan on the head, chest, and legs.

Below: *Whether a pet or a show dog, your dog will be a spirited companion.*

Guarding instinct

Suspicious; will bark warning

Temperament

Fun, mischievous, loving

Exercise

A little or a lot

Grooming

Very important: daily brushing and combing essential

Other dogs

No great problems

Summary

A great pet for old and young

Males:
10 in. (25 cm) or less

Bitches:
Slightly less

Non-sporting group

Bichon Frisé

Guarding instinct

Will warn but not a guard dog

Temperament

Happy, friendly, active

Exercise

Needs plenty to keep calm

Grooming

A deep brushing daily and a monthly bath

Other dogs

No worries

Summary

An ideal gentle dog but the coat is a priority

Ideally: 9½–11½ in. (24–29 cm)

This is an ancient breed stemming from the Barbet of the Mediterranean region from which four breeds emerged: the Bichon Maltaise, Bichon Bolognese, Bichon Havanese, and Bichon Teneriffe. The latter breed was adopted by fourteenth-century Italian and Spanish nobility and thence the French court. King Henri III (1547–1589) was so enamored of them that he carried them in baskets attached to ribbons around his neck. However, the breed went out of favor in the late 1800s, reverting to "commoner" status, and was extensively used by circus performers and street musicians owing to its lively intelligence. Eventually recognized by the French in 1934, it was given its name, Bichon à Poil Frisé, or "Bichon of the Curly Coat."

Below: *The Bichon should have a black nose and very dark, round eyes.*

Health problems

There are some eye problems under investigation. Perthe's disease and slipping patella exist within the breed.

Temperament

This dog has a lively, kind nature and is very faithful, following its favorite person like a white shadow. It is an ideal canine companion with an undiminished ability to perform tricks. A happy, friendly breed without vices, the Bichon is boisterous with a sense of humor, quick to learn, and inventive.

General care

Because of their enthusiasm these dogs need plenty of walks and things to do like interactive play in the yard. Their coat

Above: *Bichon puppies are very vivacious and love to play with you.*

must have attention daily; otherwise it tangles and knots easily and may smell. If wished, it can be kept short in a "puppy cut."

Appearance

A small dog with corkscrewlike silky curls that are always white. When trimmed correctly, the Bichon has a rounded look with the black of the eyes and nose contrasting vividly.

Miniature Schnauzer

This is the most popular of the three Schnauzer breeds, particularly in America where its final development took place. A manufactured breed with its foundation in the Standard Schnauzer, it was first exhibited as a breed by itself in 1879 in Gerrmany. It has been suggested

Left: *The long beard and hair on the legs need frequent combing.*

Left: *The Miniature Schnauzer's expression is bright and alert.*

that as well as the Wire-haired Pinscher, the blood of the Affenpinscher runs in its veins. The combination of these two breeds may well be the reason that Mini Schnauzers are the only one of the three breeds to be described as ratters. Because of their working antecedents, Mini Schnauzers are very active dogs and just love doing things, particularly fun activities with their owners such as Agility, Obedience, and Flyball.

Temperament

Immensely affable, sensitive, and intelligent, the Mini Schnauzer learns its manners very quickly, suiting all homes, especially those with children. An excellent pet dog that learns quickly what is expected of it, it is small enough to be carried but is not a toy. These dogs are very playful and they will get on well with other animals and also with children.

General care

Dogs of this breed tend to become overweight so they must be exercised. They will take as much as their owner is prepared to give although smaller amounts are acceptable. Their coat requires particular attention and should be hand-stripped about four

Health problems

Generally a hardy little dog but puppies should be bought from eye-tested parents and tested themselves in time.

times a year. The furnishings and beard must be combed out at least two or three times a week.

Appearance

A small square dog with a wire coat and profuse furnishing on the legs, a distinctive beard, and thick eyebrows. The coat color is either pepper and salt (grayish), black, or a very striking black and silver.

Below: *Intelligent and very sensitive, this game little dog makes a good companion for both adults and children.*

Guarding instinct

Slightly suspicious, good guard dog

Temperament

Loving, easygoing, happy, playful pet

Exercise

Will run ten miles, make do with less

Grooming

Hand-stripping four times yearly; furnishings combed frequently

Other dogs

Not quarrelsome

Summary

Ideal for a young active family

Males and Bitches:
12–14 in. (30–36 cm)

Non-sporting group

Boston Terrier

Guarding instinct

Very good guard; the "bat ears" miss nothing

Temperament

A tractable dog, happy and friendly

Exercise

A couple of walks a day and a bit of play

Grooming

Just a brush weekly; take care of the eyes

Other dogs

A nonaggressive dog, never seeks trouble

Summary

An easygoing character bringing pleasure

Three sizes: H
15–17 in. (38–43 cm)

Around 1865 in Cotter's tavern in Charles Street, Boston, some coach drivers, stablemen, and hostlers used to gather while their masters were attending functions. They wondered what the result would be if they were to interbreed some of the imported purebred dogs belonging to the gentry. Thus, Bulldogs were mated to Bull Terriers and then to Pit Bull Terriers, and the result was a large, handsome fighting dog. The Boston Terrier's strange beauty was recognized and fanciers of the breed then selectively bred for a smaller dog (possibly they saw a commercial advantage). In 1891 the breeders formed their own club and created a breed standard, and the Boston Terrier has now become deservedly one of America's favorite dogs.

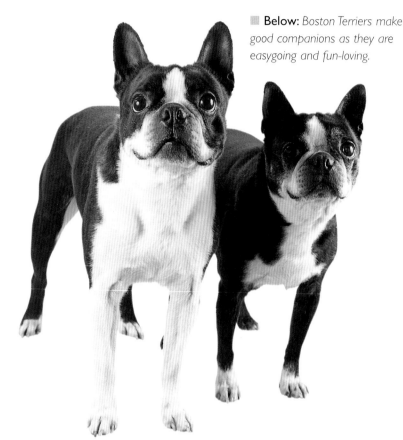

Below: *Boston Terriers make good companions as they are easygoing and fun-loving.*

Below: *The large ears are held erect and the eyes are gentle.*

Temperament

An amiable, docile dog, the highly intelligent Boston Terrier is easily trained, full of character, and a good guard dog. Although it is now just a well-behaved house pet, it was evolved as a fighting dog. A boisterous dog, it is full of fun with a liking for playing with toys.

General care

Hardly any grooming is required, just a soft brush and polish once a week. Two or three good walks a day with playtime in the yard

Health problems

Buy from eye-tested parents. There is some slipping patella.

are all the exercise a Boston Terrier needs. The protruding eyes are easily damaged so you should try to keep the dog out of bushes.

Appearance

A muscular, small, square dog with a large head and a short muzzle, the Boston Terrier's trademark is the large "bat ears." It should be brindle with white markings for preference but black with white is acceptable.

Shih Tzu

This breed was developed in ancient China; its Chinese name, Shih Tzu Kou, means "Lion dog." Its absolute origin is in Tibet where it enjoyed the status of a "holy dog" as far back as the seventh century. These dogs were often presented to visiting foreign dignitaries, which is probably how they entered China. After the death of the empress Tzu-hsi in 1908, the breed deteriorated and the best stock was sold. Outside China there was confusion as Shih Tzus were mixed with Apsos and were given different names. The first three dogs went to Britain in 1930 and by 1934 Lhasa Apsos and Shih Tzus were recognized as different breeds. Shih Tzus are first and foremost companions; they like to be out and about with their owners and to be fully integrated in family activities. However, they are extremely alert watchdogs and will not allow any strange noise to pass without noticing it.

Temperament

An amusing and independent pet that fades away without human companionship. Undoubtedly, the Shih Tzu is a fun dog – bouncy with an enthusiasm for life. An extremely intelligent and happy companion, the Shih Tzu presents no problems in the home but, craving human contact, it will dislike being left alone.

General care

Two walks a day and playing in the yard will suffice. The main attraction of the breed is the magnificent coat, but do not take on a Shih Tzu unless you are prepared for the work needed to maintain it. The hair knots and tangles easily and requires daily attention. It should be kept clean and conditioned.

Appearance

A short-legged dog with a well-muscled body under a profuse flowing coat, sometimes trailing to the floor. Shih Tzus come in

Health problems

The Shih Tzu is generally very healthy. Some pinched noses cause breathing problems; check the puppy's parents.

■ **Above:** *Shih Tzus must be groomed every day if their coats are to be kept free of tangles and in prime condition.*

any color, but a white blaze on the forehead and the tail tip are admired in particolors. Some owners keep their dogs in a "puppy clip" with the hair cut to about 2 inches (5 cm).

■ **Below:** *Enthusiastic and intelligent, the Shih Tzu is a good family pet.*

Guarding instinct

Very wary, will warn vociferously

Temperament

Outgoing character, happy nature

Exercise

A walk twice a day and plenty of play

Grooming

Gentle combing every day plus conditioning

Other dogs

Nonconfrontational

Summary

A fine family dog with a hint of the Orient

H

Ideally:
9½ –10½ inches (23–26.7 cm)

Non-sporting group

Lhasa Apso

Guarding instinct

Very suspicious; will warn of approach

Temperament

Affectionate but can be independent

Exercise

Three short walks a day or long walks

Grooming

Daily grooming and detangling.

Other dogs

Not aggressive

Summary

An unusual breed for a discerning family

Males:
10–11 in. (25–28 cm)

Bitches:
Slightly smaller

Right: These cute puppies will eventually have a heavy adult coat.

High in the mountains of Tibet, monks bred this little dog as a watchdog and companion before the birth of Jesus Christ. The Lhasa Apso may have evolved from the Central European herding dogs, such as the Pumi or the Puli. The breed was regarded as a talisman and although the dogs were never sold, they were often gifted to Chinese nobility. They were held in very high esteem by Tibetans, which made it difficult for any Westerners to acquire them. Officers who were serving in a 1904 expedition brought a few of these dogs out, followed in the early 1920s by the wife of a political officer and other ladies whose dogs formed the nucleus of the breed in Great Britain. Although in Western countries the dogs are bred as companions and show dogs, in their native land they are used as watchdogs, often sitting in a high place where they can keep an eye on the comings and goings of the monks and warning them of the approach of strangers.

Temperament

Although wary of strangers, the Lhasa Apso is loving with its human family without being too effusive. As a single dog, it will probably bond with one person very strongly but it has an independent streak and may not be as clingy as some people might like their pet dogs to be.

Left: This magnificent champion dog is in superb show condition.

General care

This tough little dog is full of energy and is able to walk long distances. However, several short walks are sufficient. The crowning glory of the breed is its glorious coat but it needs daily attention, otherwise it will tangle and mat. The coat can be kept short if you don't intend showing the dog.

Appearance

A short-legged, long dog with a profuse and heavy coat in several colors, including shades of gold, dark grizzle, smoke, particolor, black, white, or brown.

Health problems

Generally tough as befits a dog that has evolved in the harsh, cold climate of the Tibetan mountains. Some eye conditions are currently under investigation so it is wise to buy only from tested parents.

Poodle

Like so many ancient breeds, the Poodle has its origins in hunting. The breed comes from Germany; the name *Pudel* is derived from *Puddeln*, meaning to "splash in water." The French name *Caniche* is derived from "*chien-canne*," literally meaning a "duck dog," as the Poodle originally hunted wildfowl. The development of today's three varieties as pet dogs began in the 1800s. The Belgians liked big white dogs that they bred for hauling their milk carts, whereas the French bred small whites, and the Russians liked black miniatures. Although it is doubtful if any Poodles are used

Right: *Looking at the modern fashionable dog, it's hard to believe it was originally a water breed.*

as retrievers today, they still show their wildfowling antecedents by their joy in retrieving games. They are the most active of breeds and love work of all kinds, excelling in Agility, Obedience, and Flyball.

Temperament

A loving, sensitive breed possessed of superior intelligence, the lively Poodle becomes totally involved with family activities, particularly with children. It is a sheer delight for novices to experienced dog lovers. If the Poodle is trained with kindness, it will become an obedient and much-loved member of any family.

General care

All varieties have an unbounded energy and they will take more exercise and play than you can give. Poodles do not shed but they must be combed every other day to prevent tangles. Unless the owner is a hairdresser, it is better to take the dog to a groomer at least four or five times a year.

Appearance

Poodles have a springy movement and invariably look proud and happy. The Miniatures and Toys

Health problems

Standard Poodles have a low incidence of hip dysplasia (page 102). Puppies from all varieties should come from eye-tested parents. Some inherited eye problems.

look like small versions of the Standard. They come in all solid colors and the hairdressing styles vary according to taste, the lion lamb clips being most often seen.

Guarding instinct

All Poodles will bark warnings

Temperament

Gentle, fun-loving breeds, playful with children

Exercise

Should be played with and exercised frequently

Grooming

All varieties need combing every other day; should visit a groomer at least 4–5 times annually.

Other dogs

They are happy with all nondominant dogs

Summary
The almost perfect pet

H

Standard:
over 15 in. (38 cm)

Miniature:
15 in. (38 cm) or under

Toy:
10 in. (25 cm) or under

Left: *The way in which a Poodle is clipped reflects its role as a water dog and is designed to protect the joints in cold water and help buoyancy.*

Dalmatian

Guarding instinct

Will warn off intruders

Temperament

Devoted, anxious to please

Exercise

Cannot get enough

Grooming

A weekly brushing

Other dogs

Generally friendly

Summary

Ideal for an active country family

Males and Bitches:
19–23 inches (48–58 cm)

No one knows the exact origin of the breed name "Dalmatian," but almost certainly it is not from Dalmatia on the coast of what used to be Yugoslavia. Spotted dogs have been present in Europe for many centuries, as is proven by the numerous paintings and friezes of them. The breed was a farm dog and it has a strange affinity with horses. In fact, it was known as a "carriage dog" and would, by nature, run for miles under a carriage between the wheels or beside the horses.

Today, Dalmatians are companion dogs and are rarely used for work, but this was not always the case. From the eighteenth century until the mid-nineteenth century, they lived roughly in the gentry's stables, chasing rats and guarding the premises. They became renowned for riding on fire trucks, hence their name "fire dogs."

Temperament

These dogs love the company of humans and are affectionate and eager to please. Being essentially farm dogs, Dalmatians came rather late to intimate living with humans and still seem to be trying to make up for this. They have clean habits, are devoted and loyal, and get very attached to children.

General care

With their famous working past, Dalmatians obviously want and need as much exercise as their owner can give. Undoubtedly, it is preferable that they should live in the country although many are kept successfully as pets in cities. Little grooming of the short, fine

■ **Above:** *It's hard to believe that the puppies, such as this one, are born white. Their spots develop later on.*

coat is required. It does not need daily attention, and a weekly brushing will suffice.

Appearance

The Dalmatian is one of the most elegant of all the dog breeds. It is tall and slim with a smooth, shiny coat, which may have either striking black or liver-colored spots on a white background. The distinctive coat is talked about wherever a Dalmatian goes and never fails to attract attention.

Health problems

Skin allergies, urinary problems, glaucoma. Deafness is also a worry but tests are available.

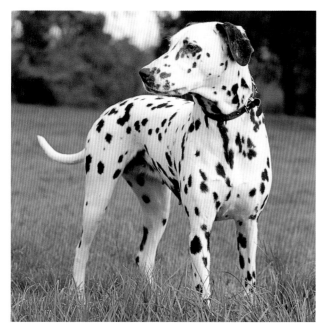

■ **Left:** *This striking, good-looking dog with its distinctive spots makes a good companion and family pet.*

Shetland Sheepdog

Herding group

■ **Left:** *Alert and tireless, the Sheltie is an extremely popular breed.*

Temperament

The Shetland Sheepdog has a sweet nature, always wanting to please and invariably willing. This is a one-man dog with a liking for outdoor activities. Even freezing cold, snow, and appalling weather conditions do not worry this tough breed. A naturally clean dog, the Sheltie is very intelligent and thus easily trained, gentle, and responsive, caring deeply for its family.

Work

This dog's standard work was to assist the shepherd in all his duties. Shetland Sheepdogs would protect their charges by keeping them from the edge of cliffs and running back to warn their owners of approaching trouble in the form of humans or animals.

General care

A tireless breed, this dog will take all the country walking that the owner can give. However, in urban situations they should have frequent walks, free running, and play. The coat will need weekly attention: deep brushing with a nylon brush is recommended and knots behind the ears are a problem. The feet, hind legs, and the hair under the tail should be trimmed with sharp scissors.

Appearance

A very pretty, perky little dog with an abundant double coat, which consists of a harsh-textured outer coat and a soft, dense undercoat. It comes in brilliant colors, ranging from gold to mahogany, tricolors, blue merle, and black and white.

■ **Below:** *The Shetland Sheepdog has an easily recognizable and abundant ruff of long hair around its neck.*

S hetland is a windswept island lying off the north coast of Scotland, and its cold, bleak look produces famous miniature livestock – Shetland ponies, cows, and sheep – so it seems natural that the dog used to control them should be small. There always were Collie-type dogs present on Shetland but they must have been crossed with dogs from visiting whaling ships or fishermen from Scandinavia and Holland. A visit from Queen Victoria, cruising the waters, probably introduced crosses with the King Charles Spaniel, producing colors unknown in Collies.

Health problems

Some hip dysplasia (page 102) and eye anomalies. Puppies should be bought from tested parents and should themselves be tested.

Guarding instinct

Suspicious, will warn vociferously

Temperament

Responsive, amicable nature, can be excitable.

Exercise

When adult, as much as possible

Grooming

Important to groom every week

Other dogs

A friendly nonstress dog

Summary

An affectionate dog suitable for a lively family

H

Males and Bitches:
13–16 inches (33–41 cm)

Herding group

Border Collie

Guarding instinct

Suspicious; will defend family and territory

Temperament

Very affectionate but energetic family dog

Exercise

Must have a great deal; needs lots of mental stimulation

Grooming

Minimal with smooth coats; long coats need frequent brushing

Other dogs

Nonaggressive, but likes to herd little dogs

Summary

Ideal for the knowledgeable, active country owner

Males:
21 inches (53 cm)

Bitches:
Slightly less

Sheepdogs have been a vital part of the shepherd's equipment since man first domesticated farm animals; without them the vast flocks of millions of sheep just would not exist. Undoubtedly, there were sheepdogs working flocks in Scotland long before the Romans invaded England, bringing with them their own breed of sheep and probably their own sheepdogs. They were interbred with the native dogs and the long process of evolution of the five sheepdog breeds began. Shepherds are naturally secretive and nobody knows which breeds went into making today's Border Collie, although some pinpoint the Newfoundland and the Borzoi. Queen Victoria fell for the Collie on her visits to Balmoral and under her royal patronage the breed prospered.

■ **Below:** *Its superb herding ability makes it the most popular working sheepdog.*

■ **Right:** *The Border Collie is always alert and responsive.*

Temperament

Always anxious to please, highly intelligent, and easily trained, the Border Collie is a good, sensitive dog although it is inclined to be headstrong. It cares deeply for its family, especially the children, and is an excellent guard dog.

Work

The most enthusiastic working farm dog, the Border Collie is very popular in Australia where it has adapted to the heat and harsh environment. In England, it's a general farm dog working cows and sheep with equal facility. Some become good show dogs, and they excel in Obedience, Agility, and Flyball.

General care

There is no doubt that this dog does need a great amount of running exercise and things to occupy it; really, an Agility course in the backyard would be ideal. The smooth-coated variety requires very little grooming – just a weekly brushing. However, the longer coat will require combing every other day.

Appearance

The Border Collie is medium-sized, always watchful, and very inquisitive. It has a fairly long body and comes in two different coats: smooth and moderately long. Any color is permissible including blue, but there should not be too much white.

■ **Above:** *The Border Collie's large eyes are set wide apart for better all-around vision when working.*

Health problems

Some low-level hip dysplasia (page 102). Genetic eye problems are being controlled but buy from tested parents and get the puppy tested. There is also some deafness.

German Shepherd Dog

This breed was produced from an amalgam of North European herding breeds. The prototype for the breed has existed in Germany for centuries. Tacitus, the Roman historian, mentioned the "wolf-like dog of the Rhineland." In the nineteenth century, a German army officer named Rittmeister von Stephanitz recognized the potential of this breed and created the *Verein für Deutsche Schäfehunde* (German Breed Club) to control its development.

Below: *The highly intelligent German Shepherd is the most numerous breed.*

Temperament

The German Shepherd Dog is highly intelligent, versatile, and steady, whether as a pet in the home or as a working security dog. When properly socialized, no breed is more caring or loyal to its human family. It is easily trained to a high standard and needs firm but kind handling.

Work

Arguably the greatest all-around working dog of all time, it is an invaluable and fearless police dog worldwide, as well as a tracker dog, a guide dog for the blind, an assistance dog for the disabled, and a patrol dog for security companies.

Health problems

Hip dysplasia (page 102), hemophilia A (page 103), Von Willebrand's Disease, eye problems, auto-immune disorders, elbow dysplasia (page 103), and digestive problems. Buy puppies from breeders who test their stock.

General care

This dog requires a lot of exercise and mental stimulation, especially games. It excels at Obedience and Agility training. Because it is so active, it needs high-quality food. A good combing followed by a brushing twice weekly will rid the coat of dead hairs and keep the German Shepherd Dog in good condition, especially when it sheds.

Appearance

A big dog whose coat consists of harsh outer guard hairs about 2 inches (5 cm) long with a thick undercoat. There is also a long-coated variety that cannot be shown. The German Shepherd's conformation gives it a far-reaching, enduring movement and an elegant head carriage. The pricked ears and bright eyes create an alert and intelligent expression for this very popular dog.

Guarding instinct

One of the best security dogs

Temperament

Loyal and affectionate

Exercise

Must have plenty

Grooming

Twice-weekly brushing and combing

Other dogs

Take care; males can be dominant

Summary

With socialization and sympathetic training, a great companion

H

Males:
24–26 in. (61–66 cm)

Bitches:
22–24 in. (56–61 cm)

Left: *The puppy's coat is fine and downy and will change color as it grows.*

Other popular breeds

There are literally hundreds of dog breeds in the world and they have been bred selectively for their ability to perform a particular job (as in working dogs), for temperament (as in pet dogs) or to produce specific physical characteristics. Consequently, the canine world is infinitely varied and interesting, and there are many breeds from which you can choose when you consider owning a dog. Here are some brief descriptions of more popular breeds plus some less well-known ones, such as the Mastiff and the Italian Spinone.

Airedale Terrier

The largest terrier, the Airedale is intelligent, loyal and good with children. Like the other working dogs, it needs plenty of exercise. It needs regular brushing and hand-stripping twice yearly.

Bull Terrier

If properly trained and socialized, this powerful dog is gentle and good-natured. It needs plenty of exercise and is easy to groom. A natural fighter, care must be taken when mixing with other dogs as it has a strong bite and won't let go.

Border Terrier

This game little dog needs lots of exercise but the wiry, weather-resistant coat needs only minimal grooming. Friendly and highly intelligent, it is easy to train and makes an affectionate family pet.

Welsh Terrier

A good companion dog and ratter, this intelligent, jaunty terrier is quite easy to train but can be stubborn. It needs regular weekly grooming and will require stripping twice a year.

Cairn Terrier

This game little dog has a typical Terrier temperament. It is easy to train and makes a good watchdog. Lively and affectionate, it will take as much exercise as you can give but needs minimal grooming.

Maltese

This good-tempered little dog in the Toy Group has a long, glossy snow-white coat which requires daily grooming. An ideal family pet, it is good with children and does not need a great deal of exercise. The Maltese is a long-lived healthy dog.

Flat-coated Retriever

This intelligent dog is often used as a gundog, picking up game. It makes a devoted, affectionate pet but will need plenty of exercise. The dense coat will need brushing daily to keep it in good condition.

Weimaraner

This striking gundog is reliable and alert. It has speed and stamina in abundance and needs free running and lead walking every day. Easy to train, the more common short-coated variety is quick to groom.

Italian Spinone

This ancient gundog is loyal and affectionate. It is a good country dog, needing lots of vigorous exercise and enjoying swimming. The rough, thick coat needs daily grooming to tease out tangles.

Curly-coated Retriever

This handsome dog loves to swim and retrieve. A reliable working dog, it is also an ideal pet if you have the time to exercise it. The curly coat does not need grooming, just dampening and massaging.

German Short-haired Pointer

This popular dog is easy to train and makes a good pet as well as an excellent gundog. It doesn't need much grooming but it must be walked daily and allowed to run. A good companion dog, it is very responsive and enjoys Field Trials.

Irish Wolfhound

This is the tallest breed of dog. A gentle giant, the Wolfhound is very affectionate and only requires daily moderate exercise, no more than any other large dog. The wiry coat needs daily combing to remove tangles and loose hairs.

Irish Setter

A racy, extrovert dog with a silky, flowing red coat, the Irish Setter makes an affectionate pet as well as a gundog. With its boundless energy, it requires lots of exercise, and the coat needs daily brushing.

Deerhound

This ancient breed makes a loyal, gentle pet. The Deerhound needs an energetic owner who will give it lots of exercise and free running over open ground. The weather-resistant harsh and wiry coat is easy to groom every day.

Welsh Springer Spaniel

This distinctive red and white Spaniel is a hard-working gundog as well as a family pet. Loyal and obedient, it is easy to train. It loves swimming and requires lots of exercise, especially free running. The coat requires daily grooming.

Afghan Hound

This elegant sight hound is highly intelligent and affectionate but does need careful handling. Its long coat must be groomed daily to prevent it matting, and it will need plenty of walks and free running to keep it fit and healthy.

Whippet

This gentle, adaptable dog makes an affectionate family pet. As well as daily walks on the lead, it must have plenty of free running. Docile and easy to train, this dog's coat needs only minimal grooming.

Old English Sheepdog

This breed demands affection. It is very exuberant and must be trained and socialized from an early age. Not only does it need plenty of exercise but also you must be prepared to spend considerable time grooming the profuse coat.

Miniature Pinscher

Looking like a tiny Doberman, this intelligent little dog makes a good companion as well as being an excellent ratter. Self-confident and affectionate, it is easy to groom and enjoys exercise.

Chow Chow

A good watchdog, the Spitz-type Chow Chow is very loyal. When provoked, it will not back off from a fight. It needs regular exercise, and the long outer coat and dense undercoat need daily brushing.

Mastiff

This large, powerful dog may look frightening but it is usually easy-going and affectionate. Because of its great strength, it needs sensible handling by an experienced owner. A good guard dog, the Mastiff must be walked regularly and will enjoy free running across country. Its short coat is easy to groom.

Bulldog

Originally bred for baiting bulls, the Bulldog can look aggressive but is actually very good natured and gentle. It needs regular but not too strenuous exercise and a quick daily brush and comb. It is very good with children.

USEFUL ADDRESSES

American Kennel Club
5580 Centerview Drive, Suite 200
Raleigh, NC 27606-3390
(919) 233-3600

American Veterinary Medical Association
1931 N. Meacham Road, Suite 100
Schaumburg, IL 60173-4360
(800) 228-7548

Canine Eye Registration Foundation
South Campus Court Building C
West Lafayette, IN 47907

Orthopedic Foundation for Animals
2300 Nifong Boulevard
Columbia, MO 65201
(573) 442-0418

National Dog Registry
P.O. Box 118
Woodstock, NY 12498-0116

American Society for the Prevention of Cruelty to Animals (ASPCA)
441 East 92nd Street
New York, NY 10028
(212) 876-7700

National Animal Poison Control Center
(900) 680-0000 ($20 for five minutes and $2.95 per minute thereafter)
(888) 4ANIHELP or (800) 548-2423 ($30 per case, credit card only)

Therapy Dogs International
P.O. Box 2796
Cheyenne, WY 82203

Canadian Kennel Club
111 Eglington Avenue
Toronto 12, Ontario, Canada

Home Again Microchip Service
800-LONELY-ONE

ACKNOWLEDGMENTS

The publishers would like to thank the following people and their dogs who gave up their valuable time to assist with the special photography for this book:
Gail Alecock and her Staffordshire Bull Terriers
Mrs. Allen and her Cavalier King Charles Spaniel
Mrs. Allum and her Cairn Terrier, Holly
Caroline Barc and her English Springer Spaniel, Maisie
Mark Barker and his Bull Terrier, Maisey
Carola, Lady Beevor and her Pugs, Clemlee Spring Fern at Butthard, Butthard the Saltcote Belle, Butthard the Dannebrog and Butthard the Beatrice Maude
Carole Brame and her dog, Simba
Enid Burch and her Dobermans, Harry and Gail
Sally Byrom and her Dachshund, Charlie Brown
Sally Cackett and her Pomeranians
Mr. Chamberline and his Old English Sheepdog, Benson
Mr. Collard and his Standard Schnauzer, Mollie
Beth Colmer and her Labradors, Bridie and Pup
Mr. Cooke and his Shetland Sheepdog, Brandy
Jo Desmond and her Rottweiler
Ms. Edwards and her Border Collie, Mij
Adrian Finbow and his Border Collie, Drake
Caroline Griffiths and her Irish Setters, Prudence and Florence
Mr. Harrison and his Jack Russell Terrier, Millie
Charlie Horrington and his Dalmatian, Amber
Mr. Houchell and his Weimaraner, Sophie
Helen Hudson and her Jack Russells, Rosie Russell and Darcy, and her cat, Ben

Kevin Jarvis and his Standard Poodle
Judy Landvik and her Miniature Schnauzer, Scooby
Kayleigh Laws and her Staffordshire Bull Terrier, Millie
Mrs. McKenzie and her Bichon Frises
Natalie Moye and her Dalmatian, Charlie
Mr. and Mrs. Noble and their Great Danes, Farrier and Jess
Simon Piers-Hall and his Labradoodle, Popeye
Mr. Player and his Beagles, Harry and Emma
Tegan Potter and her Pug, Rocky
Mrs. Reed and her Cavalier King Charles Spaniels, Baray Holly, Leelyn Red Dunster at Baray, Jirobander Juliette and Baray Crystal Lady
Thirza Rockall and her Jack Russell Terrier, Gunner, and Border Terrier, Rudi
Brenda Sandford and her Lhasa Apso, Lizzie
Mark Sexton and his Siberian Huskies, Nikita, Natasha, and Cadbury
Mr. and Mrs. Stones and their Bulldog, Louie
Mr. and Mrs. Stuart and their Lhasa Apsos, Chloe and Bridie
Lisa Taylor and her Rottweiler, Benson
Christine Ugolini and her Cocker Spaniels, Jasper and Sam
Angela Warren and her Miniature Poodle, Willow
Arron Wheatley and his West Highland White Terrier, Billy
Miss Williams and her Boston Terriers, Martha and Jessica
Mr. Williams and his Mastiff, Toby
Ken Woosnam and his Lhasa Apsos, Champion and Irish Champion Saxonsprings Tradition, Saxonsprings Silent Memories, Saxonsprings Twist of Fate and Showa Quicksilver at Pantulf

INDEX

Abscesses, 100, 121
Acure abdomen, 112
Afghan Hounds, 82, 103, 188
Agility classes, 136, 142
Airedale Terriers, 137, 186
All-breed shows, 140–141
American Cocker Spaniels, 103
American Kennel Club, 14, 15, 21, 23, 102, 136, 140, 142, 146, 147, 148, 151
Anal glands, 113
Anal regions, 22, 100
Appetite, loss of, 100
Arthritis, 117
Bad breath, 100, 104
Ballooning of earflap, 108
Barking, 59, 78
Basset Hounds, 86, 119
Bathing, 93
Beagles, 103, 160
Beds, 26
Beestings, 131
Bichon Frisés, 176
Birth, 149–150
  problems, 150
Bladder stones, 115
Bleeding, 132
Bloated abdomen, 100
Blood in stools, 111
Blood in urine, 114, 120
Boarding, 96, 97
Bone(s), 84
  marrow, 118
Border Collies, 103, 184
Border Terriers, 186
Bordetella, 110
Boston Terriers, 103, 178
Bowls, 26, 86
Boxers, 17, 103, 162
Brain, 115
  inflammation of, 115
Breeding, 144–151
Breeds,
  choosing a, 12
Broken tooth, 105
Bronchitis, 109
Bull Terriers, 186
Bulldogs, 92, 103, 189
Bullmastiffs, 89
Burns, 128
  chemical, 128
  electrical, 128
Cairn Terriers, 187
Calcium, 118
Calculi, 115
Car travel, 57
Cardiac massage, 129
Castration, 21, 144
Cataracts, 103, 106, 158

Cats, 30
Cavalier King Charles Spaniels, 17, 171
CAV-1, 113
Cerebellar atrophy, 103
Chemical burns, 128
Cherry eye, 103
Chest, 109–110
Chews, 56
Chihuahuas, 95, 173
Children, 44
Chocolate, 87
Chow Chows, 90, 189
Circulatory system, 110
Cirrhosis, 113
Clumber Spaniels, 103
Coat, 101
  types, 89
Cocker Spaniels, 17, 86, 156
Collars, 26, 65
Collie(s), 89, 103
  eye, 103
Come when called command, 72–73
Commands, 64
Conjunctivitis, 85
Constipation, 100, 111, 120
Contraception, 119
Convulsions, 115, 130
Corrosive poisons, 130
Coughs, 100, 109
Crates, 57–58, 67
Crossbreeds, 14, 22
Curly-coated Retrievers, 139, 187
Cushing's Disease, 103
Cystitis, 115
Cysts, 121
Dachshunds, 116, 117, 119, 160
Dalmatians, 17, 182
Danger zones, 64–65
Deafness, 47, 103, 182
Deerhounds, 188
Dementia, 115
Dental care, 84
Depression, 115
Destructive behavior, 59
Diabetes, 112, 124
Diabetic cataract, 106
Diarrhea, 100, 111, 112, 125
Diet, 27–28, 82, 86–87, 118
Distemper, 33, 106, 109, 112, 116
Doberman Pinschers, 17, 89, 103, 166
Down command, 74
Dull coat, 100

Ears, 22, 46, 47, 85, 101, 107–108
  foreign bodies in, 133
  grooming, 92
Eclampsia, 116, 124, 150
Ectropion, 103
Eczema, 169
Elbow dysplasia, 103, 159, 167, 185
Elderly dogs, 55, 87, 97
Electrical burns, 128
Encephalitis, 115
English Setters, 103
English Springer Spaniels, 157
Enlarged prostate, 120
Entropion, 103, 106, 158, 165
Enzyme deficiency, 112
Epilepsy, 103, 115
Equipment, 26
  for breeding, 149
  for grooming, 26, 88
Estrus, 119, 147
Excessive drinking, 124
Exercise, 39, 94–95
Extending leashes, 73, 94
Eye(s), 22, 47, 48, 84–85, 101, 106
  foreign bodies in, 133
  problems, 157, 159, 160, 167, 184
False pregnancy, 120
Feeding, 82, 86–87
  elderly dogs, 87
  equipment, 86
  postnatal, 87
  prenatal, 87
  puppies, 27–28
  supplements, 28
  traveling dogs, 96
Feet, 85
Field Trials, 143
Field of vision, 48
First aid, 128–133
Flat-coated Retrievers, 187
Flatulence, 112
Fleas, 121, 122
Flyball, 136, 142
Foreign bodies,
  in ears, 107, 133
  in eyes, 133
  in mouth, 133
  in paws, 133
Games, 35, 36, 61
  tug-of-war, 35
Genetic tests, 21, 102, 146
Gerbils, 30
German Shepherd Dogs, 17, 89, 103, 137, 185

German Short-haired Pointers, 103, 188
Gingivitis, 105
Glaucoma, 103
Golden Retrievers, 17, 103, 146, 159
Gordon Setters, 103
Great Danes, 86, 103, 167
Greyhounds, 15
Grooming, 12, 82, 88–93
  for showing, 137
  tools, 26, 88
Gums, 100
Hamsters, 30
Hazards, 31
Head collars, 68
Health care, 84–85, 98–133
Heart, 110
  disease, 109
  murmurs, 173
  problems, 162
  rate, checking, 129
Heatstroke, 97, 132
Hemorrhage, 132
Hemophilia, 103, 185
Hepatitis, 113
Herding group, 154
Herding trials, 136, 142, 143
Hereditary diseases, 102–103
Hip dysplasia, 21, 102, 103, 156, 157, 158, 159, 162, 165, 166, 167, 171, 181, 182, 183, 184, 185
Home alone, 58
Hookworms, 123
Hormonal disease, 113
Hornet stings, 131
Hound group, 154
House soiling, 54–55
House-training, 24, 66–67
Howling, 45, 59
Hydrocephalus, 103
Hypothyroidism, 103
Identity tags, 65
Indoor kennels, 32
Infectious canine hepatitis, 112, 113
Insurance, 22, 33
Intestine, 111
Irish Setters, 103, 188
Irish Water Spaniels, 143
Irish Wolfhounds, 86, 188
Italian Spinones, 187
Jack Russell Terrier 17, 168
Jaundice, 113, 114
Joints, stiff, 117
Jumping up, 60
Kennel cough, 110, 112
Keratitis, 106

Kerry Blue Terriers, 89, 103, 107
Kidney disease, 112, 114, 115
Kidney problems, 114, 156
Kidney stones, 115
Labored breathing, 109, 110
Labrador Retrievers, 17, 103, 158
Lakeland Terriers, 139
Lameness, 117
Leashes, 26, 34, 73, 77
Leash training, 34–35, 76–77
Leptospira, 114
Leptospirosis, 33, 114
Lhasa Apsos, 82, 180
Lice, 121, 122
Licking, obsessive, 100
Life expectancy, 29
Lifting a dog, 127
Liver disease, 112, 113
Long-haired dogs, 89
Lymphosarcoma, 125
Malabsorption, 112
Malteses, 89, 187
Man/dog relationship, 42
Mange mites, 108, 121
Mastiffs, 189
Mastitis, 125
Match shows, 139
Mating, 146, 148
Medicine, administering, 126
Medium-haired dogs, 89
Middle-ear disease, 108
Minature Pinscher, 189
Miniature Schnauzers, 177
Mismating, 119
Mites, 121
Mixed-breeds, 14, 22
Mouth, 22, 49, 104–105
  -to-nose resuscitation, 129
  ulcers, 105
Multifocal retinal dysplasia, 158
Muzzle, making a makeshift, 127
Nails, 85, 100
Nervous system, 115
Newfoundlands, 103
Non-sporting group, 154
Nose, 101, 107
  bleeds, 107
Nursing a sick dog, 126
Obedience Competitions, 136, 142
Old English Sheepdogs, 22, 88, 90, 103, 189
Organizations, national, 15
Osteochondrosis dessicans, 103, 165
Outside runs, 55
Overexcitability, 116
Overweight, 87
Paralysis, 116

Parasites, 121, 122–123
Parvovirus, 33, 112
Patent ductus arteriosus, 103
Paws, foreign bodies in, 133
Pekingeses, 95, 119
Perthe's disease, 169, 175, 176
Pet shops, 15
Play, 35, 61
Play-biting, 56
Playpens, 27
Pneumonia, 110, 125
Pointers, 143
Poisoning, 116, 130–131
Poisonous plants, 130
Poisons, 64, 131
Polydipsia, 112
Polyphagia, 112
Pomeranians, 95, 103, 174
Poodles, 17, 22, 88, 90, 103, 107, 181
Postnatal care, 151
  feeding, 87, 151
Pregnancy, 149
  false, 120
  feeding in, 87, 149
  signs of, 149
Prenatal feeding, 87, 149
Presentation for shows, 139
Progressive retinal atrophy, 103, 157, 158
Prolapsed intervertebral disk, 117
Prostate cancer, 120
Prostate problems, 120
Prostatis, 120
Pseudopregnancy, 120
Pugs, 56, 172
Pulmonary stenosis, 103
Puppies, 20–23, 24–39, 51, 52, 56, 58–59, 64–65
  choosing, 21, 22
  collecting, 26
  feeding, 27–28
  house-training, 66–67
  selling, 151
  showing, 139
  training, 68–79
  weaning, 151
Puppy mills, 15
Purebred dogs, 14
Pyometra, 116, 119
Rabies, 125
Registration, 23, 147
Reproductive system, 120
Rescue dogs, 15, 18
  choosing, 16, 18
Restraining a large dog, 127
Retrieve command, 75
Retrievers, 143
Retrieving dummies, 75
Rewards, 68

Rhinitis, 107
Ringworm, 121, 123
Rottweilers, 17, 165
Rough Collies, 90, 103
Rough-haired dogs, 90
Roundworms, 123
Safety, 29, 31, 61
Salivating, 104, 131
Salmonella infection, 112
Scalds, 129
Scent recognition, 49
Schnauzers, 163
  Miniature, 177
Scratching, persistent, 100, 122
Season, bitches in, 147
Seizures, 103, 115
Setters, 143
Shar Peis, 89
Shetland Sheepdogs, 89, 103, 183
Shih Tzus, 179
Shock, 131
Short-haired dogs, 89
Short-nosed breeds, 56
Show leashes, 137
Show presentation, 137
Showing, 136–141
  grooming for, 137
Showmanship, 136, 138
Siberian Huskies, 164
Sight, 47
Sinusitis, 107
Sit command, 70
Skeleton, 118
Skin, 121–122
  abscesses, 100
  inflammation, 100
Slickers, 93
Slipped disk, 117
Slipping patella, 173, 174, 175, 176, 178
Snakebites, 131
Sneezing, 107
Socialization, 24, 37, 68
Sound sensitivity, 46
Spaniels, 49, 143
Spaying, 21, 119, 144
Spinal injuries, 116
Spitz-type dogs, 90
Sporting
  dogs (gundogs), 44, 94
  group, 154
  trials, 136, 143
Springer Spaniels, 17, 157, 188
Staffordshire Bull Terriers, 170
Stay command, 71
Stings, 131
Stomach, 111
Stripping, 90
  knives, 92
Stud dogs, 146

Subaortic stenosis, 103
Swimming, 94
Tail(s),
  grooming, 92
  signals, 50
Tapeworms, 123
Tartar, 105
Teeth, 22, 84, 100, 101, 104, 105
Teething, 56
Temperature, taking a dog's, 126
Terrier group, 154
Terriers, 35, 49, 82, 90, 94
Thirst, 119
Ticks, 121, 123
Toad venom poisoning, 131
Tonsillitis, 105
Tooth abscesses, 107
Torsion, 11
Toxoplasmosis, 125
Toy group, 154
Toys, 26, 36
Training, 62–79
Training classes, 20, 82
Travel, 96–97
  boxes, 32, 57
Tumors, 105, 121
Ulcers, mouth, 105
Urinary system, 114
Uterine inertia, 150
Vaccination, 18, 22, 26, 33, 112, 114, 125
Ventricular septal "hole in the heart" defect, 103
Vocalization, 45–46
Vomiting, 100, 111, 119, 131
Von Willebrand's disease, 103, 166
Warfarin, 131
Wasp stings, 131
Weaning, 151
Weight, 101
  loss, 100, 110, 113, 124
Weimaraners, 187
Welsh Springer Spaniels, 188
Welsh Terriers, 90, 137, 186
West Highland White Terriers, 17, 169
Wheezing, 109
Whippets, 189
Whipworms, 123
Wire-haired breeds, 90
Wire-haired Fox Terriers, 137
Wobbler syndrome, 103
Wolves, 42
Working group, 154
Worming, 85
Yorkshire Terriers, 17, 89, 139, 175